THE COLD WEATHER CATALOG

LEARNING TO LOVE WINTER

The COLD WEATHER CATALOG

LEARNING TO LOVE WINTER

Edited by Robert Levine and Nancy Bruning
Designed by Paul Perlow

A Tree Communications Edition
Dolphin Books/Doubleday & Company, Inc.
Garden City, New York 1977

Printed in U.S.A.

ISBN 0-385-13494-0

Library of Congress Catalog Card Number 77-83647

Created and Produced by Tree Communications, Inc., 250 Park Avenue South, New York, NY

Edited by Robert Levine and Nancy Bruning/ Designed by Paul Perlow/ Cover Painting by Barbara Samuels/ Production Associate: Lucille O'Brien/ Production Artist: Yaron Fidler

Page 215, "Stopping by Woods on a Snowy Evening" by Robert Frost reprinted from *The Poetry of Robert Frost* edited by Edward Connery Latham. Copyright 1923 © 1969 by Holt, Rinehart and Winston. Copyright 1951 by Robert Frost. Reprinted by permission of Holt, Rinehart and Winston, Publishers.

Note: The addresses listed for mail-order suppliers are accurate at press time. The inclusion of company and/or product names in this book does not constitute an endorsement.

Much of the advice in this book is given in abbreviated form. No liability can be accepted for the consequences of accidents to readers that may occur as a result of an attempt to follow the recommendations.

ACKNOWLEDGMENTS

The editors are particularly grateful to Michael Gross, Jessica Shaktman, and Bibi Wein for their assistance — above and beyond their excellent written contributions.

Other contributors who deserve credit are David Arky, Debi Bracken, Diana Bryan, Mary Clarke, Sonja Douglas, Yaron Fidler, Linda Franklin, Frankie Freilich, Marina Givotovsky, Matthew Harris, Elizabeth Henley, Linda Hetzer, Mary Ison of the Library of Congress, Richard Kagel, Susan Keller, Silvia Kelley, Mark Kirschen, Melanie Korman, Paul Levin, Ruth Michel, Lucille O'Brien, Maggie Oster, Bruce Plotkin, Sylvia Rosenthal, Robert Schwarzenbach, Barbara Skaktman, Dick Smith, and Kenley Sprague.

We would like to thank the following for photographs: ALH, Inc., a subsidiary of Aladdin Industries, Inc., P.O. Box 7235, Nashville, TN 37210; Bernzomatic Corp., represented by Daniel S. Roher, Inc., 733 Third Avenue, New York, NY 10017; Moor & Mountain, 63 Park Street, Andover, MA 01810; Sears, Roebuck and Company, Sears Tower, Chicago, IL 60684; Swiss National Tourist Office, The Swiss Center, 608 Fifth Avenue, New York, NY 10020; Royal Norwegian Embassy, Information Service, 625 Third Avenue, New York, NY 10022; N.H. Office of Vacation Travel, P.O. Box 856 State House Annex, Concord, NH 03301; Snow & Nealley Co., 155 Perry Road, Bangor, ME 04401; Radiant Decorative Lights, 1164 Garrison Avenue, Bronx, NY 10474; Baths International Inc., 101 Park Avenue, New York, NY 10017; Norwegian National Travel Office, 505 Fifth Avenue, New York, NY 10017; Vermont Development Agency, Montpelier, VT; Government of Quebec (Tourist Branch); Frostline Kits, Frostline Circle, Denver, CO 80241; Brandon Memorabilia, 1 West 30th Street, New York, NY 10001; Mary L. Martin.

COLOPHON: The text face for this book is Goudy Old Style, set at Contempo-Type; Filmtext, Inc.; David E. Seham, Inc.; and Tree Communications, Inc. The display faces are Agency Gothic Open and Bulletin, set at Latent Lettering Co., Inc., and MKP, Inc. Halftones were made by Tree Communications, Inc. The paper used is Signature Text, made by Miami Paper Corporation and supplied by Baldwin Paper Company. The book was printed and bound by Connecticut Printers.

TABLE OF CONTENTS

Fascinating cold weather facts and recipes for heart-warming drinks and dishes are generously sprinkled throughout.

PRELUDE

L'INVERNO

Allegro non molto:
Aggiacciato tremar trà neri algenti,
Al severo spirar d'orrido Vento,
Correr battendo i piedi ogni momento,
E pel soverchio gel batter i denti;

Largo:
Passar al foco i di quieti e contenti
Mentre la pioggio fuor bagna ben cento,

Allegro:
Caminar sopra 'l giacoio, e à passo lento
Per timor di cader gersene intenti;
Gir forte sdruzziolar, cader à terra,
Di nuovo ir sopra 'l giaccio e correr forte
Sin ch'il giacoio si rompe, e se disserra;
Sentir uscir dalle ferrate porte
Sirocco, Borea, e tutti i Venti in guerra,
Quest' è'l verno; mà tal, che gioja apporte.

WINTER

Allegro non molto:
To trudge trembling down the snowy street,
Stabbed to the bone by the wind's piercing breath,
Constantly running, stamping lifeless feet,
Huddling down, teeth chattering, frozen to death,

Largo:
To sit by friendly fire, quiet and content,
While those outside are drenched by beating rain.

Allegro:
To walk on ice, with cautious step, intent
On staying upright on the icy lane,
And on frozen lake, sliding, falling down,
You climb upon the ice and run so fast,
For fear the ice may break, and you might drown,
Sirocco and Borea hurl their raging blast
Through bolted doors, and all the winds at war,
It's Winter, and the joy we've waited for!

Antonio Vivaldi's masterpiece *The Four Seasons* is a series of four violin concerti — each depicting a season by the sound of the music alone. Few people know about the sonnets, also written, it is believed, by Vivaldi, who wanted them to accompany the music. *Winter*, printed above in the original and translation, will give you an idea of what the music sounds like and will also give you greater pleasure next time you hear the concerto itself. It sums up the marvels of winter in its fourteen lines and, we hope, captures some of the flavor of this book.

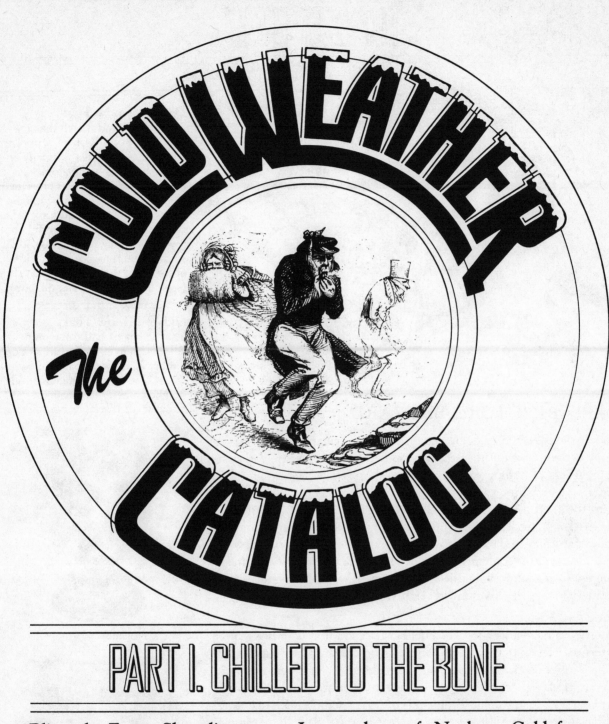

THE COLD WEATHER CATALOG

PART I. CHILLED TO THE BONE

Blizzards. Frost. Shoveling snow. Ice on the roof. No heat. Cold feet. Wind-chill. Frostbite. Thin ice. Frozen pipes. Yipes! Don't despair—you don't have to move to Mexico. Read on. There <u>are</u> flowers in the Alps.

PREPARING FOR A BLIZZARD

It's a little late to start stocking up on provisions when a blizzard has already cut you off from the outside world. But if you prepare early, the helplessness of finding your power cut off and your heating and food supplies diminishing can be considerably eased. It's crucial to think in terms of alternate ways of meeting basic needs. If your electricity is knocked out, chances are your phone, lights, cooking appliances, radios, and your furnace and its thermostat will be useless. By gathering easy-to-use, self-operating equipment that doesn't require electricity, you can ensure relative comfort while the blizzard is raging. Here is a checklist of items that are worth investing in before the blizzard season begins.

Food and Water

You should have a well-stocked cupboard of food that does not require extensive preparation, such as canned goods, instant beverages, condensed milk, crackers, cheese spread, dried fruits, candy bars, nuts, and cereals. If water pipes freeze, you will have to wait until the blizzard passes to repair them, but you can fill jars and bottles (preferably made of plastic) with water before the blizzard and store them in a cool place. If they freeze, you can thaw them out by a fire or portable stove.

Battery-Powered Equipment

A battery-operated radio or television provides contact with the outside world. Flashlights and heaters run by batteries can make up for some of the lost light and heat.

Alternative Heating Equipment

If an electricity blackout occurs, your furnace, triggered by electrical

Propane Gas Heater

Propane Gas Cooking Stove

power, and various cooking appliances can be replaced by kerosene stoves, gas ranges, or a fireplace. They each provide heat, and you can use them for cooking up some of the perishable foods still on hand.

For the Shelf
Keep matches, candles, lanterns, a fire extinguisher, and extra blankets in a dry secure place. Sleeping bags and warm clothing should be available. (You can use the sleeping bags to camp out in front of the fireplace or heater.)

Safety Tips
It may be wise, in the event of phone service being cut off, to work out signals via flashlight or flags for communicating with the neighbors. Several quick checks of batteries, fuel supplies (like gasoline or kerosene for lanterns), potential fire hazards, and your food stockpile will mean a safe, reliable backup system if you need it. Simple and portable equipment can make all the difference when you're waiting for the electricity to come back on and reconnect you with the world.

SURVIVAL TIPS: OUTDOORS

Winter camping, backpacking, or exploring can be an invigorating, worthwhile experience; but remember, there's always the possibility of becoming lost in them thar' hills. A sudden blizzard can shift the appearance of the environment enough to leave you completely confused. Severe cold can affect your judgment and cause you to miscalculate direction and distance. It is wise to listen to the Boy Scouts: *Be Prepared.*

Preparations
First and foremost: do not travel alone. You should also let someone know where you are planning to go and the length of time you intend to spend on your journey. It stands to reason that the sooner someone realizes that you are missing, the sooner rescue operations can get underway. It is also a good idea to inform local authorities— game warden, sheriff, forest ranger— whoever has responsibility for the area. They are probably the ones who will have to go after you if you are lost, and a fair idea of your destination will make their job of finding you much easier.

Second, it takes only a few minutes to call the local weather service to determine if your plan is wise at the time. There is nothing to be gained by purposely pitting yourself against severe weather conditions, and the possible outcome might be disastrous. If you are advised to delay your trip, by all means do so.

Packaged survival kits are available, or you can make up your own. The kit should include: waterproof matches (available at camping equipment stores); some sort of tinder— cotton balls, cardboard, anything you can use in the event that wet weather makes dry tinder unavailable; bouillon

FROST
Frost is the process which forms ice crystals as well as the crystals themselves. When the temperature falls below 32° Fahrenheit (0° C.) frost may form. While this seems straightforward enough, here are some terms related to frost which may be of interest to home gardeners and crystal gazers alike:

Hoar Frost
This is also known as white frost, and it is not the frozen facade on a house-of-ill-repute, but rather the latticework of scales, needles, fans and feathers of ice that forms from the condensation of damp air.

Ground Frost
A temperature just above ground level (grass temperature) of 30.4° Fahrenheit (-1° C.) that is harmful to vegetation.

Killing Frost
This is sometimes called hard frost or black frost, and is a climatic condition that blackens the landscape with damaged organic material. It is caused by a dry freeze (when crops are unprotected by snow or hoar frost insulating layers). The agricultural growing season is measured from the last killing frost of spring to the first killing frost of autumn.

Rime
Milky-white layers of ice crystals formed from low clouds or fogs (called rime fogs) which may resemble a light snowfall.

cubes, dry soup or cocoa mix, tea bags—some source of energy that can be prepared with hot water; several safety pins to repair torn clothing; and a few bandages. All of this should be packed in a watertight can with a plastic lid. The can may then be used to melt snow for preparing hot drinks. This is the most basic survival kit to which you can add other items you think necessary, such as a plastic sheet to use as shelter, wire from which to improvise a snare, a single-edged razor or knife. Naturally, if you have a two-way radio, that should be the first thing that you pack.

Don't Panic

If you find that you are lost, *stop* and determine exactly what the situation is. Probably the single most important factor in survival is being able to maintain morale and a degree of calm clearheadedness. The great outdoors can generally provide you with what you'll need to sustain life — if you are rational enough to investigate calmly. It is crucial that you avoid any initial tendency to panic and run. Take stock of the situation, determine your most immediate needs, and proceed with seeing that these are met.

Devise a Signal

Make your position known as soon as possible. For daylight, smoke is highly visible over long distances and will be investigated immediately. At night, fire will alert officials who often survey large areas by air. If maintaining a large, steady fire proves too difficult, try to keep a small flame burning that you can fuel up if you hear an airplane approaching. Another long-distance signal device is a piece of glass, a mirror, or shiny can lid. Sweep this across the horizon *often*; even if it is hazy or overcast, this reflected signal can generally be seen from an aircraft.

If all else fails, do whatever is necessary to alter the natural appearance of the landscape. Trace out a large S.O.S. signal in the snow and fill it with dead leaves. Spread a colored cloth on the ground, and keep all metal surfaces exposed and free of snow. Make a crude flag and keep it waving. Blink a flashlight on and off. In short, make your whereabouts known, using *any* means available, short of starting an uncontrollable fire.

Frost Action or Frost Heaving
This is the expansion of freezing water in the ground and can cause heaving and shifting of the earth's surface. This action can result in damage to crops.

Frost Hollow
Not a Washington Irving story but valleys where the temperature may be up to 20° Fahrenheit (−7° C.) colder than on the neighboring slopes. Frosts occur more often and more severely in frost hollows and are possible even when the air temperature is above 32° Fahrenheit in most of the surrounding area.

Frost Day
Any day during which the temperature falls below 32° Fahrenheit.

Air Frost
This has nothing to do with the branch of the armed services in which airplanes are used. It is, rather, when the temperature at thermometer level as well as ground level is below 32° Fahrenheit.

Jacula Prudentum
"Every mile is two in winter."
— *George Herbert (1593-1632)*

If you are traveling by car, snowmobile, or any vehicle, stay close to it. Often it's the vehicle that is spotted long before the person. If the temperature drops very low, or if the vehicle is not well ventilated, it is not recommended that you remain inside. If there is shelter to be found at a distance from the vehicle, try to leave some sort of message indicating your location, even if it's just an arrow carved into the paint or devised from twigs and placed out of the wind. Do not rely on your footprints to show directions; they may disappear in a matter of moments.

Shelter

Use whatever shelter is available: rocks, logs, a cave, even a snow bank will break the wind somewhat. A layer of snow over a blanket will increase warming insulation significantly. Conserve your energy — don't try to build a fortress. Staying as warm as possible is the name of the game; you won't win any points for neatness.

Hypothermia

The body is losing more heat that it can generate — this is the biggest danger you face. If all that's available is clear ground, dig a hole and lie in it, covering yourself with leaves or bark to help trap body heat and increase visibility. If you begin to show signs of hypothermia (intense, uncontrollable shivering; difficulty with speech,

ALL-TIME COLDEST TEMPERATURES

Most weather-observation stations have been recording temperatures for only the last 100 years, but some of the figures they've come up with make chilling reading.

It's All Relative

In winter, your house may make you feel like you're camping out at the North Pole, but unless you keep a home in Vostok, Antarctica, you don't know what cold is. The Russian station at that particularly uninviting place recorded a temperature of -127° Fahrenheit (-53° C.) on August 24, 1960. (Yes, August.) That's the lowest temperature ever experienced on earth since weather stations began studying highs, lows, and everything in between. You may want to keep away from a couple of other places that are al-

15

and sluggish thinking; skin beginning to turn blue or puffy) take steps *immediately*. Hypothermia can be fatal. Do anything you can to increase warmth and remain alert. Melt snow and drink the steaming water. Do not make the mistake of eating snow directly from the ground. Eating snow can chill your body enormously; always melt the snow and drink it as hot as you can tolerate. Walk, sing, jump, keep your limbs moving and your mind working. The symptoms will quickly reverse themselves if treated efficiently and swiftly.

Remember that perspiration will cool the body as it evaporates and that wet clothing is a real danger. If you begin to perspire, loosen garments to allow your skin to dry quickly. If your clothing does become very wet, let it freeze and beat the ice crystals off with a branch. It is absolutely essential that extremities be well protected. You can lose half of your generated body heat through the top of your head, and hands, feet, ears, and your nose are quickly prone to frostbite.

Snow Blindness
Protect your eyes by wearing sunglasses, improvising a visor or mask from bark or cloth, or rubbing soot around your eyes to cut glare.

In all likelihood, your survival emergency will prove to be of short duration. Most wilderness areas are patrolled regularly to check for fires and other problems. If you have taken the precaution of alerting friends and local officials before your trip, it may only be a question of surviving for a few hours until rescue. However, it is important to remember that even an hour in severe cold can be quite dangerous, and you should begin immediately to put your survival measures into operation.

Above all, remember that man is a tough, resilient creature and can withstand ordeals few would believe possible. Remember, too, that man survived the wilderness for centuries using what nature provided in the way of shelter, food, and water—in short, all that's needed to sustain life.

SURVIVING A BLIZZARD IN YOUR CAR

You know how long a trip by car can take when snow and ice cover the road, but if a blizzard hits while you're driving, you may have to forget about moving altogether and pull off the highway. When a blizzard is starting, *before it reaches its full force*, look around for a safe place to wait out the storm. Head for a smooth area, where the snow follows the contours of the roadside. Concealed ditches or deceptively banked snow can create problems. If you inadvertently park on a snowdrift, you may experience a curious sinking sensation—it's not fear, it's your car descending into near oblivion.

While your car is providing you with shelter from the elements, run the motor and heater sparingly, do not keep radio or lights on constantly (this will drain the car's battery); be sure to leave a window slightly open for

most up there with Antarctica in the competition for all-time cold weather. In Siberia, on February 6, 1933, a temperature of −90° Fahrenheit (−32°C.) was recorded, and in Greenland, on January 9, 1954, it was a crisp, refreshing −87° Fahrenheit (−30°C.).

Welcome, Alaska!
Residents of North America may feel they can't match such incredibly cold temperatures, but the Canadian Yukon area has come pretty close with −81° Fahrenheit (−27°C.). Since Alaska joined the Union, citizens of the United States can boast, or fret, about the fact that their country has experienced −80° Fahrenheit (−27°C.) on several occasions.

SNOW BOUND
No cloud above, no earth below—
A universe of sky and snow.
—*John Greenleaf Whittier*

Weather Prophecies
The saying goes that the groundhog interrupts his winter sleep on February 2, and steps outside to stretch his limbs a bit. If he sees his shadow (that is, if it's a sunny day), he goes back to sleep and we can expect six more weeks of winter. Incidentally, on the other 364 days of the year, he's known as the woodchuck.

BLIZZARD BOX FOR YOUR CAR

Putting together a Blizzard Box of emergency equipment *before* leaving home is the way to ensure relative comfort if you're stuck in your car during a blizzard. Some larger items in your trunk will also prove handy.

Food items such as chocolate bars, crackers, C rations, and dried fruit are energy sustaining.

Matches and candles can keep you warm for hours. Just remember to keep a window open for air.

An old blanket supplements clothing.

Flashlight, flasher, emergency lights, flares — these can be seen even in a blizzard and can warn off rushing traffic if you're parked near a highway.

Paper towels, window scrapers are useful for cleaning windows and maintaining a view of the situation. You may want to keep larger items on hand if you have a good-sized trunk:

Booster cables, tow chains, tire chains, for when you want to get moving again.

A shovel and a bag of sand may provide you with the means of getting traction when the storm has abated.

ventilation. Shift around in your seat periodically to avoid getting cramped. Foot stomping and hand clapping will help keep circulation going.

If you have any doubts about the safety of moving out on foot, don't. If you try to push your car, shovel snow, or look for help in an isolated area, you risk overexertion and overexposure. The storm will probably subside in a matter of hours. Until then, remember that your car is far more visible than you are; so stay close to it.

RECORD U.S. BLIZZARDS AND SNOWSTORMS

Date	Place	Depth
1717, Feb. 19-24	New England	60-72 inches
1888, March 11-14	Boston, New York, Philadelphia, Washington, D.C.	40-50 inches
1899, Feb. 11-14	Washington, D.C.	35.2 inches
1901, April 19-21	Watertown, Ohio	45 inches
1913, Nov. 7-11	Ohio, Pennsylvania, West Virginia	3-36 inches
1918, Jan. 11-14	Illinois, Indiana, Ohio	20 inches
1921, April 14-15	Silver Lake, Colorado	95 inches
1921, Nov. 17-20	The Dalles, Oregon	54 inches
1922, Jan. 27-29	Washington, D.C.	28 inches
1928, April 27-28	Bayard, West Virginia	34 inches
1930, March 25-26	Chicago, Illinois	19.2 inches
1933, Jan. 18-19	Giant Forest, California	60 inches
1935, Jan. 20-24	Winthrop, Washington	52 inches
1940, Jan. 18-22	Watertown, New York	69 inches
1940, Jan. 23-24	Louisville, Mississippi	15.5 inches
1940, Nov. 11-12	Iowa to Minnesota	————
1944, Dec. 11-12	Erie, Pennsylvania	26.5 inches
1946, January	Stampede Pass, Washington	192.9 inches
1946, Nov. 2-6	New Mexico	36 inches
1947, March 2-5	Readsboro, Vermont	50 inches
1947, March 2-5	Peru, Massachusetts	47 inches
1947, Dec. 26-27	New Jersey, New York	25-30 inches
1949, Jan. 1-6	Colorado to Dakotas	7-30 inches
1950, March 25-27	Dumont, South Dakota	60 inches
1950, Nov. 23-28	Ohio, Pennsylvania, West Virginia	35-37 inches
1951, March 10-14	Iowa City, Iowa	27.2 inches
1955, April 2-5	Colorado to Dakotas	30-52 inches
1956, March 16-17	New England, New York, Pennsylvania	20 inches
1958, Feb. 13-19	North Carolina to New Jersey	36 inches
1958, March 19-22	Virginia to New England	17-30 inches
1959, March 11-13	New England, New York	20 inches
1960, Feb. 18-20	Maryland to New England	20-36 inches
1961, Jan. 10-20	North Carolina to New York	10-30 inches
1961, Feb. 3-5	North Carolina to New England	10-36 inches
1964, Feb. 2-5	New Mexico, Oklahoma, Texas Panhandle	18-36 inches

Date	Place	Depth
1966, Jan. 29-31	Virginia to New England	12-36 inches
1966, March 2-5	Nebraska to Dakotas	12-36 inches
1967, Jan. 26-27	Chicago and Midwest	23 inches
1969, Feb. 9-10	New York and New England	15 inches
1969, February	Mt. Washington, New Hampshire	172.8 inches
1969, Dec. 26-28	New Jersey to New England	6-36 inches
1973, Feb. 10-11	Georgia and Carolinas	15-21 inches
1974, Dec. 1-2	Michigan, Ohio	17-20 inches
1975, Jan. 9	Adams Center, New York	54 inches
1975, Jan. 10-12	North Dakota, South Dakota, Nebraska, Kansas, Montana, Minnesota, Wisconsin	8-15 inches
1975, Feb. 8-10	Oswego, New York	44 inches
1975, April 2-5	Illinois, Pennsylvania, New York, New England	12-48 inches
1977, January	Buffalo, New York	126.2 inches

AVALANCHES

Anyone who participates in winter sports such as skiing, mountain climbing, or winter camping should be on guard against avalanches or snowslides. However, the danger from this form of natural disaster is not restricted to the winter sportsman. Homes have been destroyed and cars swept off the road by these masses of snow and rock sweeping down the side of a mountain at speeds of up to 200 mph.

Causes

Whenever the weight of the surface layer of snow overcomes the frictional resistance of the surface on which it lies, you have an avalanche. The conditions that determine when this is most likely to occur include the steepness of the slope as well as its shape (naturally the steeper the slope the greater the likelihood of a slide occurring), the vegetation it supports, its exposure (the direction it faces), and, of course, the weather.

The triggers (direct causes) of avalanches vary. Sound waves often can and do trigger avalanches. An airplane's sonic boom can have the same effect as a ski patroller's pistol. If dangerous avalanche conditions prevail and nothing is momentarily in the path of the potential slide, courageous, highly trained and experienced mountain rescue teams will set hundreds of tons of snow and rock hurtling into a valley so that the chances of an unsuspecting skier being trapped are diminished.

Be Prepared

If you are likely to be traveling in avalanche country this winter, these safety precautions could save your life.

1. Travel on windward slopes.
2. Look for small slides or sloughs. This may indicate that conditions are ripe for larger ones.
3. Travel as high on slopes as possible, not in the valleys beneath.
4. Stay behind natural barriers such as ledges, trees, or rock outcroppings.
5. Loosen your gear for quick removal.
6. Carry an avalanche cord. This is a colored cord, ⅛ inch in diameter and 30 to 50 feet long, that you trail behind you so that if you are caught in a slide, the rope will rise to the surface as you are swept along. This colored cord will provide visibility for searchers.

If You Are Caught in a Slide

1. Use a swimming motion to stay as close as possible to the surface.
2. Try to end up on your back to facilitate digging yourself out.
3. Keeping your hands near your head will create air pockets and help prevent your hands from being pinned.
4. Dig slowly. You can tell which way is up by suspending any object that will hang (a parka cord or a watchband).
5. Breathe slowly, and do not shout until you are sure someone will hear.

DEGREE DAYS

This term indicates an accumulated temperature record used by engineers to compute the heating (or cooling) needs of buildings over the course of a season. In winter, 65° Fahrenheit (18° C.) is taken to be the temperature at which no heat is required, and the difference between the average daily temperature and 65° becomes the number of degree days for that day. For example, if the average temperature on a given day is 43° (5° C.), that gives you 22 degree days for that day. The next day's total is added to that, and each day a new total is computed. Totals may be given by the week, month, or year to give fuel suppliers and civic engineers a picture of how this year's heating needs are comparing with last year's, and current trends and directions.

Did You Know . . .

. . . the cold mass of air over the Antarctic ice cap determines most of the weather for the half of the world south of the equator? This, in turn, affects the weather all over the world. Extreme changes in the Antarctic, such as an earthquake, will affect the weather *wherever* you are.

No one knows exactly where these dogs came from, but they apparently originated in Asia and were brought to Europe by conquering Roman armies. For the past 150 years or so, they've been specially bred, but never in recorded history did St. Bernards need special training to do their work.

THE WINTER OF 76/77

It was a winter that brought snow to American cities that had never seen it before. All-time low temperatures were recorded in places across the country, from Miami Beach (32° Fahrenheit [0° C.]) to Cincinnati (−25° Fahrenheit [−4° C.]). Buffalo, New York, was buried under an accumulated 126.2 inches of snow.

Strange Contrasts

It was a winter that had ironic twists: in areas used to cold weather and blizzards, relatively mild skies kept Anchorage, Alaska, at 45° Fahrenheit (7° C.) and Rocky Mountain ski slopes dry, while citizens of southern states rushed to their windows to watch the first winter storms in memory. America had gone through what is sure to be remembered as a legendary winter.

Modern technology didn't ensure automatic services: fuel supplies and transportation systems were just about as endangered as they had been in the winter of 1888. But, as in other days, people used their ingenuity to cope with the deep freeze. Citrus growers in Florida placed night-heaters in their groves, hoping that the freezing temperatures in places like Ft. Lauderdale wouldn't wipe them out. Wise vacationers avoided traditional Florida resorts and headed for Arizona and California, while people forced to remain in their hometowns made do. Elderly women were spotted scattering kitty litter on their front steps when the stores sold out de-icers. A young man in Pennsylvania spent an eve-

THE ST. BERNARD

Until a great tunnel was cut through the Alps in relatively recent times, travelers had to make their way on foot over snow-clad mountain slopes, where they frequently lost their way or were overtaken by blizzards. The Augustinian friars of the famous Hospice of St. Bernard de Menthon took on the responsibility of rescuing these poor travelers, and have been doing so for more than 1,000 years. How long they've had the aid of their incredible St. Bernard dogs, no one knows.

ESP in Dogs?

St. Bernards have remarkable pathfinding abilities and a sense of smell that enables them to locate humans buried under snow. They're also reputed to have a sixth sense that warns them of approaching avalanches, and dogs have been known to move suddenly for no apparent reason from a spot that, moments later, was buried under tons of snow and ice.

Teamwork

There are records of thousands of lives saved by these loyal, courageous, intelligent animals. Running in packs of three or four, the dogs would make lone patrols during or after a storm in search of lost travelers. When they came upon a victim, two of the dogs would lie down in the snow on either side of him to warm him with their bodies, while a third would lick his face to restore consciousness. Meanwhile, the fourth dog would be on his way back to the monastery to get help.

WINTER OF 77

ning in the warmth of his local laundromat's king-size dryer.

Frozen Imagination
There were some who took it all calmly. North Dakotans long used to cold wore buttons proclaiming: Minus 40 Below Keeps The Riffraff Out. Police stood by while the robbers who held up the Cleveland Trust Co. frantically tried to escape in their getaway car, the spinning tires digging deeper and deeper into the snow.

With waterways frozen, schools and factories closed, and thermostats turned down, perhaps the comment of a Georgia mountaineer sums up best the winter we just passed through: "It is so cold, my imagination is frozen."

THE BLIZZARD OF 1888

There have been heavier snowfalls, stronger winds, and lower temperatures, but the blizzard that struck the Northeast on March 12, 1888, was to become a legendary combination of all three. The forecast was for "clouds, light rain, and a clearing." The light rain became a downpour, the downpour became a hurricane wind and a blinding snowstorm. The citizens of New York woke to an eerie sight: the wind was piling up snowdrifts along one side of the street, while the other side remained smooth and icy.

Workers made their way to offices and shops, not realizing what they were in for: clocks had stopped, telegraph wires had frozen and snapped, and New York Harbor was full of ships so blanketed in snow they resembled the work of a winter sculptor.

New York City Drama
New York City was hardest hit, but the blizzard fanned out to New Jersey, Pennsylvania, and parts of New England. It took trains six hours to go two blocks—the few commuters who arrived from outlying districts found Grand Central Station silent and empty.

Thirty members of the Wall Steet Exchange showed up to buy and sell, bankers automatically extended outstanding loans, and prisoners refused offers of freedom—they preferred the security of jail cells to waist-deep snowdrifts on the city streets. New York's great department stores had one or two custom-

ers apiece; their employees watched strange parades of citizens dressed in blankets, carpets, and rubber boots form single-file lines in attempts to cross the street.

All Work and No Play...
But enterprising merchants, barkeepers, and cabbies were raking in money for their respective services: shopowners sold out every piece of cold weather clothing in stock, cabbies doubled their fares, and saloons kept citizens fortified with hot rum and whiskey.

March 13 saw signs of a thaw: the temperature climbed from one degree below zero (−19°C.) to 23° Fahrenheit (−5°C.) by afternoon. Workers carted and shoveled snow, wire service was restored, trains began running. (The Mayor took the opportunity to press for underground trains for future travelers.) The Blizzard of 88 was over in four days. It left a path of destruction, a record of people helping each other survive, and the Blizzard Men, a group who met for years afterward, swapping stories and perpetuating the legend of that incredible winter.

A BLIZZARD IS ...

According to the National Weather Service, a snowstorm is officially designated a blizzard under the following circumstances: Winds are 35 mph or more, visibility is less than ¼ mile due to falling or blowing snow, and the temperature is 20° Fahrenheit (−7°C.) or less.

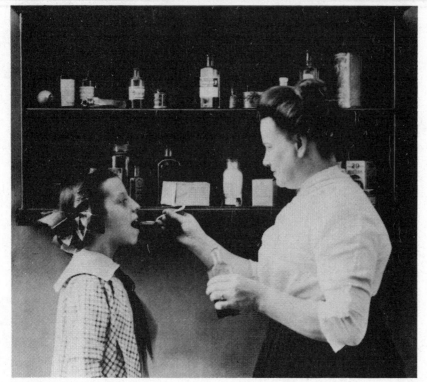

COLDS AND FLU

Perhaps the most difficult thing about having a cold is trying to drum up a little sympathy from those around you, and that's because the common cold is just that: common. At any given time, there are probably enough people suffering with the bug to populate an area the size of Michigan. If you find yourself similarly afflicted, there may not be much solace in the fact that it remains uncurable. However, chances are your best bet is home care and, if you're lucky, at least one understanding friend.

"Take Two Aspirin, Rest, and Drink Fluids"

This advice has become a cliché that seems to symbolize medical neglect and irresponsibility. In fact, however, this approach is probably the most reasonable and effective method of dealing with minor colds and flu. There is an abundance of cold remedies to choose from on the market, but most are expensive and relatively ineffective. Before rushing out and buying the contents of your local pharmacy, it is suggested that you try this simple regimen for the following reasons:

1. Aspirin will generally help relieve headaches, muscle aches, and soreness and will lower the fever of a cold or flu. The usual dosage is two aspirin every four hours, particularly in the afternoon and evening, when symptoms are most intolerable. If you find that aspirin upsets your stomach, try taking it with food or milk, or try one of the aspirin substitutes (Tylenol, Datril) on the market.

AMERICAN FOLK REMEDIES FOR COLDS AND FLU

The frequency of the common cold and the frustration in treating it have created a vast collection of old wives' tales and a variety of therapeutic maneuvers, ranging from the ridiculous (tying the skin of dead fish to your feet) to the sublime (drinking concoctions of tea, honey, and whiskey). These folk remedies may not cure your cold, but reading about them may make you somewhat more content to just lie in bed (blissfully removed from the odor of fish flesh).

An Organic Wardrobe

It was believed that strips of raw pork wound around the neck would induce perspiring (undoubtedly, it would) thereby relieving coughs. Another prescribed necklace was one of salted herring, supposedly in ensemble with your scaly slippers. To complete this organic wardrobe, you were to bind cabbage leaves across your chest (being sure to change them when they became transparent), wear one sock filled with black pepper, and one stuffed with split onions (bouillabaisse, anyone?).

Hearty Appetite!

To take internally, you had your choice of kerosene (with or without sugar) or one tablespoon of turpentine in a cup of melted lard. It is assumed that if your cold didn't improve, you could at least shine up your floors with your medicine. Watermelon was said to reduce fever and chills, and diced turnip roots were the rage for sore throat. Most likely the sore throat didn't seem too bad when the sufferer was faced with a pot of turnip roots.

Cure by Osmosis

It was also advised that a flat whiskey bottle filled with crushed rock candy, linseed oil, and whiskey be

COLEMAN'S "WINCARNIS"

2. Drinking plenty of liquids is particularly necessary if a fever is present as the body will require more fluids at that time. Fluids help to liquefy mucus, break up congestion, and will aid in preventing complications such as bronchitis and ear infections. Hot liquids—particularly heavily spiced chicken soup—are especially effective congestion relievers.

3. Rest is desirable simply because you'll feel better if you avoid the burdens of excessive or even normal activity. If you have a bad cold, you may not have a great deal of choice in the matter; sitting up to take your aspirin may prove to be all the exertion you can handle. In general, some reduction of your own level of activity is recommended—the reduction depending upon the severity of your cold and the type of activity you normally engage in. Boredom, frustration, and anxiety from too little activity are the risks involved in too much bed rest—use your own good judgment to arrive at a reasonable personal compromise.

4. If you have a painful sore throat, try gargling with warm salt water every three hours or so. This is the safest, cheapest treatment, and none of the lozenges, gargles, rinses, pills, or syrups you can buy are really very much better.

5. Maximum effectiveness in treating a stuffy nose can be obtained by using a simple nonprescription nasal spray. A note of caution, however: prolonged use of a nasal spray will diminish its effectiveness, and there might arise the tendency to rebound with more severe symptoms after each dose wears off.

6. For your sore, tender nose (suffering from too much rubbing or blowing) try using a simple petroleum-based ointment and a little gentleness.

7. Finally, try patience and fortitude. Your body will rid itself of the virus and repair the damage—if left to its own devices and if you are basically in good health. Most people will feel better in a week or two regardless of, or despite, what they do.

placed near the cold sufferer. It can only be hoped that these individuals devised some method of extracting the whiskey during their illness and were allowed to remain somewhat intoxicated throughout their ordeal.

In any event, cleaning up this paraphernalia was not difficult, as one was also required to strap bars of soap to the feet when down with the bug.

It is small wonder that Molière remarked, "Nearly all men die of their remedies, and not of their illnesses."

HOW NOT TO TREAT A COLD OR FLU

Colds are viral, and antibiotics such as penicillin do no good and may produce serious side effects.

As of this writing, it has not been proven that large doses of vitamin C either cure or prevent colds. (Advocates recommend 250 mg. daily as a preventive measure. This may be supplemented by 1,000 to 8,000 mg. over the course of the day at the first sign of a cold. Drinking plenty of citrus-fruit juices, which are high in vitamin C, will help keep up your fluid intake as well.)

If symptoms persist, or if you develop pain in your ears, or produce bloody- or rusty-looking sputum when coughing, it is no longer wise to treat yourself at home. Contact your physician.

God Bless You

The association between sneezes and demons is worldwide. The popular Christian custom of saying "God bless you" after someone sneezes has its origin within this association. This practice started during the sixth century, while an epidemic was raging throughout Italy. Pope Gregory the Great ordered that this special form of prayer or wish be instituted to ward off the evil demons of the pestilence who were making their presence known by the sneezing of their victims.

An ancient Persian prayed after sneezing believing a fiend to be departing from the body. In the *Sadda*, the sacred book of the Persians, the sneeze was supposed to be the sound of Satan's wings as he hovered overhead.

HERBAL TEAS FOR COLDS AND FLU

There is nothing quite as soothing to a cold-sufferer as a cup of delicious, hot, aromatic tea. Herbal teas, known as tisanes, have been used to treat minor ailments for hundreds of years, and are still prescribed widely in parts of Europe for a variety of medical complaints. In the U.S., where the tendency is to reach for a pill or spray at the first sniffle, these delightful tisanes are overlooked in favor of expensive, advertised cold-relief products. These products certainly don't cure the cold or flu, and often don't make you feel any better at all. A couple of aspirin, a warm blanket, a good book, and a mug of freshly brewed herbal tea will probably make you feel better than all of the capsules and potions available.

The Easy Way

For convenience, most herbal teas are available in tea bags or in loose form for use with a tea strainer. For the die-hard traditionalists, dried herbs are also available in their natural form. But be advised: working with stems, flowers, leaves, and roots may take more time and effort than you're willing to devote when you're coughing, sneezing, and wiping your sore nose.

The following list explains the function of several tisanes that are generally used for the treatment of colds and flu:

CHAMOMILE: A soothing tea for a sore throat, can be drunk hot after meals or used as a gargle at room temperature.

COLTSFOOT: Taken with meals, this tisane is an excellent source of vitamin C and also acts as an expectorant.

WIND-CHILL FACTOR

The temperature of the air is only one factor to be taken into consideration when deciding how best to dress for comfort and safety when venturing outdoors in winter. The velocity of the wind at any given moment plays a large part in how cold your body gets. In fact, wind affects temperature so greatly that men in Antarctica have been known to play ball outdoors in light clothing in zero temperatures on a calm day, but the slightest breeze would force them to run for the warmth of their shelters.

A formula was developed to compute the wind's effect on the rate of the body's heat loss. This loss of heat is caused by the wind replacing warm air around the body with cold air and is known as the wind-chill factor. The wind-chill factor may result in exposed flesh freezing at a temperature of +20° Fahrenheit (−6°C.), if the wind is over 50 mph. On a calm day (wind velocity less than ¼ mph), a temperature of −130° Fahrenheit (−90°C.) would be necessary to achieve the same effect.

One to One

The wind-chill factor, as given in your local weather report, is a

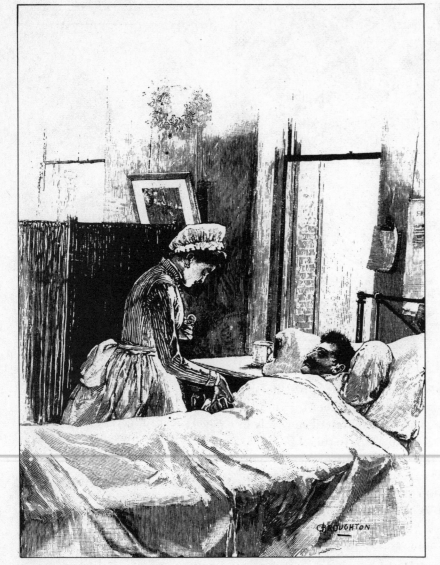

BROUGHTON

ELDER: This tea has a sedative effect (most herbal teas are caffeine-free), and a hot cup at bedtime will ease your aches and pains and reduce chills.

HYSSOP: Taken hot or cold, hyssop tea will calm your cough.

LIME: Add a dash of lemon, and enjoy this refreshing tea at bedtime. It is a mild expectorant and also helps ease chills.

ROSE HIPS: An excellent source of vitamin C, a hot cup of this fragrant brew is a favorite among tea lovers.

This partial list will introduce you to the pleasures of tea, certainly the most satisfying, comforting cold treatment around. One word to the novice herbal tea drinker: milk is a no-no, but lemon and/or honey will enhance the natural flavors enormously.

simplified version of these complex equations and is given in degrees. In milder temperatures with moderate wind speeds, the wind-chill factor can be computed as one degree of heat loss per one additional mph of wind. In other words, if the temperature is 0° Fahrenheit and the wind velocity is 10 mph, your body will lose heat at the same rate as it would on a calm day with a temperature of −10° Fahrenheit. This home computation method becomes more inaccurate at lower temperatures and higher wind speeds (−40° Fahrenheit + 35 mph = −113° Fahrenheit rather than −75° Fahrenheit).

Because of the unpredictability of wind gusts, it is always a good idea to dress slightly warmer than the temperature alone indicates, striking a balance between allowing body moisture to get out (perspiration increases the wind-chill factor by 10) and preventing the wind from getting in. As the song says, "Button Up Your Overcoat When The Wind Is Free..."

Nothing to Sneeze At

During the sixteenth century, it was customary to release patients from hospitals, and abandon treatment for those at home, as soon as the sufferer had sneezed three times. It was believed that complete recovery was then imminent. On the other hand, ancient Hebrew rabbis declared that, by God's law, every person sneezed but once — and having sneezed, died. Jacob, an ancestor of the Israelites, objected to this undignified and sudden farewell, and so he prayed that another gesture of final leave-taking be instituted. His prayers were answered, and Jacob became the first human being to sneeze and live to tell about it.

TOOLS FOR SNOW REMOVAL

Winter, unfortunately, is not all fun and games. While that first snowfall is admittedly a thing of beauty, it also represents a potentially back-straining job of removing the snow from walkways and driveways. The right tools can make this unpleasant task easier for home owners and shopkeepers who, for one reason or another, can't do the easiest thing—which is to hire someone else to do it.

Snow Shovels and Pushers

With the invention and increasing popularity of lightweight, low-cost snow throwers, the lowly snow shovel is fighting extinction. If, however, you are in reasonably good physical condition and snowfall in your area is light, you may not want to invest in even an inexpensive machine, since it will probably sit in storage most of the year. For small walks and driveways a snow shovel is still the most efficient method of snow removal, particularly if the snow accumulation is light.

Snow shovels or snow pushers (shovels that are deeply concave, made for pushing snow aside rather than lifting or throwing) can be made of either aluminum or steel. Aluminum shovels are adequate for most light jobs and add little weight to that of the snow. A good aluminum shovel should have a steel edge to add strength and to prevent the blade from curling. Ribbing increases the strength of the blade. For heavier removal operations, the all-steel models offer more strength and durability. Both aluminum and steel shovels should be coated with nonstick Teflon or

SHOVELING SNOW SAFELY AND EFFICIENTLY

If you have any doubts at all about the shape you are in, don't shovel. Overexertion in the snow can cause collapse, especially if you are middle-aged, overweight, or have a heart condition. You're better off hiring someone to do it or using power equipment. The main object is to remove snow and slush before they turn to ice, but if you think it's going to be too big a job for you, don't start shoveling.

Doing It Yourself

If you do decide to tackle the job with a hand shovel, use a relatively small one, and push or scoop the snow to the side rather than lift it. Do the work in stages, and take frequent rests. If the shovel is made of steel-edged aluminum, you can cover the blade with a thin coat of hot paraffin or paste floor wax. This keeps the snow from sticking to it and makes the removal job easier. Don't heat paraffin or other wax directly; use a double boiler if you have one, or heat the blade itself—if it's made of metal—and use the hot blade to melt the paraffin. In this way you can obtain a thin, even coating, which is preferred.

Remember not to push yourself too hard when you decide to shovel. If you've put in an hour or so and the temperature is dropping, don't hurry to finish the whole sidewalk. The American Medical Association can tell you how unwise that is.

It Snows

" It snows!!' cries the schoolboy,
'Hurrah!' and his shout
Is ringing through parlor and hall,
While swift as the wing of a swallow,
   he's out,
And his playmates have answered
   his call."
— *Sarah Josepha Hale (1790-1879)*

When Father Frost is nipping at your toes on a winter's morning, try this for a nourishing, thawing-out breakfast.

Comack

2 slices bacon
1 can condensed tomato soup
2 eggs
pepper (optional or to taste)

Cut the 2 slices of bacon into large dice, and fry in a skillet until medium crisp. Now toss in the can of condensed tomato soup. Let this come to a slow boil, and drop in the 2 eggs. Immediately stir them round and round into the soup. Continue stirring until the eggs are cooked and all is a thick amalgam. Add a touch of pepper, if you like, and put the Comack on a slice of bread or toast and eat with a fork. Unusual and satisfying. Serves one.

Did You Know . . .

. . . scientists believe that the perfect weather for work and health is 64° Fahrenheit (18°C.), with 65 percent humidity? It as also shown by an early twentieth-century study that human beings produce their greatest mental activity at 38° Fahrenheit (3°C.).

silicone so that wet snow will slide easily off the blade. A narrower, more deeply scooped shovel is best for drifts, heavier accumulations, and ice chips.

Snow Throwers or Blowers

For those with weak hearts or backs and no teen-age offspring to press into service, a powered snow thrower may be the answer. The size and type you buy should be determined largely by the amount of snowfall you expect and the type of terrain to be covered. Using a mechanical snow-removal device when a shovel would be adequate will result in far more work.

There are basically two types of snow thrower: single stage and two stage. Single-stage machines may come in lightweight and super-lightweight varieties but lack the throwing power of a two-stage machine. If your driveway is very wide, a two-stage machine may be necessary to avoid throwing snow back on the drive.

Lightweights and super lightweights: If the snowfall in your part of the country is light and you have a relatively small area to cover, you may want to consider one of the new lightweight or super-lightweight model snow throwers. Lightweight may sound like a misnomer for machines ranging from 95 to 195 pounds, but this is in comparison with the heavy-duty throwers which can weigh 300 pounds or more. The super lightweights may weigh as little as 23 pounds, making the shovel maneuverable enough to clear steps or dig out cars. Even large drifts can be tackled one layer at a time with these lightweights. These relatively inexpensive machines (180 to 280 dollars) require very little storage space. Shovel models

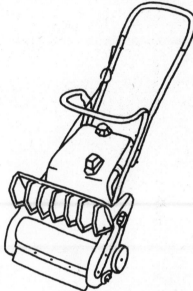

SAFETY PRECAUTIONS FOR SNOW THROWERS

can be hung on the wall, and some of the walk-behind models have folding handles for storage under shelves and other small spaces.

There are, however, some disadvantages to these lightweight snow throwers. The light weight is due to plastic parts, which can be easily damaged. Small wheels and light weight combine to limit traction, causing these machines to override packed snow. If you have major snow-removal chores every winter, you will probably need a heavier snow thrower.

Self-propelled machines: If your driveway is gravel or crushed rock, you will need a self-propelled machine. It should have more than one speed to help compensate for wind, snow depth, and terrain variations. You will also find reverse gear helpful in deep snow when it becomes necessary to pull the snow thrower back every few feet to clear the blades. Outfitting a self-propelled machine with chains will help prevent slippage when you are faced with large drifts or a layer of ice.

Chutes: The type of chute should not be overlooked when you are purchasing a thrower. The chute should be rotatable through 180° to compensate for wind direction and to direct the snow to the desired deposit area. It should have a vertical adjustment as well to determine the distance the snow will be thrown.

Whether you buy a heavy-duty or super-lightweight thrower, make sure that the spark plug, carburetor, and carburetor linkage are sufficiently shielded from the snow and ice. This will prevent stalling and damage.

These then are the tools of the trade. If they are unable to make snow removal a pleasure, they will at least take some of the drudgery out of this unpleasant winter chore.

Assuming you have a strong back and heart, there is little likelihood that you will hurt either yourself or anyone else with a snow shovel. A snow thrower, on the other hand, can be dangerous unless certain precautions are taken.

1. No one should ever stand in front of the chute while the motor is running. Loose stones, pieces of ice, and other debris may be picked up and ejected with tremendous force.

2. Do not try to clear jammed blades and chutes before shutting off the engine. As an added feature, some models have safety-grip handles that automatically shut off the motor if the operator leaves the controls while the blades are engaged.

3. Don't walk in front of a self-propelled machine while the motor is running even if the clutch is disengaged. The clutch can slip, causing the machine to lurch forward unexpectedly.

4. Never leave a running machine unattended.

5. Let the motor cool down before refilling the gas tank.

DE-ICING ROOFS AND PAVEMENTS

Roofs

You can spot snowy sidewalk or driveway problems at a glance, but melting snow on your roof, though not readily visible, may cause problems as well. An invisible "ice dam" can form along the roof's edge, causing water to back up under the shingles and leak into the house. When gutters become clogged with ice, accumulating water simply has no place to go but down — into your living room. Low-pitched roofs are more prone to this problem than steep ones, and roofs with little or no overhang are subject to greater interior leakage. But, if weather conditions are right, ice-clogged gutters can be a problem on any type roof.

The safest and most practical solution to this problem is to install electric heating cables as a preventative measure. These cables produce just enough heat to prevent ice from forming and can be turned off to conserve energy when not needed. Some are controlled by a thermostat that automatically turns the cable on when the temperature dips to 40° Fahrenheit (4°C.). These cables can be bought in lengths of 20 to 200 feet for 120-volt or 240-volt circuits.

The best time to install a heating cable is during warm weather, of course. However, if you didn't get around to buying one until after the

ICICLES

The freezing of dripping water causes one of winter's most beautiful phenomena, the icicle. Snow melting off a rooftop gives birth to rows of jagged, crystalline teeth along the eaves. The apparent paradox of snow melting and water freezing simultaneously is easily explained. Heat from the sun and the inside of the house melts the snow. The air temperature, however, remains below freezing, allowing icicles to form.

Weather Prophecies

Certain farmers examine their cornhusks in late summer and early fall for a weather forecast; the thicker the husk, the colder the winter.

freeze set in, unroll the cable fully on the ground and plug it in to allow it to warm up. This will make it more pliable and easier to install.

Installation of the cable requires special clips that are used to secure the cable in zigzag fashion along the lower edges of the roof. The clips are pushed under the shingles, and the shingles are then pressed down so that small spurs in the clips become embedded in the roof. For slate roofs, a thick roofing compound is used to fasten the cables. A set of instructions, which will explain installation steps fully, will come with your purchase of an electric heating cable.

Pavements

If someone slips on your property you may be sued. To get rid of ice (and prevent further ice build-up) on driveways and pavements, spread sand or gravel over the surfaces and then apply rock salt (sodium chloride). These old reliables are the safest effective way to keep your walkways clear. Although you may read advertisements for some wonder chemical that will remove all snow and ice, no matter how deep, most chemicals are best used by your local highway department for making roads easier to plow. When used on your sidewalk or steps, these chemicals may be effective in clearing snow and ice but may also cause damage to shrubs and lawns and even to the pavement itself (as with the use of ammonium nitrate or ammonium sulfate). In addition, these chemical products are very expensive to use over large surfaces.

Comparison shop and check the ingredients on various ice/snow removers. Common rock salt is often given a fancy name and sold at high prices, so know what you're paying for. Don't expect anything to magically erase winter from your home. Salt, sand, chemicals—all do their best in limited amounts on thin ice coatings. Overuse may ruin the ground underneath and create even more problems come springtime.

THE CELSIUS-CENTI-GRADE/FAHRENHEIT CONTROVERSY

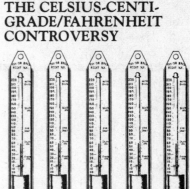

Whatever happened to good old Fahrenheit? One might say it was good enough for my grandfather, and it's good enough for me. But it's not so. The metric system of measurements is far more exact (that's why it is used in scientific studies), and the rest of the world has always used, or recently converted to, metrics. So get in step and learn how to think in Celsius (or Centigrade).

The name is beautifully logical. *Centi* means hundred in Latin. Between 0° and 100° there are 100 gradations—hence, centigrade. However, since 1948, the official designation has been Celsius, after Anders Celsius, who devised the system.

The formulae for conversion are:

$$C = \frac{(F-32) \times 5}{9} \qquad F = \frac{C \times 9}{5} + 32$$

Here's how it works. Say it's 77° F. Subtract 32 from 77. Multiply your answer, 45, by 5. Next divide that answer, 225, by 9. The temperature on the Celsius scale is 25.

TEMPERATURE CONVERSION TABLE

°C	°F	°C	°F
−30°	−22°	+10°	+50°
−20°	−4°	+20°	+68°
−10°	+14°	+30°	+86°
0°	+32°	+40°	+104°

...YOUR PIPES FREEZE

One day during an exceptionally cold December, a friend dropped by to avail himself of a neighbor's shower. It seems that the water had frozen in his pipes, and while trying to thaw them, he had succeeded in bursting one. The plumber was due, but in the meantime he was using his friend's plumbing. Before *you* lose any pipes or friends, you will want to follow a few steps for preventing and thawing frozen pipes.

Prevention

1. When building a house, check with **your** local weather bureau about the frost line in your area. The depth of underground pipes will depend on soil composition (sand, clay, loam) and the level of the frost line.

2. When installing new pipe, make sure it runs closer to the inside wall of the house than the outside wall. Even pipes well insulated with fiberglass must be as close as possible to a heat source, or they will freeze.

3. If freezing weather is expected, shut off the water supply to outside faucets, and turn on the taps to drain them of excess water.

4. If the pipes are close to a power source, wrap specific trouble spots in electrical tape or cable. This tape may come with an automatic thermostat that switches on below 35° Fahrenheit (1° C.).

5. Apartment dwellers may find that leaving their taps running just a trickle at night will ensure water in the morning. If you don't own your own home, the only other preventive measure would appear to be mailing a copy of these hints to your landlord or building superintendant.

Cure

Even if you have followed all these instructions to the letter, you may awaken one morning, turn on your faucet, and get—nothing. Don't panic. Before you put your house up for sale, try these relatively simple

Nothing to Sneeze At

In the West Indies, it is believed that if you sneeze, it means that someone is saying nasty things about you. (Of course, if you sneeze all over someone, this would be entirely logical.)

In rural areas of the American South, it is thought that if you sneeze while eating, you will hear of a death. (If you sneeze your meal all over your dining companions, the death may be your own.)

In Germany, it is considered unlucky to sneeze while putting on your shoes (well, you could fall over while balancing on one foot), but sneezing during an argument lends veracity to your position.

In Estonia, it is believed that if two pregnant women sneeze together, their offspring will be female; if their husbands sneeze in unison, the offspring will be male. What happens if the husband of one and the wife of the other sneeze in concert is anyone's guess.

methods of thawing your pipes. Heat is the key word, and there are many ways of applying heat, but caution must be exercised to avoid ending up with burst pipes.

1. Open the tap so that water and steam may escape as you melt the ice. Always start heating at the tap and work back toward the source. Starting in the middle will cause steam, prevented from expanding because of ice on both ends, to burst the pipe.

2. If there is another water source available, the cheapest, easiest method involves hot water and any material that will hold heat (thick towels, burlap bags, sand, bricks, or a combination). Wrap or surround the pipe with the material and pour on hot water, once again starting at the tap and working toward the source. Use a pot or pan to catch the excess water.

3. A propane torch is quick and especially useful if no water is running. It is less messy than hot water but one must be careful to avoid setting fire to the house. This may be avoided by placing a piece of asbestos behind the area being torched. Keep the flame moving quickly, especially over soldered or welded joints. Protective glasses should be worn.

4. If water backs up from a frozen drainpipe, hot water down the drain should do the trick. Should you need to get closer to the ice blockage, insert a garden hose into the pipe until it hits solid ice and feed in hot water with a funnel. Until the ice melts, the hot water will back up toward you; so be careful—you don't want to scald yourself.

5. If an outlet is handy, heat lamps, hair driers, and electric irons offer slow but effective ways of thawing troublesome plumbing. Also it is not too late to wrap pipes with heating cable as a curative measure.

If everything that you try fails, there is nothing left but to call the plumber—who will come and collect an enormous fee for thawing your pipes with one of our methods you forgot to try. Until then, you may still be lucky enough to use a neighbor's shower.

METHODS OF PREDICTING WEATHER FROM AMERICAN FOLKLORE

If many rural Americans are right, it may not be necessary to listen to the radio, watch television, or read newspapers to find out about coming weather conditions. Forecasting weather may be as simple as learning to read the signs that nature provides. Here is a list of natural weather forecasts which may help you anticipate winter weather:

If the smoke from your chimney sinks to the ground, there will be a heavy snowfall within 30 days, and the winter will be severe throughout.

If your outdoor fire snaps and pops, expect a snowstorm within three days.

The number of days old that the moon is on the night of the first snowfall of winter is the number of snowy days to expect.

The later the first frost, the harder the winter will be.

There will be a snowy day in winter for every foggy one during the month of August.

An overabundance of thunderstorms during late autumn means a harsh winter is on the way.

If the snow on the ground doesn't melt in three days, a new snow will cover it.

A long, hot summer warns you of a long, bitter winter to come.

Old Winter
"Let him push at the door,
in the chimney roar,
And rattle the window-pane;
Let him in at us spy with his
icicle eye,
But he shall not entrance gain."
— *Thomas Noel (1799-1861)*

THE COLD IS BRUTAL ENOUGH TO CAUSE FROSTBITE

Frostbite does not only affect those who spend the winter in the great outdoors. Even if you never leave the city, a walk to the store or a long wait at a bus stop in high winds and freezing temperatures can expose you to the risks of frostbite.

What Frostbite Is

When insufficiently protected skin areas (particularly extremities—toes, fingers, ears, or the tip of your nose) come into contact with high winds and winter cold, the tissues in the skin can become frozen. As circulation decreases you'll feel a stiffening, numbness, or stinging sensation in the affected part. This is the first stage of frostbite—when crystals of ice are forming between the body's cells. As the condition advances, the frostbitten area will change in color—from pink (in the initial stages) to white, which indicates a more serious phase. Blistering of the skin may also occur as the tissues harden.

Preventive Measures

Checking on weather conditions and dressing appropriately are crucial steps toward avoiding the risk of frostbite. Wearing a well-insulated outer garment, mittens, wool socks, and cap will greatly reduce the chance of frostbite occurring. If your hands become particularly cold, hold them against your body for heat. Exercise fingers and toes by wriggling them around to generate a little warmth.

It is hard to avoid all the holiday parties (and cups of Christmas cheer that go along with them), but be advised: alcohol and cold weather do not mix. Alcohol contributes significantly to the risk of developing frostbite because it hampers circulation and can make your body insensitive to the degree of cold. If you've overindulged in holiday spirits, you may be completely unaware of developing frostbite symptoms. Drinking hot coffee, tea, or cocoa would be a wiser choice. If your precautions haven't worked, and frostbite does set in—what do you do?

Treatment

No matter what you've heard, do *not* rub snow into frostbitten skin: this only increases the danger of breaking the skin and destroying tissue. As soon as you can, get indoors, cover the frozen area with woolen material, and have a warm drink. Do not massage the area; it requires gentle treatment. You should immerse the affected skin in water that has been heated to about body temperature. Don't overdo the heat treatment by exposing the skin to a roaring fire or hot stove—this amount of heat can damage the skin.

Gently exercise the area as it returns to normal feeling and color. If, for some reason, you must go outside again, a large sterile dressing over the area should help protect it. If frostbite persists, call a physician.

...THE ICE IS THINNER THAN YOU SUSPECTED

While ice fishing, ice-skating, or ice boating, one must keep in mind that under the ice is water—*very cold* water. If you or someone near you should miscalculate the thickness of the ice, it could result in an instant and unwanted membership in the Polar Bear Club.

Ice is thinnest and should be avoided at the bend of a river, near a dam in a pond, or any place where the current runs rapidly. If at any time the ice should bend beneath you, immediately lay flat and spread-eagled. This distributes your weight so that you can wriggle on your stomach like a snake to thicker ice or solid ground.

What to Take with You

It is an excellent idea to carry a pair of awls or ice picks if you are going to be on an ice-covered body of water. In the event that you should fall through, kick your legs to raise your body to the surface level, and use your picks as claws to pull yourself out of the water and on to stronger footing. If someone else falls through, throw him a rope, making sure you stay as far away from the opening as possible. A long branch or a ladder may be used, or if none is available, form a chain of bodies. No matter what method you use, always remain flat for maximum traction and weight distribution.

Once out of the water, the person should be taken indoors, dried and warmed by being placed near a heat source or placed in a tub of *warm* (not hot) water as quickly as possible. If the time of exposure is longer than a few minutes, be sure to check for symptoms of frostbite.

"Love, and a cough, cannot be hid."
— *George Herbert (1593-1632)*

COLD WEATHER
The CATALOG

PART II. WARM AS TOAST

Candlelight. A roaring fire. Trimming the tree. Holiday feasts. The warmth of a quilt. The heat of a sauna. The rewards of indoor gardening. Sachet, potpourri. And what exactly <u>is</u> a three-dog night?

PAUL BUNYAN, MOVE OVER...

So you've decided to forego the convenience of purchasing your firewood from a dealer. Before you sling a double-edged axe over your shoulder and head out for the wood, read on. Without the proper knowledge and equipment, chopping your own firewood can prove to be exhausting, time-consuming, and dangerous.

When to Get Started
Although the act of chopping wood will warm you up tremendously, doing so during the winter when it's icy and bitterly cold will make the job

"Wood heats you twice; once when you cut it, and once again when you burn it."

—H.D. Thoreau

Weather Prophecies
When chipmunks carry their tails high in September, it's an indication of a cold winter ahead.

WEATHER PROPHECIES FROM AMERICAN FOLKLORE

Many animals are reputed to have some sort of sixth sense that enables them to anticipate coming weather conditions. Rural Americans have often relied upon their furry and feathery neighbors to indicate the approach of severe winter weather. We can't vouch for the accuracy of these methods, but there are those who swear by them. We'll leave it up to you.

A severe winter is approaching if:

Crows gather in trees and other birds group together on the ground.

Squirrels start to gather their winter store of nuts in September, and their tails grow very bushy by October.

A screech owl's hoot sounds like a woman weeping.

Rabbits grow thick fur around their feet.

Even insects can predict the approach of a bad winter. You'll know severe weather is on the way if:

Hornets build their nests close to the ground.

Anthills are taller than usual.

You find a worm in your home in October.

Butterflies swarm together in midair.

The woolly worm has a black head.

Crickets nest in your chimney.

You notice a great number of spiders and black bugs during the autumn.

more difficult. Late autumn, when the weather is crisp and exhilarating, is a better time, and there is the added advantage of not having to trim off leaves; Mother Nature has already done that work for you. If you really enjoy working up a sweat, try chopping wood during the summer. If you fell a tree or two during the hot summer months, you can let the leaves remain intact for a few weeks — they will absorb some of the tree's moisture, thereby reducing the seasoning (drying) time necessary before the wood can be burned. No matter what season you decide on, remember that the wood will have to be stacked for drying for some time to come.

Tools

Using a chain saw is the most efficient (and noisiest) method of felling trees. A 12-inch-class model is adequate for nearly any job you might tackle and is less expensive and far easier to handle than the large models. Whichever model you choose, make sure that you are thoroughly familiar with its operation and always keep the chain saw in tip-top condition. Keep the blade sharp, the parts lubricated, and *your mind on the job!*

A curved bow saw is an inexpensive tool and is just dandy for two people who want to develop their muscles. Each person, on opposite sides of the tree, takes turns pulling the saw toward him. Doing the sawing this way, rather than both persons pulling and pushing the saw, cuts the effort in half.

A hatchet can be used to remove twigs and small branches from the felled tree, but this tool must be used with extreme care. The sharp blade head may slip or ricochet from the force of a blow — the possible danger of this does not have to be explained. It is not recommended that you use an axe to chop down a tree. The possibilities of injury are simply too great for the inexperienced woodsman

How to Bring the Tree Down

Check the lay of the land before you make your first cut. If the forest is fairly dense, you had better clear a fall path or you'll have to hire a crane to get your tree untangled. It is extremely difficult for the inexperienced to determine exactly which way a tree will fall. The best advice is to keep your eyes open, and make sure that there is plenty of room on all sides for you to get out of the way. Once your area is cleared, you're ready to begin. Make your first cut on the side you want the tree to fall on. Continue this cut straight into the tree trunk about one third of the way through. Then, cut from above this at a downward angle until the two cuts meet. Remove this wood wedge, and move to the other side of the tree. Start cutting here

at the same level as the bottom of the previous wedge. The weight of the tree will shift its center of gravity towards the wedge side (hopefully), causing the tree to fall in the intended direction. Once again, it is important to state that the direction of the fall cannot be predicted with 100 percent accuracy—be alert to the first signs of the fall. In addition, as the tree falls, the trunk, at the point which you've cut through, may jump up and back. Move well out of the way to avoid getting knocked in the head or chest.

Cutting the Tree into Logs

You may choose to cut logs (this is called bucking) for firewood right where the tree falls, or you may decide to cut the tree into transportable chunks and do this work at home. This, obviously, depends on what kind of transportation you have. In either event, the first step in bucking the tree into fireplace or woodstove logs is to remove all of the small branches and limbs. If possible, keep the tree on flat ground or brace it from beneath to prevent it from sagging as you saw (thereby pinching the blade and making everything more difficult). Determine the length of the logs you want, and then measure them off down the trunk, marking the sections off with a light hatchet blow or chain-saw nick. Then, just start at one end and go!

Splitting the Logs

Setting the logs on a hard flat surface will facilitate matters tremendously. Soft ground will diminish the force of the blow, making you work harder for the same results. Once you get the knack of log splitting, you'll be able to handle most jobs with a single try. Use a strong, overhead swing to the center of the log when you're using an axe. If you decide to use a steel wedge and a sledgehammer, less force is necessary. Tap the wedge into the center of the log and hit the wedge itself with the hammer. If you really want to take it easy, use your chain saw. Whatever method you decide to use, set up a system and pace, which keeps exertion to a minimum and establishes a smooth rhythm.

Stacking the Firewood

The point of stacking your firewood is to allow it to air dry for burning; so don't defeat the whole purpose by stacking it in an unsheltered area. Keep the bottom layer of logs off the ground (they will rot and be unburnable otherwise) by devising some sort of platform that allows air to circulate. The exact pattern you use to stack your wood is really a matter of choice, but keep in mind that the more air that reaches the logs, the better the seasoning process will be.

All of this may sound like an overwhelming amount of hard work, and indeed, chopping wood requires a fair amount of labor. However, when the woodshed is filled, when the flames are dancing in the fireplace, when the woodstove is warming the kitchen, you can sit back and say, "I did it!" And that makes it all worthwhile.

Café Diable
2 cups hot strong black coffee
1 cup cognac
6 cubes sugar
6 whole cloves
peel of 1 orange (no white pith)
peel of 1 lemon (no white pith)

Use a chafing dish or warmed silver bowl. Put in the cognac, peel, and cloves. Warm a ladle and dip up a few tbsps. cognac. Put in a couple of lumps of sugar. Ignite the mix and ladle it into the chafing dish or bowl. Add the rest of the sugar as you dip up and down with a folding motion. Gradually add the hot black coffee while you fold and spoon the mixture until the flames die down. Serve in demitasse cups. Serves about six.

41

FIREWOOD

Using a fireplace for supplementary heating in your home makes a great deal of sense. When you burn wood, you are using a renewable resource — new trees can be planted, assuring a plentiful supply for coming generations. In many instances, using wood as fuel actually helps the local environment by reducing the accumulation of dead trees.

You may find that you can obtain firewood from local dumps and landfills, since many areas no longer permit open burning of scrap lumber. Industrial sources, such as sawmills, paper, and power companies may be only too happy to provide you with slabs of wood for a very small charge.

In addition, several state parks and forests will allow you to cut your own wood from designated areas. To find out if such a service is available to you, write to your state forester at the state capital. And remember, you can always trim branches from trees on your own property, being careful to allow healthy limbs to thrive.

Of course, it may be necessary to buy your firewood commercially. Firewood is sold by the cord, a stack measuring 4 feet by 4 feet by 8 feet. You should expect to pay anywhere from $30 to $90 per cord, depending upon the type of wood you order. Naturally, how many cords of firewood you should purchase for the season depends upon your specific needs. See how far one cord goes, and make future decisions accordingly.

Types of Wood

The next question is what kind of wood to buy. Once again, this depends upon your needs. Softwoods, such as spruce, fir, and pine, are very easy to ignite and will burn quickly with a very hot flame. This very

GET YOUR AX TOGETHER
Be Sharp
A sharp ax will make chopping wood easier and safer. Working from the face to the blade, file one side until it shines brightly, then turn the ax over and repeat. Now, using a grit stone, hone the bit from toe to heel (heel to toe on the flip side).

Proper Handling
The handle should fit tightly into the head. A wooden wedge will help, but should the wood dry out, it will shrink and loosen. Linseed oil will swell it again, or in a pinch, soaking it in water will accomplish the same thing.

Keep Covered
Make sure that your ax is always masked (the sharp edge covered) when not in use. A leather sheath is best for carrying. If you are taking a break while chopping wood, bury the edge in a log (never in a live tree).

❄✳❇❄❉❄✳ ❄❄✳ ❍❄

Snowflakes
"Whenever a snowflake leaves the sky,
It turns and turns to say 'Goodbye!
Goodbye, dear clouds so cool and gray'
Then lightly travels on its way."
—Mary Mapes Dodge (1838-1905)

speed of burning may make softwoods a less desirable choice than other types. Such a fire will need almost constant attention and replenishment. If, however, you want to be able to produce a quick warm-up fire to take the chill off the evening, or until the old furnace gets cranked up, softwoods may be ideal for you.

The hardwood species, such as oak, ash, or maple, burn more slowly than softwoods; the flame is less vigorous, but more constant. The best firewood for all-around heating purposes is a combination of the two. If you are ordering from a dealer, make sure that he can provide you with a mixture of woods, as requested, in a variety of log diameters.

It is extremely important to efficiency and economy that the wood you burn is dry. You can improve the heat given off by a log by as much as 45 percent simply by allowing it to air dry before burning it. If you are cutting your own wood, start chopping a few seasons early to assure plenty of ready fuel when needed. Ideally, wood should be allowed to air dry through the summer to ensure optimum burning efficiency.

Knowing the BTUs (British Thermal Units) of various woods will give you an indication of their heat-producing qualities. BTU is a measure of heat energy, and, naturally, the higher the BTU content, the more heating power in the wood.

Wood	BTUs Per Cord	Expect to Pay (Approx.)
White Oak	22,700,000	$60-$70 per cord
Beech	21,800,000	$60-$70 per cord
Hickory	24,600,000	$65-$80 per cord
Sugar Maple	21,300,000	$55-$65 per cord
Red Maple	18,600,000	$45-$55 per cord
Elm	17,200,000	$45-$55 per cord
Yellow Pine	18,500,000	$45-$55 per cord
White Pine	13,300,000	$40-$50 per cord

This is a very limited list, merely meant as a guide. There are hundreds of available woods to chose from, and you should realize that firewood prices, like anything else, are unpredictable.

For an aromatic fire, try using fruit-tree wood added to your supply of firewood. Generally, wood smoke's scent resembles the fragrance of the tree's fruit. Apple, pear, and black cherry wood all have beautiful aromas (apple wood is probably the best fuel of the three). Hickory and pecan have lovely aromas, and both burn quite well.

WEATHER PROPHECIES

American folklore tells us to check the forest and our own gardens for these signs of a harsh winter to come:

Trees have an abundance of green leaves in late autumn.

Grass is particularly dark green and lush during the summer.

Heavy moss abounds on trees.

Onions develop more layers than usual.

Carrots are deeper orange than normal.

Trees grow more acorns, berries, and pine cones than usual.

Bark on trees is thicker than normal and is particularly thick on the north side of the tree.

Leaves drop off the trees while still green.

Keep your eyes open for opportunities to get free firewood. If a building goes up in your neighborhood, chances are that trees are coming down. A heavy storm may leave an ample supply of kindling and logs on the ground—an entire tree may have fallen across the roadway. Beg or borrow a chain saw and get out there—quick. No matter how you go about developing your woodpile, you'll still find that using wood for fuel can constitute a healthy savings in the long run.

ONCE YOU'VE GOT YOUR WOOD . . .

There is nothing more discouraging than a fireplace flame that simply refuses to stay lit. Nobody likes to sit around the hearth staring at thin wisps of gray smoke and a few live cinders. The following tips should help you build and maintain a roaring fire:

1. To burn correctly, firewood must be dry. To be sure of this, strike the log with a hammer before burning; if moisture appears, it's still too wet.

2. The fireplace floor should have at least an inch of ashes for insulation, to catch embers, and to keep the heat near the logs. Setting the logs on a grate will allow air to circulate beneath the logs.

3. To lay a fire, put a generous amount of crumpled newspaper on the hearth; then arrange a crisscross pile of kindling over the paper. Dried bark, twigs, or pieces of split shingle work fine as kindling. It is better to lay down more than enough kindling than to have your fire go out. (You will have to empty the fireplace and start again.)

4. Put your major logs in next, positioning the longest and thickest log across the rear. Do not position this log directly against the back of the

GAMES AROUND THE FIREPLACE

Whatever your feeling about family togetherness, it tends to be a greater fact of life during the winter months. Short days and inclement weather conspire to keep adults and children indoors together for long periods of time, and nerves may be worn to a frazzle. The following games may prove to be just the thing to establish harmony in the family. (A fireplace is nice but not essential.)

Mystery Person
Parent or child thinks of a well-known character and gives clues in the form of questions. For instance, parent thinks of LBJ and asks, "Who lifted his dog by the ears?" Or a child thinks of Goldilocks and asks, "What housebreaker also ate and slept in the house?" One purpose of playing these games is to wean children away from the tube, although parents may find that television provides the only common ground with their progeny, as in "What wife called her husband Sonny?" (Cher.)

Awry
More active children will enjoy this game. Two teams are chosen. One team leaves the room while the other team busies itself exchanging articles of clothing, resetting clocks, and turning pictures upside down. After an agreed-upon period of time, the first team returns to the room and attempts to determine what is "awry." Points are awarded for each item they discover and subtracted for the ones they miss. In addition to providing controlled activity for restless, shut-in family members, this game will increase powers of observation. Be sure to closely supervise the younger participants so that the emphasis is on rearrangement, rather than destruction.

Rhyming Words
One person says, "I'm thinking of a

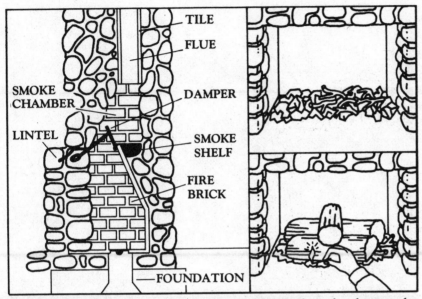

fireplace; at least ½ inch of air space is necessary. In fact, the closer to the front of the fireplace you lay the logs, the more heat will enter the room. Place a split log, flat side down, in front of the first log, and a third log across the two, forming a pyramid. Setting the logs on a grate will allow air to circulate beneath the logs.

5. When the fireplace is not in use, the damper should be closed to prevent your home's heat from escaping up the chimney. However, before lighting a fire, make sure that the damper is open to allow smoke to escape. Once the fire is going, adjust the damper as necessary so that the maximum amount of warmth and the minimum amount of smoke will enter the room.

6. To keep the fire burning brightly, make sure that there is plenty of air supplied. If you've sealed your house for the winter, it may be necessary to open a window a few inches to keep the air circulating. If possible, open a window located opposite the fireplace rather than off to one side (opening a side window can create a smoky cross draft).

There are a great many fireplace accessories on the market, many of which you can do without—unless, of course you feel that you just cannot live without a chartreuse flame and a screen that depicts the major battles of the Civil War. Some sort of screen *is* necessary; cleanup will be easier, and even more important, a fully closed screen will prevent live cinders from floating out onto rugs and furniture. Grates (as previously mentioned) and andirons will perform the important function of allowing air to circulate among the logs, thus helping to keep the fire blazing.

If you're ready for the fire to stop before *it* is, use your fireplace tongs to stand any unburned logs on end in the rear corners of the firebox. The logs will burn out quickly. Make sure that you keep the damper open and the screen fully closed as long as there is anything burning.

word that rhymes with came." Participants must then think of words that rhyme with came and give their definition in the form of a question, as in "Does everybody have at least two?" "No, it's not a name." "Is it what we're playing?" "Yes, it's a game." The rules are flexible from this point on—you may want to award demerits if the person thinking of the original word is stumped.

Think Tink
If your family enjoys rhymes and puns, this is your game. Players give definitions such as a fat fish. The response must be two "rhyming" words—stout trout. Clever insects are wise flies. Depending on the age and sophistication of the players, think tink can go on to two communists sleep in a...red bed, or an award to a cabby is a hack plaque. Experts go on to two-syllable words. If everyone is a certified genius, try three-syllable words.

Once the children are safely tucked away in their beds, the grown-ups may want to graduate to drinking games such as:

Bump
Players are all served the drink of their choice and sit in a circle. A number from one to nine inclusive is chosen. This number and all its multiples become the "bump" numbers (i.e. if the number is 7; 7, 14, 21, 28, 35, become the bump numbers). Players count off around the circle calling out "bump" every time their number is a bump number. A player who calls out a bump number instead of bump must down his or her drink. Make sure that the bump number is not the same as, or a multiple of, the number of people in the circle, or the same person will always say bump! A variation involves one person pointing to each player in the circle consecutively while the rest count off silently, only speaking if their number is the bump number. Play continues until bedtime.

BUILD-YOUR-OWN-FIREPLACE KITS

Those of you who thought that having your own fireplace was an idle dream have cause to rejoice. Until recently, having a fireplace meant locating a mason to construct the stone hearth, and paying for this service was generally no mean feat. Because of new mobility in design, the construction and architecture of the dwelling no longer determine the feasibility of installing a fireplace. Preassembled fireplace kits are now available, and what they may lack in picturesque authenticity, they more than make up for in economy, efficiency, and aesthetic value.

Fireplace units come complete with firebox, chimney, flue, and damper and require neither masonry

walls nor a special supporting foundation. Installation is reasonably simple for the skilled handyman or woman. Styles are virtually limitless, ranging from do-it-yourself, built-in models (which can mimic the traditional masonry fireplace), to free-standing styles, to designs that can be suspended from the ceiling or hung on the wall. Sizes are varied so that you can put a fireplace

in just about any room you wish. Most models range in price from $250 to $500 (not including whatever installation costs come up); you have only to compare these prices with those of a custom masonry job to see how reasonable the kits are. It may be necessary to hire a carpenter to help with the initial framing for a built-in model, but the completed cost will still be far below the traditional variety.

Most built-in units have multi-wall construction so no special insulation is required, and they can be

inserted into walls made of wood, plaster, or other combustible materials. Before work begins, check that dimensions fulfill requirements of local building codes and whether or not a building permit is necessary.

Despite the undeniable charm of a crackling wood fire, limited wood supply or your own choice may make it wiser for you to investigate the gas or electric units available. Gas fireplaces have many safety features that will prevent any leakage and some even come equipped with thermostatic controls. The only thing necessary to install an electric fireplace is an electrical outlet to plug it into; it is therefore extremely mobile and inexpensive.

WARM YOUR FEET

Sometimes cold feet come from over-action of the brain. In such cases use the brain less and the feet more. Many persons suffer from cold feet simply from a neglect to keep them clean. Warmth may be brought by washing and rubbing the feet in warm water every day. After the skin has become soft, a good washing with warm water twice a week during cold weather will greatly contribute to a healthful condition of the feet as well as to the personal comfort. Warm stockings or shoes that compress the feet and render the separate action of each toe impossible will not keep the feet warm.

—From Scammel's 1891 *Treasure House of Universal Knowledge*

WOOD-BURNING STOVES

Not long ago, the wood-burning stove was thought of as a rusty antique used by never-say-die romantics who lived out the winter in the back hills. However, the fact is that if you have a good, solid wood burner, you not only have an unusually attractive stove to warm yourself by on a chilly winter's evening, you also have an efficient way to help heat your home.

Caveat Emptor!

Let the buyer beware! The recent nostalgia craze and the clamor for energy-saving devices have combined to make the wood stove a practical reality for many Americans. Unfortunately, this has also resulted in many unethical dealerships. Know what you're looking for when you go shopping, or you might end up with a huge hunk of metal that produces neither

Stewing Dried Apples or Peaches

When the animals are bedded down for the winter, and the fresh fruit is scarce, dried fruit makes a most satisfying dish—herewith a recipe.

Wash fruit in two or three waters, and put them to soak in rather more water than will cover them, as they absorb a great deal. After soaking two hours, put them into a preserving kettle in the same water, and with a lemon or orange cut up; boil them till very tender; when they rise up in the kettle press them down with a skimmer or spoon, but do not stir them. When they are tender, add clean brown sugar, and boil fifteen or twenty minutes longer. Dried apples are rendered tasteless by being strained or stirred so as to break them up; and they are also injured by soaking over night. If they are to be used for pies, there should be more sugar added than for sauce, and a small piece of butter stirred in while they are hot. Nutmeg and clove are good spices for dried apple pies. Dried peaches are done in the same way, only the lemon and spices are omitted.

—*The Young Housekeeper's Friend*
(1859)

warmth nor romance. It takes time to learn the difference between acceptable and unacceptable products, and a wood-burning stove may be a little too complex an apparatus for you to purchase without assistance. You may be lucky enough to know someone who is "into" wood-burning stoves who can help you out. But if you cannot find anyone to assist, and you really don't know anything about the subject, be sure to buy your stove from a reputable dealer who allows you to test the stove before you buy it, answers your questions in detail, and is willing to install it for you.

Some Tips to Keep in Mind

1. Steer clear of stoves made of sheetmetal. At best they are inefficient; at worst, they are downright dangerous. Sheetmetal can be heated to red-hot, creating a fire hazard for nearby walls and floor. In addition, the repeated opening and closing of the stove door may cause this metal to weaken, resulting in leaks, which waste the heat you are trying to preserve. Hold out for a steel-plated or cast-iron model. Either kind will heat more evenly, last longer, and smoke less than a sheetmetal stove.

2. Make sure the firebox is tightly fitted and has an adjustable damper to allow wood to burn slowly.

3. Check to make sure that the body of the stove is a *solid* mass of metal. This enables the stove to absorb heat and radiate it back into the room.

Checking out these features will help you avoid a complete disaster.

Sauerbraten
When the weatherman says, "It looks like a long siege of snow and cold," prepare this European dish and settle in for a warming sojourn.

1 four-pound eye-of-the-round pot roast
1 pint red wine
1 cup sliced onion
2 carrots
1 bay leaf
10 peppercorns
1½ tbsps. salt
6 whole cloves
2 tbsps. sugar
5 gingersnaps
½ cup sour cream

Sprinkle the meat with the salt and put into a large bowl. Pour over the meat the red wine, and add the onion, carrots, bay leaf, peppercorns, cloves, and sugar. Boiling water to cover is added, and the entire pot is covered and allowed to stand four days. Turn twice a day. Keep in the refrigerator. At the end of the alloted time, remove the meat from the marinade and dry thoroughly. Sauté meat in a Dutch oven until browned all over. Add the marinade and vegetables to the meat. Don't let the liquid come more than halfway up the meat. Cover and simmer until meat is fork tender. Add more liquid as the meat cooks. It will take 2 to 3 hours.

Remove meat from liquid and prepare gravy. Mash up the gingersnaps very fine, and mix with the sour cream. Stir into the liquid from the meat and serve with potato dumplings.

Irish Tea

Irish whiskey
Irish tea
honey or jam
lemon

Add a shot of whiskey to a cup of tea. Sweeten to taste with jam or honey. Top with a slice of lemon.

However, nearly any wood-burning stove is going to require repair work. Some problems can be easily corrected at home, while others will leave you with an ice-cold conversation piece.

Look for these Features When You Shop:

CRACKS IN THE FIREBOX: Small cracks can be repaired by welding and thin fissures sealed by stove cement, but any crack which is large enough to be obvious will allow excessive amounts of smoke to escape into your home. This is not only messy but can be quite dangerous. Don't fall for that beautifully shiny, chrome-plated stove; chrome can hide a lot of cracks.

RUST, ESPECIALLY ON CAST IRON: Stove polish can take care of small rusty patches, but only a foundry can repair massive corrosion; having this done can easily double your initial investment. Use a flashlight to examine the surface of the stove; if pinpoints of light are visible in abundance, keep shopping.

SEAMS: They should be smooth and even. Spot welding indicates trouble spots and any stove that has been so repaired should be avoided.

DOORS AND TOPS: You must have a well-fitted stove. Any gap that exceeds ⅛ inch is out of the question, unless you are prepared to melt down and refit warped parts.

Because the law of supply and demand is not working in your favor, you may find that by the first snowfall, there is not a good wood-burning stove to be had for love or money. It is a good idea to start checking local dealers as early as summer—prices are likely to be lower as well.

OPEN-FIRE COOKING

Although other people may use gas or electricity, scout troups and summer campers have never stopped cooking with fire. But if you can hold a long-handled fork, or even a sharpened green stick loaded with franks or marshmallows, you, too, have mastered the principles of the first 90,000 years of cooking history. Though par for the course, outdoor campfires, bugs, trips to the bushes, and scary stories are all unnecessary equipment for open-fire cooking. Any fireplace can be your stove.

Different Methods for Different Fireplaces

There are four kinds of fireplace cooking: (1) food is skewered, or held on long-handled heavy wire utensils and cooked in or just on top of the flames; (2) food is buried in the hot ashes or embers at the sides of the fireplace; (3) food is put in pots and cooked above glowing coals, embers, or flames; (4) food is arranged on the hearth in pots, on gridirons or griddles, and cooked in the reflected and/or radiated heat of the fire. The size of your fireplace and the depth of your pioneer spirit will determine how and what you cook.

If you live in a house, chances are your fireplace will be at least 2 feet

---

FOOT WARMER

An ornamental yet useful article can be made out of an old box; if possible, it is preferable to have it round; line it neatly with some woolen fabric and cover it on the outside with silk or other light material of the same shade and color as the lining or of a contrasting color; the outside covering may be embroidered; or 3 or 4 ruffles of lace may be sewed on; the lid should be made to fit and covered and lined the same as the box; it should be fastened on by bows of ribbon or brass hinges; a bright silk cord finishes the edge of both box and lid neatly; inside of this place the hot bricks, or, better still, a rubber bag filled with hot water.

—From Scammel's 1891 *Treasure House of Universal Knowledge*

CANDLEMAS

February 2 has been an important weather prediction day since ancient times. The pagan version comes down to us as Groundhog Day, but like many other pagan customs it was incorporated into early Christianity. Today Anglicans, Eastern Orthodox, and Roman Catholic churches bless all the candles to be burned in the coming year on Candlemas day.

Secular and Religious

A clear Groundhog Day means that the animal will see his shadow and we will have six more weeks of winter. A similarly clear Candlemas day has a similar meaning to religious farmers as indicated by these ditties:

"If Candlemas Day be fair and clear
There'll be five winters in the year."

"When Candlemas Day is fine and clear
A shepard would rather see his wife
on her bier."

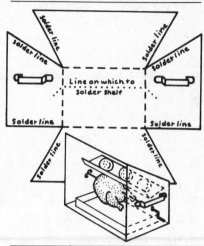

TIN KITCHENS

If you really want to get into fireplace cookery, and if your fireplace is large enough to hold a good fire for several hours, one of the most interesting ways to cook is with a reflecting oven or "tin kitchen." Any cooperative tinsmith can make one to your specifications. The purpose of the tin kitchen is to reflect the radiated heat of the fire, thereby cooking whatever is on the shelves or spit(s) within. Have one made that is at least as wide as the distance between your andirons or the width of your fire basket, and cut your bannock-baking plank so that it will fit inside. Biscuits, potatoes, little meat pies, Cornish hens, even TV dinners and other goodies can be cooked on the shelf. Chickens, roasts, and large shish kebabs can be spitted (always put a drip pan underneath). The baking time of bannocks will be reduced by placing the plank within the reflecting oven.

Cleaning the oven isn't fun, but don't allow the oven to rust or the reflecting power is lost.

Did You Know...
... thin people are particularly prone to winter ailments, since they have less insulation against the cold than their heftier friends?

deep and about 3 feet wide and have a damper. It is big enough for several kinds of fireplace cooking. If you live in an apartment, your fireplace (and it's sometimes a kindness to call it that) may be less than half that size and not have a damper. A long-lasting supply of glowing embers is nearly impossible to achieve in such a small fireplace, and a roaring hot fire can be very dangerous. But the apartment fireplace can be used for skewered food—grilled hot dogs, split by the heat, and perhaps wrapped with a strip of bacon (fastened with a toothpick), or beef shish kebab with partially precooked chunks of potato, carrot, and whole small onions. Your mini-fireplace is also fine for keeping prepared food warm in enameled or iron pots. Sets of heavy-duty outdoor barbecue or roasting utensils, forks and grills, plus long-handled wire bread toasters are available new, used, and antique. Wear a pot-holder, glove, sit on a stool in front of the fireplace, have your ingredients ready, lock the cat in the bathroom, and have fun.

One-Pot Dishes

With a larger fireplace you can try practically anything, but one-pot dishes in which everything is cooked together are traditional favorites. Some of these long-cooking pot dishes—roasts, stews, and thick soups—date back 600 years and are the easiest for the twentieth-century fireplace cook. Use either a large earthen pot or a cast-iron pot with a close-fitting lid. For cooking in iron pots, let the fire die down, rake the embers so that they form an even bed, and set the filled pot on a couple of bricks placed among the coals. Or rest the pot on the log supports of the andirons.

To Stew a Rump of Beef

(*A 1753 recipe brought up to date*)

3 pounds beef rump roast
2 tsps. nutmeg
2 tsps. freshly ground black pepper
2 tsps. salt
½ cup red wine vinegar
2 cups dry red wine
6 cups water
3 large onions stuck with whole
 cloves
2 cloves minced garlic
1 tied bunch fresh sweet herbs,
 or dried basil, marjoram, dill,
 thyme, and parsley to taste

Sprinkle the roast with nutmeg, pepper, and salt. Lay the meat fat side down, or if there is no fat, lay a strip of suet under the roast. Add the vinegar, the wine, and enough of the water to just cover the meat. Put in the onions, the garlic, and the fresh or dried herbs. Put the lid on and stew for 4 or 5 hours. If you are using a Dutch oven, place some of the glowing embers on the lid so that the heat will surround the pot. If you wish to serve in the eighteenth-century manner, lay the sliced roast on sippets (which are toasted, fried, crustless pieces of bread).

Obviously there are many variations that can be devised by anyone with a modern cookbook, especially one written for slow-cookers. Smaller pieces of meat or meatless stews require much less cooking. Chicken, peas, and

potatoes cooked in broth, or veal and oysters make good one-pot fireplace dishes. Serve with crisp green salad and perhaps some bannock bread cooked on a plank in front of the fireplace.

Bannock Bread

3½ cups flour
(mixture of unbleached wheat and corn flour)
½ cup wheat bran
½ cup softened butter (1 stick)
1½ cups milk
½ tsp. salt
3 tsps. baking powder

Mix the ingredients into a soft dough. Roll to a thickness of about ¾ inch. Cut into large 3- or 4-inch rounds with the rim of a coffee cup

or a large cookie cutter. Slap firmly onto a plank, prop about 20 inches or so from the fire, on the hearth, and bake for 20 to 40 minutes, depending on the heat. (Makes about 20.) *Do not turn over* as the bannocks will not stick on the cooked side. These are delicious served with apple sauce or apple butter.

Also try: toasted cheese sandwiches held in a toaster over the fire; baked potatoes—sweet or white—pushed into the hot ashes at the far side of the fireplace; roasted corn, wrapped in aluminum foil and buried in the ashes.

Positively Irish Coffee

Into a stemmed glass put 1 tsp. sugar, granulated or Demarara; then add 2 ounces of Irish whiskey. Fill to within an inch of the top with strong *hot* black coffee. Float lightly whipped cream on the surface and add a dash of nutmeg. *Super!*

 THE SEASON TO BE JOLLY

HANUKKAH, THE FEAST OF LIGHTS

It was an ancient winter custom in the Middle East, practiced not only by the early Hebrews but by the Egyptians and other peoples as well, to kindle ceremonial lights that burned all night or for a number of nights in succession. The significance of these practices varied with the culture, but the rites generally occurred during the winter solstice, the darkest time of the year, when days are short and nights may seem interminably long.

The Hebrew ceremonies were accompanied by prayers that expressed the yearning of man's soul for light in the season when cold and darkness had, and still have, a tendency to fill the spirit with doubt and despair. A seven-branched candelabra called a menorah was kindled in the Temple, and this ancient symbol of light — a metaphor for faith and freedom of body and spirit — is still the universal symbol of the Jewish people.

The Maccabee Triumph

The importance of the menorah became permanently fixed in Jewish life by historical events that transformed a minor ritual into a holiday of major cultural, if not religious, significance. In 162 B.C., during the reign of the tyrannical Syrian King Antiochus, who was considered a madman even by his friends, the Great Temple of Jerusalem was desecrated and virtually destroyed, and the Jews were persecuted and slaughtered en masse in a three-year period of sickening carnage. Finally, a small number of guerilla

Aunt Gussie's Potato Pancakes
4 medium to large potatoes
1 large onion
2 heaping tbsps. flour
3 eggs
salt
pepper
Peel and grate the potatoes into a large bowl. Drain off the water that accumulates. Immediately grate the onion into the bowl; this will keep the grated potatoes from turning black. Add eggs, flour, salt and pepper. Mix well and dollop into a well-oiled frying pan or onto a greased griddle. Brown both sides until crisp. Serve with sour cream and/or apple sauce. Makes 15-20 pancakes.

Apple Sauce
Simmer apples in water until tender. Strain or blend them into a purée and return puréed apples to the pot. Add sugar to taste and cook about 3 minutes. For extra flavor, lemon juice or vanilla extract may be added.

troops under the leadership of Judah Maccabee miraculously defeated the vast, powerful legions of experienced Syrian soldiers.

The Miracle

On the 25th of Kislev, the day of the traditional winter-solstice rites, and exactly three years after the desecration of the Temple, the victorious Hebrews gathered in Jerusalem to rededicate the Temple. Although the building and its artifacts had been substantially restored in the preceding days, apparently no one had had time to check the supply of holy oil for the lighting ceremonies, and at the last minute, the priest responsible for kindling the lights discovered that only one jar of the specially prepared oil—enough for only 24 hours—remained unbroken. Miraculously, this oil burned not only for a single day but for eight days and nights. The joyous feelings of renewal inspired by this miracle were still further increased by the fact that the eighth day symbolized the beginnings of a second creation—since God created the world in only seven days.

An eighth branch was added to the traditional seven-branch menorah, followed later by a ninth, the *shamas* (helper or servant), with which the other candles are lit. The festival of lights was given the name Hanukkah (meaning dedication), and now symbolized the victory of the light of spiritual faith over tyranny and persecution. But although it was decreed an annual eight-day holiday, no precise rules were specified for its observance, and the story of Hanukkah does not appear in the Old Testament, but only in the Apocrypha in the Book of Maccabees. In the absence of written law, rabbis argued for hundreds of years until the present proce-

MUMMERS' PARADE

No matter what the weather on New Year's Day, Philadelphia's Mummers will make their annual four and a half mile march up Broad Street, and at least a million spectators willing to freeze their toes and other vulnerable parts will be out to watch them. The seven-hour pageant starts at 8:30 A.M. and includes string bands, fancy-dress figures and events, elaborately decorated floats ridden by comics, clowns, and acrobats, and of course the female impersonators in various states of chilly undress. Real females are strictly excluded, but the lore is filled with tales of women, frequently disguised as men disguised as women who've attempted to make the march.

Seventeenth-Century Tradition

Mummery is one of America's oldest holiday traditions, dating back to the seventeenth century when various rabble-rousing Christmas and New Year's customs were brought to the South Philadelphia area from England, Sweden, and Germany. By the late 1900s, groups of rowdy New Year's Eve celebrants had banded into clubs, and in 1901 the city invited such organizations as *The Hardly Abels*, *The Mixed Pickles*, and *The Energetic Hoboes* to get together for the first official parade.

Today, mummery is as much a family affair as ever, and competing for substantial cash prizes, club members and their families spend the entire year preparing for the parade. On New Year's Day, they start gathering before dawn. It takes an early start to get into a satin cape with a 200-foot train, and to coordinate the 130 costumed pages who will carry it—possibly through knee-deep snow. To be sure they'll make it on time, many Mummers still do as their grandfathers did: they go directly from an all-night party to the parade.

dure for the lighting of the candles was established. Other Hanukkah traditions — including gift-giving, parties featuring special foods, and the gifts of coins or *Hanukkah gelt* to children — evolved differently in various parts of the world.

"A Miracle Happened There"

Aside from the menorah itself, the only Hanukkah symbol stemming directly from the original celebration is the dreidel, a small four-sided top embossed with four letters of the Hebrew alphabet (standing for the phrase "A miracle happened there"). During the reign of Antiochus, when the study as well as the practice of Jewish law was forbidden, the Jews gathered in clandestine groups and studied anyway, as they always have. But they always kept a dreidel in the center of their circle so that when the Syrian soldiers made their rounds, the students could quickly hide their books and appear to be gathered for an innocent gambling game with the top or with the playing cards they also kept handy. It was a simple ruse that saved many lives.

CELEBRATING THE NEW YEAR

Man began greeting the New Year with some sort of festivities even before consistent methods of measuring time were established. The celebration of New Year's is probably the oldest and most universal of holiday customs, observed in eastern, western and primitive cultures throughout the world. Since various kinds of calendars — or none at all — are used, it's obviously not celebrated everywhere on the same day, or even at the same time of year. Yet the meaning of New Year seems consistent. It symbolizes the victory of life over death, the present and future over the past, and the triumph of the regenerative forces of nature over the period of suspended animation or death manifested in the winter season.

A Religious Occasion

Originally, the arrival of the New Year was a religious holiday established on the basis of natural phenomena — in some places the winter solstice, in others the fall equinox at harvest time. March 25 is still a common New Year's Day, and it was the first day of the year in non-Catholic western countries, including the American colonies, until 1752.

Our own way of celebrating the New Year in the United States has come to seem virtually devoid of religious content or spiritual connotations, but it is in the very orgiastic quality of our partying, drinking, and brawling, that we are perpetuating some of the same things people have always done everywhere on the New Year, and probably for the same reasons.

Basically, New Year's rites have always been rituals of purgation and exorcism. Even the old and widely practiced customs of settling quarrels, renewing friendships, forgiving and forgetting grievances of the past,

THE MORNING AFTER THE NIGHT BEFORE

Hangover cures can be classed, if you will, into two basic groups: pleasure (including various hairs of the dog) and pain.

Pleasure

In the 30s, guitarist Eddie Lang proffered the ultimate hair-of-the-dog-type remedy. It began "Take the juice of 1 quart of Scotch...." In varying degrees all such remedies are alike, but be warned—drinking to get over the effects of excessive drinking can start a dangerous cycle.

The hangover joins the common cold in the science-stumpers hall of fame. Aspirin may aid your head but will hurt your ailing stomach (aspirin substitutes are better). Inhaling pure oxygen, if you can get it, has been touted, but it appears that sleep and rest are the only surefire remedies. Small comfort!

Pain

The guilt that often accompanies a hangover has given rise to countless self-punishment panaceas, including the ancient Greek remedy of literal self-flagellation. Some dandies are: raw owl eggs, bitter almonds and raw eel, swallow's beak and myrrh, boiled cloves and olive oil, warm mashed potatoes, sauerkraut juice, salted cucumber juice, rubbing half a lemon under your arm, and reading the Bible.

HAPPY NEW YEAR!!!

Hot Spiced Rum

When you've just come in from the cold, one of these will set you right.

Two lumps of sugar, two wineglasses boiling water, one wineglass Jamaica rum, a little butter—about as much as you can put on a dime; cloves and allspice. Serve in small bar glass.

—*La Cuisine Creole* (1885)

have this quality. So do New Year's resolutions. In the Korean version of this practice, people seek to rid themselves of their distresses by painting images on paper, and writing over them their troubles of body and mind, then giving the papers to a boy to burn.

Away with the Evil Spirits!

The idea of purging the past and purifying one's life of evil spirits and influences is at the core of the most common and universal of New Year's rites: noise. The boisterous use of every imaginable kind of noisemaker, firecracker, or explosive, including the shooting of guns into the air, is one of the earliest customs known to man. This practice probably originated in ancient Babylon and is found today in such varied cultures as Cambodia, Bohemia, primitive Africa, and of course, the United States. Once the demons and evil spirits have been terrified away by all the racket, the new year and a new life can commence afresh.

The archetypal American New Year's celebration in Times Square in New York City would not be altogether alien to peoples who would find our automobiles, our homes, our dress, our manners, utterly bizarre. The pealing of bells, tooting of whistles, wailing sirens, blowing of car horns, shooting off of firecrackers and rockets may reflect our need to expel our own "demons," whether they be primeval relics of our ancient past or very current and real problems. This need may also account for the feeling most of us get at this time, a feeling of wanting to do something special. We feel an urge to be part of something larger than ourselves, even if that larger entity consists of only one other person with whom we spend the evening quietly.

However we choose to celebrate, the traditional din of New Year's Eve not only promises new and better things, but echoes the most distant reaches of our past.

Wine Flip

Take 6 new laid eggs; separate the yolks from the whites, and beat up the former with a fork until thin; take 1 qt. sound port wine; pour it into a clean saucepan, and put over a gentle fire, with a few cloves, a little nutmeg, 1 or 2 blades cinnamon, a little sliced lemon peel; add sugar to taste; simmer a short time; take it off, and pour into a bowl in which are the eggs; stir briskly. Have the whites of the eggs beaten to a froth, and put this over the crimson fluid in the bowl, which will present a snow-capped appearance.

Happy New Year! love, Carol + Jim

California and Florida Navel and
Valencia oranges
Winter pears
Puerto Rican pineapple
Florida tangerines

Vegetables
California artichokes and green
beans
Broccoli
California and Texas brussels
sprouts and carrots
Green, red, and white winter
cabbage
Cauliflower
New York and Pennsylvania
mushrooms
Onions
Winter potatoes
Collard, dandelion, turnips, and
kale greens
Acorn, butternut, and Hubbard
squash
Radishes
Spinach
Watercress
Florida bibb, romaine, head
lettuce

This partial list should serve to
prove that winter need not be a
season of deprivation for any
gourmet.

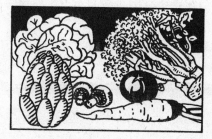

SEASONAL FOODS

Many delicious foods are in season
during the winter. A knowledge of
the varieties of fruits, vegetables,
and fish that are good buys during
the cold months will enable you to
prepare many tasty, economical
winter feasts.

Fresh-Water Fish
1. Best buys at the start of the
season:
Lake and river carp
Great Lakes pickerel
Lake smelt
Great Lakes chub
2. Best buys during peak of the
season:
Lake herring
Great Lakes sauger

Salt-Water Fish
1. Best buys at the start of the
season:
Atlantic sea bass and striped bass
Atlantic and Pacific large cod
Atlantic fluke flounder
New England gray sole and
haddock

2. Best buys during peak of season:
Mackerel
Fresh sardines
St. Lawrence smelt

Shellfish
Shelled crab
Atlantic mussels
Atlantic deep sea scallops
Florida Gulf shrimp
Atlantic clams

Fruits
Cranberries
Florida grapefruit and limes
California grapes
Lemons

The Traditional Swiss Cheese Fondue

In Switzerland, no skiing venture is complete without an après ski cheese fondue. No one can be cold after this. You may not have the Alps at your doorstep, but you can gather some friends together and yodel over a Fondue au Fromage.

1 clove garlic
½ pound Emmenthal cheese, shredded
½ pound Gruyère cheese, shredded
2 tbsps. cornstarch
2 cups dry white wine
1 tsp. dry mustard
3 tbsps. kirsch
dash of nutmeg
salt and pepper to taste
a long loaf of French or Italian bread torn into bite-sized pieces with a bit of crust left on each portion

Rub a caquelon or any heavy earthenware casserole with the cut side of the garlic. Then dredge the cheese with cornstarch. Pour the wine into the caquelon and let it warm (never boil) to the point where air bubbles are forming. Now start tossing in the cheese by the handful, stirring constantly with a wooden spoon. When the cheese is melted, stir in the kirsch mixed with the mustard and nutmeg, and salt and pepper to taste. Remove the casserole from the fire and set it over a spirit lamp placed in the center of the table.

Each guest spears a bread cube and twirls it into the fondue pot, scraping the bottom of the caquelon, which gradually becomes encrusted with the cheese — delicious.

As the fondue becomes thicker, add a little heated wine to thin to an agreeable proportion.

Serves about four.

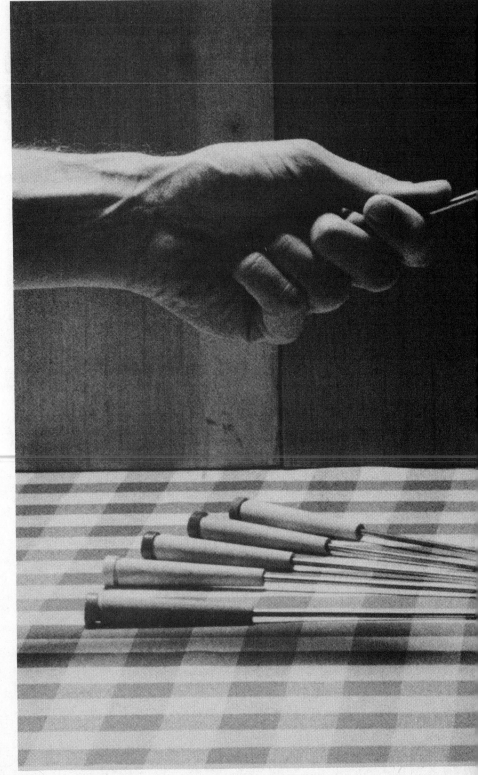

Fondue Bourguignonne

On a chilly wintry night or when an energy crisis has hit and you have no heat, a Fondue Bourguignonne is fun and rib warming.

Cut 2 pounds of lean tender meat into 1¼-inch cubes. Half fill a fondue pot (not ceramic) with peanut or vegetable oil. Set over a heating element at the table, one that will keep the oil at a low bubble. Be sure the pot is deep enough so the oil will not spatter out.

For the service, each guest has a plate large enough for the sauces, two forks (one a long-handled fondue fork if possible), and a plate with the prepared meat. A nice touch is a finger bowl with a serviette. Around the table, within convenient reach, are the sauces, various condiments, and salts and peppers.

Each person helps himself to the sauces and condiments, then spears a piece of meat using the fondue fork. Pierce the cube so that the fork goes all the way through, extending about ¼ inch on the opposite side. The tines of the fork rest on the bottom of the pot and prevent the meat from sticking. When done to the guest's taste, the meat is dipped into the sauce or condiments and eaten with the second fork. Do not use the fondue fork—it's too hot! Serves four or five.

The following sauces are traditional with the fondue, or you can concoct your own.

Béarnaise sauce
Chili Sauce
Sour cream mustard sauce
Horseradish
Curry mayonnaise
Chutney
Caper sauce
Mushroom sauce
Sweet-and-sour sauce
Roquefort sauce

Jerky

If you have a few strips of jerky in your pocket, or a block of pemmican in your glove compartment, and if you are caught in a blizzard, not to worry. There's great nourishment in these two foods, and you can make out, hopefully, until someone finds you.

Cut very lean meat (beef, squirrel, deer, rabbit) into strips 1 inch wide, ¼ inch thick and about 5 to 6 inches long. Weave onto sticks (green wood) or skewers, and dry out over a slow-burning campfire. Another method is to put the strips on grids into a very low temperature oven—140°. Leave the door ajar. If the strips are sprinkled with salt before drying, dehydration is hastened. Worcestershire sauce and soy sauce are good flavoring agents. Jerky may also be eaten au naturel, sliced very thin and sauted, or cooked in fresh water, patted dry, and sliced.

Swiss Chocolate Fondue

¾ pound semisweet chocolate
¾ cup heavy cream
3 tbsps. of one of the following: cointreau, kirsch, cognac, or crème de menthe.

Break the chocolate into pieces. Combine chocolate and cream in a chafing dish or small pan. Stir over low heat until the chocolate melts. Stir in whichever of the liquors or liqueurs is preferred.

For each guest, provide an individual plate, wooden skewer or fondue fork, and an assortment of the following to be dipped into the fondue:

Ladyfingers or sponge cake cut into bitable chunks
Bananas sliced in ½-inch sections
Strawberries
Fresh or canned pineapple in bite-sized portions
Seeded green grapes
Serves five or six.

Pemmican

This is very nutritious, and will keep you from starvation if you're lost in a snowdrift. (If you happen to have it along.)

1 pound finely ground jerky (see above)
4 tbsps. powdered dried fruit, berries, and herbs, according to preference
sugar to taste, if desired
enough animal fat to make a solid block (see below)

Mix all the ingredients together and press into a solid block.

If It's Too Cold to Wait for a Proper Bouillabaisse, Try this Quickie

one 13-oz. tin ready-to-serve onion soup
two 15-oz. tins condensed fish chowder
one 4½-oz. tin (drained weight) tiny shrimps
6 sprigs parsley, chopped
1 bay leaf
½ tsp. thyme
¼ cup dry white wine
freshly ground black pepper, 8 turns of the mill
finely chopped scallions (optional)

Combine all the ingredients and simmer until thoroughly heated. If desired, sprinkle the chopped scallions over each serving. Serves six.

Hot Rum Buttered

One tsp. brown sugar, 1 strip of lemon peel, 1 tsp. lemon juice, 5 whole cloves . . . put all together with a spoon into a double old-fashioned glass. Add 2 ounces dark rum and boiling water to taste. Stir, and add 1 tsp. butter, sliding it on top of the mixture. Sip slowly as the butter melts. Guaranteed to help anything in cold weather—from redness and swelling of extremities to frostbite.

Super Wheat Bread

When winter winds numb the soul, this whole wheat bread, warm from the oven and slathered with butter, is a spirit-uplifting experience.

2 cakes yeast
⅔ cup warm water
1 tbsp. brown sugar

Dissolve the yeast in the warm water and add the brown sugar. Allow this mixture to stand while mixing the following:

2 cups warm water
½ cup brown sugar
1 tbsp. salt
2 tbsps. butter
6¾ cups whole wheat flour

Then mix all together thoroughly. Let rise for 1½ hours in a warm place. (An oven with a pilot light is a good spot.) Turn out, knead, and divide into three loaves (for one-pound loaf pans). Let rise for 1 hour; then bake at 385° F. for 15 minutes. Lower temperature to 350° F. and bake for 35 minutes. Remove at once from pan and cool on racks.

Heavenly and warming. Makes three loaves.

"The" Onion Soup

7 onions, about 2½ inches in diameter, sliced very thinly
6 tbsps. cooking oil (not butter)
2 tsps. Dijon or Dusseldorf mustard

2 tsps. flour
1 tin concentrated beef bouillon or consommé plus
½ tin water
1 pint dry white wine (or leftover champagne if you have it)
salt and pepper

Put the cooking oil into a casserole, preferably enameled cast iron. Then add onions and salt and pepper. Cook slowly until the onions are a very dark brown. This is a most important step and can take ¾ to 1 hour. Keep scraping the onions as they stick to the bottom of the pan. Use a wooden spoon or spatula for this, not metal. Now add the flour and mustard, stirring in until well incorporated.

Add the wine, bouillon, and water, bringing all to a boil. Stir well, lower the heat, and simmer for

about ½ hour. This is a thick soup and goes well sprinkled with Parmesan cheese.

A different touch from the usual "bread with cheese and under the broiler" are croutons dusted with Parmesan. To make them, butter both sides of regular white bread. Dust with grated Parmesan or Gruyère cheese, cut into ½-inch cubes. Put in a pan and place in a moderate oven until lightly browned. Then strew over the soup. Serves four to six.

Gram's Swiss Steak

If you're snowbound, make a batch of this steak. It tastes super even to the fourth and fifth day.

2 pounds chuck steak about 1 inch thick
5 medium onions
cooking oil
flour
water
salt and pepper

Cut steak into approximately 2-inch squares. Dredge the meat with plenty of flour and salt and pepper. With the edge of a saucer, pound the meat thoroughly on both sides until the flour has almost disappeared into the meat. It should now be about ½ inch thick. Set aside.

Pour cooking oil into the bottom of a cast-iron casserole or Dutch oven, enough to cover the bottom to a depth of about ¼ inch. Add onions and cook until fairly brown. Remove the onions and in the same pan quickly brown the meat, a few pieces at a time. (More oil may be necessary.)

Now put all the meat back into the casserole, put onions over the top, and add boiling water to cover. Cover the pan snugly and cook at a slow simmer approximately 45 minutes or until done — tender when pierced with a fork. More water may be necessary during the cooking. Serves six to eight.

Uncle Charlie's Christmas Taffy

2 cups sugar
½ cup light corn syrup
½ cup water
1 tsp. vanilla
⅛ tsp. salt

Mix together the sugar, syrup, salt, and water. Cook over moderate heat to 272° F. on a candy thermometer or until a few drops will crack when dropped into cold water. Pour out onto a buttered tin. When the mixture cools enough to handle, lightly oil your fingers, and pour the vanilla into the center of the taffy. Gather it together, folding the edges over so the vanilla is incorporated into the mixture.

Form the taffy into a ball. Pull it out into a long rope, twist it slightly, and double it back on itself. Pull out, twist, and double back a few times until the taffy is quite white and rather porous looking.

Now roll the candy out on a greased surface so it resembles a long rope. Twist slightly and cut into pieces about 1 inch in length. (The rope should be no more than ¾ inch in diameter.) The scissors for cutting should be dipped frequently into cold water to prevent sticking.

Various essences may be substituted for the vanilla flavoring: peppermint, wintergreen, lemon. The taffy may also be colored with vegetable dyes. Makes about one pound.

Mother's Oatmeal Yeast Bread

*"The North Wind doth blow,
And we shall have snow,"
But who cares when one is warmed
with this hearty cereal bread.*

1 cup milk and water (half and half)
1 tsp. salt
1 tbsp. fat
2 tbsps. molasses
1 cup rolled oats (not the instant type)
1½ cups flour
2 cakes compressed yeast (½ tbsp. dry yeast may be substituted)
¼ cup warm water

Scald the liquid and add the salt, fat, and molasses. When lukewarm, add the yeast, which has been softened in the warm water. Add the flour and knead. Allow the dough to rise until double in bulk. Knead again and put into baking tins. When the loaves have risen about to the top of the tin, bake in a moderate oven (350° F.) 40 to 60 minutes, depending on the size of your tin. Makes two or three loaves.

Vermouth Beef Stew à la Pinky

½ pound salt pork (bring to boil in pan of water before using)
    or
½ pound bacon may be used in place of salt pork
2 pounds well-trimmed chuck in bite-sized pieces (any cut of good, lean meat is suitable)
1 tbsp. flour
½ tsp. pepper
1½ cloves garlic, chopped
1 bouillon cube
12 peppercorns
3 whole cloves
¼ cup chopped parsley
1 cup water
½ cup dry vermouth
1 bay leaf

Cut the briefly boiled salt pork into thin strips and sauté slowly in a large skillet. When fairly crisp, remove and put aside. Brown beef in pork fat at high heat. Add fried pork, flour, and peppercorns. Bring remaining ingredients to boil except for vermouth and pour over meat. Simmer, covered, for 3 hours. Stir occasionally and add extra water if necessary. After 3 hours, turn off heat, stir in vermouth, place stew in casserole or bean pot, and refrigerate—preferably overnight. When ready to serve, reheat in 300° oven for about an hour. This is superb served with noodles. Serves four to six.

Blue Blazer

Combine a wineglass, each, Scotch whiskey and boiling water; put into a mug and ignite the liquor, and, while blazing, pour from one mug to another, five or six times; sweeten with white sugar, and add a piece of lemon peel.

ST. NIKOLAUS

Everybody knows who Saint Nicholas is, right? He's the jolly, fat, impish fellow (also known as Santa Claus) who slides down the chimney every December 24th, leaving toys and goodies for all good little boys and girls. The fact of the matter is that Saint Nicholas really existed, but it is highly doubtful that he ever performed any such act. In America, the name was gradually modified to Santa Claus.

The Giver of Dowries

Saint Nicholas, who died in the year 343, was a Greek Orthodox bishop of the city of Myra. He is most often associated with the story of his kind gifts to three poor sisters, to each of whom he gave a sack of gold for their dowries so they could attract the good husbands they yearned for.

Miracle Man

The miracles attributed to Saint Nicholas were numerous. He could bring the dead back to life, redirect threatening storms at sea, save people from drowning, and he reputedly once saved the entire city of Myra from starvation by miraculously producing boatloads of grain. He became the patron saint of children, maidens, and merchant mariners. Good Saint Nicholas' fame spread, and he was made patron saint of many cities and countries, including Russia. From Russia, his popularity spread to the Laplanders, and by the time these northern people elaborated his holy deeds and introduced him to the Dutch, he came equipped with a sleigh and reindeer.

St. Nick in the New World

The Dutch, who called him Sinterklaas, brought the legend of Saint Nicholas to the New World in the

early 1600s. The ascetic old European saint took on a different personality in the New World—robust and jolly. His connection with gift giving resulted in his gradual domination of the Christmas festivities, and by 1800, Washington Irving described him as the spirit of Christmas: chubby, good-natured Santa Klaus.

Our present image of Saint Nick originated with Thomas Nast, the great political cartoonist of the late 1800s. He published a collection of drawings of the jolly saint dressed in an ermine-trimmed red coat, which we would all recognize today as the classic Santa Claus.

MISTLETOE
Have you ever wondered why you're permitted to steal kisses under the mistletoe branch at Christmastime? It might surprise you to know that this romantic holiday custom has its basis in Norse mythology.

This Promise
Balder, the popular Apollolike god of the Scandinavians, received a prophecy of his own death. His mother, Frigga, the queen of the gods, upon hearing of the prophecy, exacted an oath from every person and thing in the land to ensure that no attempt would be made on Balder's life. She traveled far and wide, receiving this promise from every person, stone, animal, and plant—except for the pretty mistletoe. Frigga could not see how this harmless little plant could inflict any injury on her beloved son, and therefore, she passed it by. Loki, the evil sprite who continually plagued the gods and goddesses with his mischief, was lurking nearby when Frigga decided to overlook the mistletoe. He formed an arrow from the stem of the plant, and during a competition in which Balder participated, he put this arrow into the hands of a blind spectator. He guided the innocent man's hand and launched the arrow, which struck Balder, thus resulting in a mortal wound.

Balder Reborn
Balder was restored to life, fortunately, by the combined efforts of the gods and goddesses. Frigga then declared that the mistletoe would never thereafter be used as an instrument of evil. Because she was the goddess of love, she expressed her joy and gratitude for the return of her son by bestowing a kiss upon those who passed beneath the mistletoe.

Although the church has never sanctioned the use of mistletoe as a religious decoration, it has accepted this charming custom, which has been preserved through the ages as a sign of peace and love during the holiday season.

GIFT WRAPPING

Commercially produced gift-wrapping paper is available today in astonishingly beautiful designs, colors, and textures. Unfortunately, the prices can be equally astonishing. If the cost of your wrapping paper equals the cost of your gift, you may want to investigate some colorful, creative methods of making your own coverings.

Found Materials

You may already have suitable materials on hand. Shelving paper, fabric, wallpaper, butcher paper, or road maps all make potential wrapping paper. Some felt spots, appropriately arranged on plain white paper, turn cube-shaped boxes into dice. Brown bags may be cut up and decorated with découpage decals for a rustic look.

Newspapers and Magazines

Foreign-language newspapers provide attractive hints of the presents to come. What better way to wrap an oriental vase than in a Chinese newspaper? French newsprint for French cookbooks and Yiddish or Hebrew newspapers for Hanukkah presents make perfect sense.

Tissue-Paper Designs

Aluminum foil can be dressed for the occasion with colored tissue paper (available at five-and-ten-cent stores or art-supply stores). Cut or tear the tissue paper into holiday shapes and place them on the foil. Using a 1-inch-wide brush, apply a mixture of acrylic polymer gloss (not matte) and water to the tissue paper. This acts both as glue and protective coating. After each application, rinse the brush thoroughly to remove any color it may have picked up, thus preserving the acrylic's transparency.

YULE LOG

In pre-Christian Europe, the Teutonic and Celtic peoples held a festival when the sun climbed high in the heavens, after its long winter's rest, and the days began to lengthen with the approach of spring. This festival celebrated the turning of the wheel of time which symbolized the progression of the seasons. This wheel was called the *Houl* or *Hioul*. It was believed by many that the sun stood still during the 12 days of the festival, and this point was considered to be the time when the sun changed direction and began its climb in the horizon. Druid priests selected a Yule log during this special, mystical period, and it was proclaimed that this holy log must be kept ever burning.

Perennially Aflame

Just as the old year consumed itself, to be born anew during the winter solstice festival, the Yule log was kept perennially aflame, a brand from the old log being used to kindle the new fire. As Christianity spread throughout Europe, the Yule season became associated with the Christmas holiday. In many northern countries, this 12-day period of Christmastime is still referred to as Yule, and the burning of the Yule Log has become one of the many Christmas holiday traditions.

Block Printing

If you hand-print your Christmas cards, you can print matching gift wrap at the same time. Or make your own printing block using adhesive-backed foam weather stripping. Cut up lengths of foam and stick them to wood blocks in various designs. (You can use foam carpet padding by applying it to the blocks with glue.) Put some acrylic paint in a dish and thin it to the consistency of India ink. Dip the block into the paint and print. Try not to get any paint on the block. If you want to do a repeat pattern, start at the top of the paper. Mark the upper right corner of the block, and print again. (Dip the block in the paint as soon as the impression starts to fade.

A Gift Bag

Burlap or felt makes great bags in which to place odd-shape gifts. If carefully constructed and decorated, the bags themselves can become a second gift. Cut two rectangles of material the same size and sew them together on three sides. (Seams may show or not, as you prefer. To hide them, reverse the material before sewing and turn it inside out afterward.) To make a drawstring top, stitch a hem at the top of the bag. Draw a piece of string, yarn, or leather thong through the hem, putting it in at the side seam.

How to Wrap a Package

If you have your own handsomely decorative, personalized Christmas wrapping paper, how do you get it on the package? First, make sure that you start with enough paper. Place the package on the piece to be used. The paper should be wide enough to overlap on top of the package and long enough to allow for the final flap. Fold the sides of the wrapping paper over the box and tape them securely. Fold the top corners down. Then fold flaps A and B in toward the box. Bring the resulting flap up and tape it to the box. Turn the box around and repeat this procedure on the other end. You can tie a ribbon on the package if you like.

Did You Know

. . . Ulan Bator in Mongolia has the dubious distinction of being the coldest established city on earth? Its average annual temperature is a chilly 24.8° Fahrenheit (−4°C.). Anchorage, Alaska ranks way down at 28th place, with an average temperature of 35.2° Fahrenheit (2°C.)

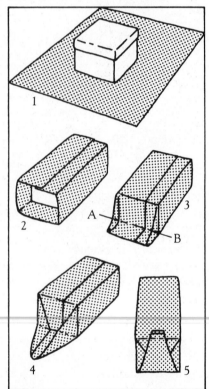

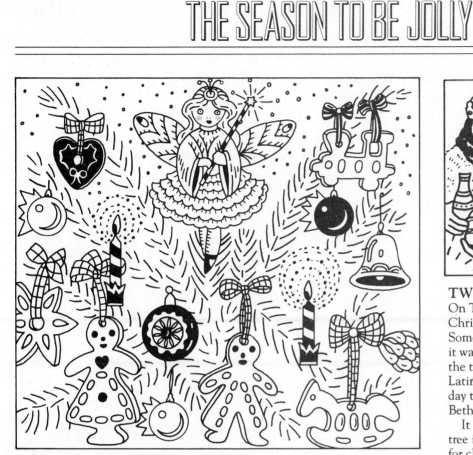

TREES AND TRIMMING

As Sherlock Holmes might have said, "Elementary, my dear Watson. Before you trim the Christmas tree, you must *choose* it." Here's how.

Balsam Fir

The balsam fir is the best and most popular tree for indoor use. Shiny foliage, classic pyramid shape, strong branches to support heavy lights, the balsam gets it all together. Also, its needles are soft. Decorating the tree is so much fun you don't want the occasion spoiled by hurt fingers. And maybe the balsam's best trait is that it doesn't shed (at least not as much as other varieties). With proper care, the Balsam fir should keep indoors for two to three weeks.

Douglas Fir

Next best is the Douglas fir. However, its branches aren't as sturdy as the balsam's so your decorations must be lighter in weight and fewer in number. If that's not a problem, the Douglas fir does well indoors. Other good trees you might select include the Norway pine, spruce, cedar, and arbor vitae. The Douglas fir will keep well indoors for three to four weeks. Just watch out for sharp needles.

Prepping Evergreens

Growers say an evergreen should be prepped before being brought indoors for trimming. If you're lucky enough to have a back porch or backyard, store the tree outdoors until a few hours before tree-trimming time. The

TWELFTH NIGHT

On Twelfth Night, January 6, the Christmas season officially ends. Sometimes called Three Kings Day, it was, until the twentieth century, the traditional gift-giving day in Latin countries, for it was on this day the Magi presumably reached Bethlehem and presented their gifts.

It is also the day the Christmas tree is dismantled and so a sad day for children. To comfort them for this loss, a King's Cake is baked. Hidden in the cake is a bean, and the child who gets the slice with the bean gives a party the following week.

❄❄❄❄❄❄❄❄❄❄❄❄

PUT YOUR FIRST-FOOT FORWARD

In Scotland and the north of England they still observe a custom known as "first-footing." On January 1st, the first person to enter the house must be a dark stranger; he carries a piece of coal which he places on the fire, and sometimes a sprig of mistletoe. The residents give him food and drink to ensure that they themselves will have enough bread and wine in the coming year. The whole ceremony takes place without a word spoken, until the end when the stranger wishes the family a Happy New Year.

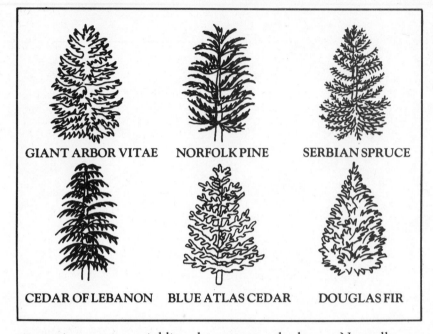

GIANT ARBOR VITAE   NORFOLK PINE   SERBIAN SPRUCE

CEDAR OF LEBANON   BLUE ATLAS CEDAR   DOUGLAS FIR

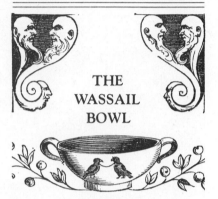

THE WASSAIL BOWL

Drinking ale or mead from a communal bowl or loving cup on Christmas and Twelfth Night was a sixteenth-century custom. The poor carried an empty bowl from house to house to have it filled with a hot punch of beer mulled with spice, roast apples, and toast. Naturally, they drank to their benefactor's health; hence, our expression to "toast" someone or to drink his health.

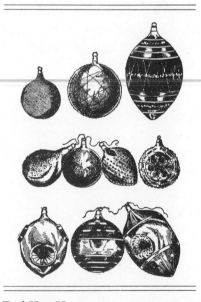

Did You Know . . .
. . . those beautiful apple blossoms would not be so beautiful if they didn't hibernate in temperatures below 45° Fahrenheit (7° C.) for 900 to 1,000 hours?

more rain or snow sprinkling the tree gets, the better. Naturally, you should protect it from hard winter winds or sun, both of which will scatter needles.

Before you decide you can't wait any longer, before the anticipation and excitement of decorating the tree become too much for the children in the family (including the older ones!), acclimate your tree. Let it have a short stopover in the basement or the garage. If that's not possible, turn the thermostat way down low and open the windows. And before the tree leaves the lot, be sure that the base of the trunk is cut on a long diagonal or a V. You want to make sure that as much of the surface as possible is exposed to the water or wet sand in the tree stand.

A spot near the window is a good location for the tree (passersby enjoy it too) as long as that's not also the location of the radiator. And, of course, you won't put the tree near a fireplace or television. Set it up as close as possible to a wall outlet so unsightly extension cords aren't necessary.

Tree Lights
That brings us to the important question of lights, how many you need for a really splendiferous effect and how to place them. First, decide whether you're going to use large lights or miniatures. If you've a store of treasured old lights in fanciful shapes, augmented by large modern globes, here's your rule: 3 times tree height x tree width = the number of standard-sized bulbs you'll need.

When using the miniature lights that twinkle like stars or candles, this is the rule: 4 times tree height x tree width = the number of mini-bulbs you'll need.

There are three ways you can arrange the lights on the tree. One is an

elegant and formal effect that follows a tepee pattern. For this, string your lights vertically from the top down to the base of the tree. Tape the wires together at the top of the tree, and anchor them at the bottom to a circle of cardboard or a wooden square you've placed under the tree stand. Taping at the top and anchoring at the bottom will keep your lights straight; the tepee pattern is especially pleasing in a room with modern and clean-lined furniture.

If your living room is traditional or eclectic, you'll probably prefer a spiral design. This involves placing the lights closer together and overlapping. It's done by running two strings of lights diagonally around the tree, one clockwise and one counterclockwise. And if this is your first home or apartment and it's mostly early hand-me-downs, there's the very old-fashioned, tried-and-true method of hanging lights in wavy loops around the tree.

Once the lights are in place, garlands are next. Follow the same pattern that you used with the lights — vertical, spiraled, or loose garlands. If you're using garlands of various widths, the narrowest should be at the top of the tree and the widest at the bottom.

Adding Tinsel

The most important rule of all for trimming the Christmas tree is certainly the hardest to enforce on the decorating committee. Don't throw the tinsel. You'll spoil all the good work. Instead, hang four to eight strands over a branch to create that shimmering icicle effect. Take care that the tinsel doesn't get caught in the bulb sockets.

Finally, place all your ornaments on the tree just as you did the garlands, with the heaviest on those sturdy bottom branches. And have a wonderful holiday.

That year that Christmas day falls on Sunday,
Winter shall be good, spring windy, summer dry,
Vintage good and plenty of sheep and of honey,
There will be peace and the mortality of old folk will be high.

That year that Christmas day falls on a
Monday, winter shall be unrewarding and spring good,
And summer windy and tempests shall occur,
Feebly vintage, men shall fare well but beasts shall die.

That year that Chritmas day falls on Tuesday,
Winter shall be watery, spring windy, summer
rain and tempest; men and women shall suffer high mortality,
And kings shall perish, vintage (will be) perilous and
Many ships shall perish.

That year that Christmas day falls on Wednesday,
Winter shall be hard, spring evil and windy, summer
good, vintage hazardous and young folk suffer a high mortality,
Chaffering shall be troublesome.

That year that Christmas day falls on Thursday,
Winter (will be) good, spring windy, summer good, vintage good
And plenteous, there shall be peace and princes shall die.

That year that Christmas day falls on Friday winter (will be)
Changeable, spring good and plenteous, vintage good,
(And) sore itching sheep shall die.

That year that Christmas day falls on a Saturday,
Winter wearisome, spring windy, selling troublesome, old
Men shall suffer high mortality and sheep perish, houses shall burn.
—*From a manuscript in Samuel Pepys' Library.*

THE TASTE, SMELL, AND LOOK OF CHRISTMAS

They all come together in cookie baking. Crisp sweet stars, bells, fat snowmen are easy to bake, easy to decorate. Tangy with ginger and cinnamon, they're easy to eat. But if you can resist, they can be made in advance and stored in a tin container.

Cookies

⅓ cup butter or margarine
½ cup dark brown sugar
⅔ cup molasses
1 egg
1 tsp. vanilla extract
1 tsp. ginger
1 tsp. cinnamon
4 cups flour
4 tsps. baking powder

Cream butter and brown sugar. Add molasses, egg, vanilla, ginger, and cinnamon. Beat until fluffy. Mix flour and baking powder; sift into butter mixture gradually. Roll in ball, wrap in wax paper, and chill. Cut dough in four parts and roll out each quarter to ⅛-inch thickness on a floured board. Cut into different shapes with cookie cutters. Pierce a good-sized hole with a needle or skewer so you can hang the finished cookie on the tree. Space cookies 2 inches apart on cookie sheet and bake in 350° preheated oven for 8 to 10 minutes or until firm and golden. Let cool before frosting.

Frosting

1 pound confectioner's sugar
2 egg whites
1 tbsp. lemon juice

Decorative toppings: chocolate and multicolored sprinkles, dragées (silver balls), angelica, candied fruit, green and red granulated sugar. Mix sugar, egg whites, and lemon juice. Add food coloring if desired. Beat for a few minutes until thoroughly mixed and smooth. Spread on cookies with knife or spatula. Use fingers, tweezers, fork, or spoon to make designs. Add decorative toppings.

CHRISTMAS CARDS

In the eighteenth century, children demonstrated the progress of their penmanship by giving samples of their handwriting to their parents each year at Christmas time. These Christmas "pieces," as they were known, became the forerunners of today's Christmas cards. Inasmuch as children had a hand in creating the Christmas tradition, it seems only fair that they play a part in restoring it. What better way to fight the commercialism of the modern holiday season than to join your children in making your own personalized Christmas cards.

Materials

Acrylic paints are an amateur's delight. They come in easy-to-use tubes and are reasonably priced. They provide brilliant color and can be used for printing or painting. Best of all, thinning and clean-up require only tap water.

At least one large brush (Japanese writing brushes work fine) and a few smaller brushes are sufficient for application. Be sure to clean brushes or put them in water as soon as you finish using them (even if it is only for a few minutes).

Scissors and an ordinary steak knife are all the cutting tools needed for most projects. Some glue or rubber cement and some paper complete the list of things you are likely to have to buy. Construction paper offers the most possibilities in terms of texture, durability, and color for the price, but any paper from rice paper to brown bag is suitable.

Printing

If you are planning to send more than one or two cards, you will probably want to avoid having to draw separate pictures for each card. Printing will save you much time and effort without sacrificing the personal touch.

Anything can be used to print with. Look around the house for different shapes and textures. Beer cans, spools, corrugated cardboard, fruits, vegetables—anything to which you can apply paint and press on a piece of paper.

CARD-CARRYING COLLECTORS

It might surprise you to learn that saving this year's Christmas cards for 50 or 60 years could provide you with a lucrative dotage or a handsome legacy for your heirs.

The fact is that a 1910 penny postcard depicting Santa Claus (such as the one at left) can easily cost $30 at your local antique shop. Cards from the 1880s (similar to the one at near left) have been known to fetch over $100 at auction.

Among collectors the names of Louis Prang and Kate Greenaway signify artistry in design and quality in workmanship that gives their cards a value over and above that imparted by age and rarity.

Milk Punch

1. Steep yellow rinds of 18 lemons and 6 oranges 2 days in: rum or brandy, 2 qts.; lemon juice, 1 qt.; loaf sugar, 4 lbs.; 2 nutmegs, grated; boiling milk, 2 qts., Mix well, and in 2 hours strain.
2. 1 tablespoonful fine white sugar; 2 tablespoonfuls water; 1 wineglass cognac brandy; ½ wineglass Santa Cruz rum; ½ tumblerful shaved ice; fill with milk. Shake the ingredients well together, and grate a little nutmeg on top. To make it hot, use hot milk, and no ice.

Did You Know . . .

. . . you may be contributing to your post-holiday letdown by overindulging in holiday goodies? All of those starchy, carbohydrate-laden, sweet foods can leave you feeling sluggish and out of sorts and may cause your blood sugar level to drop, which may result in feelings of hostility and depression. In addition, finding that you've gained ten pounds in one afternoon is hardly likely to cheer you up!

Potato Printing

Potatoes can be used to make relief prints. Just cut a large potato in half and paint a simple design on the white, exposed face. Then, using an ordinary steak knife, cut around the design and cut away all the excess potato to a depth of about ¼ inch, leaving a raised relief of the design. Apply paint to the raised part and print away. Reapply paint after each printing and recut the design after you have made about eight or ten cards. If you use letters in your design, remember they will print in reverse so carve them backwards. Also be sure to slant cuts away from the design; undercut designs will collapse. When changing colors on the same potato, you may have to slice off the old color. Interesting effects can be obtained by blending colors right on the potato.

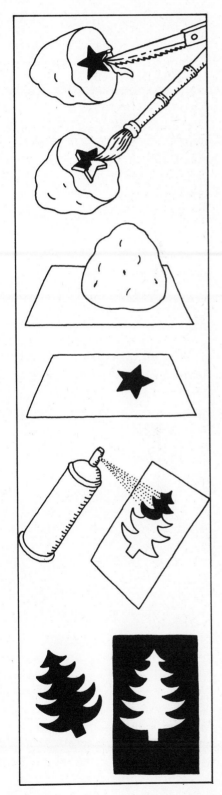

Stenciling

Spray painting the paper through a lace doily provides a beautiful background on which to write your holiday greetings. Other textured backgrounds may be achieved by applying thinned paint to an old toothbrush and scraping the bristles with your finger or a small stick, splattering the paint onto the paper (messy but fun). Spray painting or the toothbrush technique can be combined with any objects or cut-out shapes placed on the paper. When the shapes are removed their outline will remain against a background of sprayed or speckled color.

Collage

If you have a year's worth of magazines lying around collecting dust, you can put them to use as material sources for collages. Christmas scenes can be pasted together out of the most unlikely pictures. Photos of various flowers can be cut and pasted into the shape of a Christmas tree, conveying the Christmas spirit while anticipating the spring to come. A hint: if you use rubber cement to construct the collage, make sure you have thinner available to pull loose any mistakes.

Lettering

Lettering your message can be done by hand, stencil, or one of the commercially available transfer types. (These are sheets of wax paper with the alphabet in capitals and small letters. You rub the front of a letter to transfer it to paper.)

You may use any of the above techniques in combination. Should you or your child create a fantastic design that you are unable to duplicate at home, consider taking it to a professional printer to be reproduced. You may have to sacrifice color and all your friends will get the same card, but the design will be one you are proud of, and most important, it will be yours!

Materials are inexpensive, the techniques are simple, ideas are the hard part. This is where children have the advantage. From their incredible imaginations spring concepts and avenues of approach that can turn ordinary paper and paint into works of art celebrating the holiday season.

MAKING CHRISTMAS DECORATIONS

This winter, why not spend some time making your own decorations?
You may have all the materials you need around the house. If not, you
can buy them at the five-and-ten.

Decorated Spools

If you have empty thread spools, you can make interesting tree ornaments. Use glue to secure snippets of silk, velvet, or satin to the spools.
Then add gold stars or Christmas seals. Bits of lace or sequins can be used
to trim the top and bottom, held on by a drop of glue. To make a hanging
cord, loop a piece of yarn or ribbon around the spool and knot it. You can
cut the ends for a fringed look.

Making Garlands

Evergreen garlands are an extremely versatile Christmas decoration. You
can wind them around front-porch pillars, loop swags around the windows, and heap them on a fireplace mantel. To make the garlands, cut a
piece of clothesline cord to the length you need. Use pieces of greenery no
more than 4 or 5 inches long for best results. Wrap them together and
attach them to the cord with fine wire. Be sure the greens overlap as you go
for the full foliage effect, and keep all the greens facing in one direction.
It's easier to work with the cord if you tie the ends of the clothesline to a
chair or doorknob before you begin. For best results make sure there is no
slack. You can add touches of color with bows, frosted pine cones, gilded
nuts, and fruit.

A Miniature Tree

If your apartment is too small to contain a normal-sized tree, but you love
the smell of fresh evergreens, you can make your own miniature tree with
branches begged or bought at the Christmas-tree lot. They will keep ten
days or longer if you put them in a container of wet sand. Place the container in the designated spot before you put in the sand (wet sand is extremely heavy). Fill it two-thirds full of dry sand, put in the branches, and
saturate with water. A basic arrangement is one large branch with two or
more smaller branches filling out the base. Wire the branches together
with 24-gauge wire. Use small ornaments so the tree isn't overloaded.

Styrofoam Decorations

Styrofoam comes in many shapes and sizes, offering a wealth of decorative
possibilities. Cones can be studded with lollipops to make a lollipop tree.
Styrofoam balls of various sizes can be covered with candy, sequins, rib-
bons, or simply painted. Children enjoy stringing popcorn and cereal into
garlands (one for the tree and one for me!), but consider the hazards of
insects and pets first.

Making your own decorations not only saves you money but also offers
hours of imaginative recreation for you and your children.

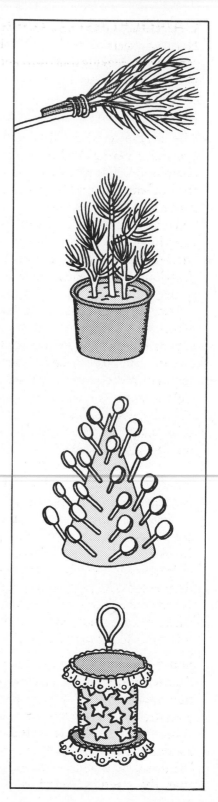

CANDLELIGHT, YOUR OWN WAY

Nothing cheers up a wintry evening quite like the warm, soft glow of candlelight. Making your own candles at home is a pleasant, inexpensive project; all that's needed are a few easily obtainable materials and some imagination.

Materials

The simple hand-dipped method of candlemaking will result in graceful, tapering candles that are ready for use just a few hours after completion. The materials you'll need are: wax, wicks, a container for the hot wax (dip tank), a pan for heating water, a second dip tank for cool water, wax paper, and paper towels. In addition to this basic list, you may need to purchase some stearic acid. This is desirable if you are using low-quality wax—the stearic acid (use about 3 tbsps. per pound of wax) will ensure that the wax hardens correctly and burns evenly. Stearic acid is very inexpensive and is available at most craft and hobby stores.

Beeswax has a lovely natural fragrance but may be a little too expensive to buy in bulk. You may choose to add some beeswax to less expensive wax for a delicate scent, or you can purchase scented oils to mix in. Paraffin, which is man-made wax from a petroleum base, is generally an economical choice and will produce candles that burn cleanly and evenly. Candle dyes are inexpensive, and can be obtained in packages of assorted bright colors. Braided wicks are stronger than twine or string, easier to work with, and will burn cleanly. Use 15-ply braided wicks for candles of up to 3 inches in diameter, 24-ply for 3-to-4-inch candles, and 30-ply for candles greater than 4 inches in diameter. Avoid using lead-core wicks, particularly if children are participating in the project; the lead contained can be quite dangerous.

After deciding upon the length of candles you'd like to make, select containers that are a few inches taller than the length of the candles to use as dip tanks—one for melted wax, and one for cool water. Coffee or soup cans are fine; just remove the paper labels and clean thoroughly. A deep-sided skillet or bread pan can be used for heating water, as long as it is wide enough to set the dip tank in without splashing water over the sides. After spreading a cloth over your work area (to prevent dripping wax from becoming a clean-up chore) you are ready to begin

Hand-Dipped Candles

Set the pan of water on the stove and heat to boiling. Reduce the heat so that the water will simmer without bubbling. Place chunks of wax into your dip tank, and place the tank directly into the pan of hot water. (Using indirect heat to melt the wax is to prevent the hot wax from suddenly bursting into flame or spattering on hands and clothing.) While the wax melts, cut the wicks. Make them about 3 inches longer than the intended length of your candles so you can hold the end

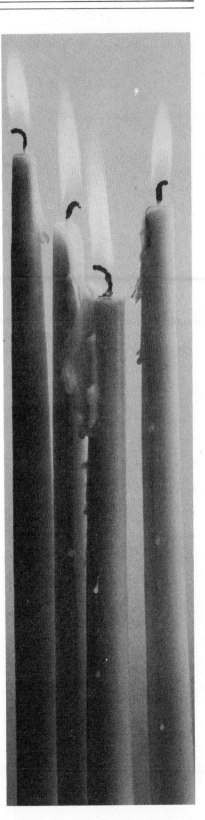

comfortably while dipping the wick into the hot wax.

When the wax has melted, dip each wick, one at a time, into the dip tank until it is thoroughly saturated with wax. Hold the wick above the dip tank until it stops dripping; then dip it into the cool water for a few seconds. Dry the wick gently with paper toweling, and lay it on a sheet of wax paper. Be sure to keep the wick as straight as possible; this will determine the shape of the candle when completed. Repeat this process with each wick until all have had their first dipping. Then start again with the first wick—dip it into the heated wax, drip, dip into cool water, drip, dry, and back to the wax paper. Each time this is done, a new layer of wax will form, gradually increasing the diameter of the candle. If you find that the candles begin to curve, roll them gently on the wax paper until straight. Be sure to check the straightness of the candle after each dipping so that any irregularities can be easily corrected.

WHAT'S A THREE-DOG NIGHT?

We asked an old-time resident of Maine to set us straight on this, and here is his report.

"Well . . . up here in the wintertime, it gets kind of cold. Now . . . if you're a bachelor like myself, what you need on a seriously cold night is a little warmth. Preferably it oughta have a self-contained source of power so it won't go and get cold on you during the night (you're lookin' for an advantage here over a hot-water bottle). It should have kind of a soft pleasant aspect to it so's you can abide bein' real close, and it oughta be mobile so you can get it under the covers with you. Now I don't know what choices you people got available to you down in the big cities, but up here, about the only thing that fits the bill is the family dog.

"If it ain't too cold an evening, I might get by with, say, just that little terrier of mine curled up near my feet. But when the season really gets a grip on the country up here, I find myself being more than usually friendly to my fine young collie. I can usually coax her to take up alongside my back, and with that and the terrier at my feet, I make out O.K. Worst fight I ever had with my sister when we were kids, by the way, was over a big, black Labrador retriever. We raised such a ruckus that the animal finally decided to take up with our grandmother for the night, which was a pretty good thing because otherwise the old lady might not have made it.

"Long about yesterday, I saw the way the temperature was fallin' and I started lookin' at this other dog I got around the place. He's a mean old critter, and I ain't paid much attention to him since he took a bite out of one of the few callers I do get up this way. But as the sun went down, he started to look a little different to

You will find that wax will build up at the base of the candle. You may prefer this shape, but if you wish to keep the candles uniformly narrow, simply shave the base as needed with a paring knife or vegetable peeler while the candle is warm and easy to trim. Shave the bottom surface of the candle to just where the wick begins.

If you have decided to add scented oils or dyes, you can economize by adding them to the wax only for the last two dippings. The candle will still have a lovely aroma, and the color will be nice and bright on the outer surface. Of course, you can add the scent and dye at the outset for stronger fragrance and uniform color.

When the candles are of the desired width, let them cool for several hours (the actual time necessary depends upon the width of the candle). Once thoroughly cooled, they are ready to be lit or stored until the next gloomy evening.

Molded Candles

You may wish to try molded candles. If so, why not use the snow on your front porch to make your own one-of-a-kind mold? Simply scoop up the snow into a bucket, pail, or can, and dig out the shape you'd like your candle to be. When you've created the desired mold, pack the snow firmly around the sides and bottom so that there are no holes for the wax to leak through. Melt the wax as for dipped candles, adding the desired scent or dye at the outset. Pour or ladle the melted wax carefully into the mold. When the wax is fairly firm, insert a straightened wire coat hanger directly through the center, making a tunnel through which you can later thread the wick. When the wax is opaque and ready to be taken out of the mold, simply scrape the snow away. Run the wick through the tunnel, and carefully spoon melted wax into the hole to fill in any gaps. Cut the wick to the bottom of the candle, using a fingertip of melted wax to seal it to the surface.

How to Care for Your Candles

To keep your candles burning correctly without smoking or excessive dripping, just remember these few pointers: 1) Keep the wick trimmed (about ½ inch), and make sure that it is straight. 2) If the flame is too low, pour off accumulated wax; if too high, trim the wick and be sure that the candle surface is free of accumulated debris. 3) Even the best-made candle will smoke and drip if set in a draft or if not set completely upright in its holder.

If, by the way, you find that your candle's surface is rough or dull, polishing it with an old nylon stocking dipped in salad oil will smooth the surface and restore luster. You should store your candles in a box or dark closet to keep the colors from fading.

Your local crafts shops usually carry candlemaking supplies. If you cannot locate all the necessary materials, several mail-order suppliers are listed in the last section of this book.

3 Dog Night (cont'd)

me, and I gave him a good meal and commenced to pattin' on his head a little. He seemed agreeable after a while, and then I called to the other two and we settled down under the covers for the evening. And that, sir, is what we call a three-dog night."

Candles
"They light with joy the wintry scenes—
The candles of the evergreens!"
– Arthur Wallace Peach (1886-?)

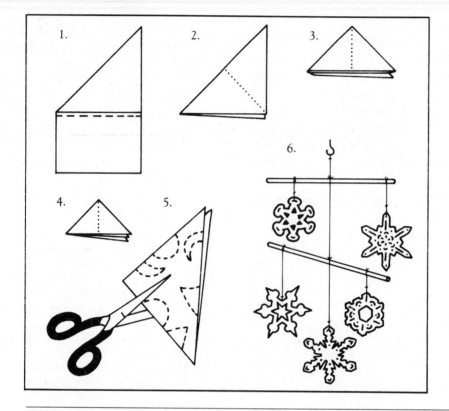

PAPER SNOWFLAKES

Maybe you live in Maine and just can't get enough snow. Or perhaps you've moved from Vermont to Florida and miss all the white stuff. In either case, you can make your own snowflakes using only paper and scissors.

Since most paper is rectangular, you will need to make a square. Start with a piece of paper that is at least 3 inches long on its short side. Fold the short side over to the long side. Cut off the excess paper. The result is a square with the first fold already made. Fold this triangle in half once. Then fold it in half again . . . and again. Cut small pieces out of the folded paper. The more cuts you make, the more intricate the design will be. When you finish cutting, unfold the paper and you will have a lovely snowflake. For variety, you could use colored paper, or hang several snowflakes together to make a mobile.

HOME SCENTS
Sachet

A sachet is a small bag containing powdered herbs and/or flowers. It is one of the simplest and most pleasing ways to perfume clothes, note papers, or stored bedding and rugs. A small sachet can be tucked into a pillow or behind sofa cushions — virtually anywhere you'd like to add a touch of fragrance.

Many large pharmacies sell the dried flowers and herbs necessary for the sachet, or you can purchase them fresh and allow them to dry at home. To make a winter sachet to use in storage closets and among woolens, mix equal amounts of rosemary and mint leaves, one fourth part thyme, and a tablespoon or so of ground cloves.

There are no rules in sachet making (except that materials must be completely dried before filling);

whatever fragrances you enjoy make perfect sachets. You might like to try using orange flowers, patchouli leaves, ground mace, oakmoss, white sandalwood, rose blossoms, lavender, or heliotrope — any combinations which appeal to you.

Small pieces of silk make the best sachet bags. You may be lucky enough to find a prettily embroidered silk handkerchief at home; if not, most thrift shops have dozens for sale. Fold the handkerchief in half, inside out, and sew up the sides, forming an envelope. Turn it right side out and add the filling. Make sure that the sachet ingredients are completely dry, or mildew may form.

By adding lace or trimming to the completed sachet, you can make a lovely personal gift, which will be much appreciated during the long winter months.

Pomanders

Pomanders are perfumed balls that can be stored in closets, pantries, or drawers to impart lovely aromas to clothes, linens, or room areas. These fragrant balls have been in use at least since the first century A.D., when Pliny described one made of cassia, cinnamon, betel nut, saffron, myrrh, balm, and honey.

As cities grew in size, and health hazards became greater, various fanciful medicinal properties were attributed to these scented spheres, among which were pomander recipes to make your breath smell sweeter, and pomander cures for sleeplessness.

Thomas Wolsey, the sixteenth-century English cardinal, is said to have carried a homemade pomander of fruit shells filled with spices. From his basic idea comes an easy recipe for you to try at home: punch holes in a large, fresh orange using an ice pick or sharp knife. Put a whole clove into each hole until the orange is completely studded with the spice. Roll the fruit in cinnamon (you may add other spices as desired to the cinnamon), using about 1½ tablespoons of the powdered spice for each orange. Wrap the prepared fruit in foil or tissue and allow to dry for several weeks. When completely dry, you can decorate the pomander with ribbon, making a loop by which it can be hung. Pomanders make charming gifts, and can be easily adorned with holly, flowers, or leaves as seasonal offerings.

Potpourri

Potpourri (from the French, meaning "pot rotten") is a blend of scented ingredients in a decorative jar with a loose-fitting lid. When the lid is removed, the heady fragrances trapped within the jar will linger in the room for hours. Delightfully aromatic flower petals, sweet and pungent herbs, and essential oils are the ingredients used to create this visually lovely home perfume. Making your own potpourri requires your choice of ingredients, a few weeks of patience while the potpourri cures, and a desire to make your home a pleasantly scented place.

Potpourris are made by either the dry or moist method. A dry potpourri contains completely dried ingredients (cracker dry) to which es-

sential oils are added to help the flower fragrances along. All of this is cured for several weeks before use. A moist potpourri uses semi-dry ingredients, is fermented with salt, and is combined with essential oils. Making a dry potpourri is an easier project but may be less lastingly fragrant than the moist. Following are two traditional recipes, one using the dry method, one the moist.

Dry Potpourri

8 cups rose petals (dry)
4 cups rose leaves (dry)
6 cups lavender buds (dry)
⅔ cup orrisroot powder (a fixative to prevent petal oils from dissipating)
4 tablespoons allspice (coarse ground)
¼ cup cloves (coarse ground)
4 tonka beans (ground, this adds a sweet vanilla scent)
4 drops oil of roses
4 drops oil of lavender

Combine all the dry ingredients (treat them gently, or they may crumble), and add the oils a drop at a time. Mix the ingredients, and seal in a large jar. Store the jar in a dry, dark closet for 6 weeks. While it is curing, shake the jar gently once a day to keep the fragrances mixed. After six weeks, put the potpourri into your prettiest glass jars and place around the home. Open the lids whenever you want to give your room a breath of spring.

Moist Potpourri

9 cups fresh rose petals
1½ cups coarse salt
1½ tsps. cinnamon (ground)
¾ tsp. cloves (ground)
8 dried lemon verbena leaves
½ cup dried rosemary
¾ cup dried lavender buds
½ cup orrisroot powder
1 cup dry flowers of your choice for color (zinnias, pansies, larkspur, marigolds, and delphiniums all have rich, deep colors)
4-8 drops oil of roses

Put the rose petals on a screen, set in a warm, dark, well-ventilated place for about 8 days, until the rose petals dry to a soft, leathery texture. Layer the rose petals with the salt in a large crockery jar. Place this jar in the same place in which you dried the rose petals for about 10 days. Mix the rose petals and salt daily. When the mixture has dried completely, blend in the other ingredients, and turn the contents into your chosen glass potpourri jars.

❉❀❉❀❋ ✳❀✳❀✳❉❀❉❀

Snowball

This is an old English-Scottish drink, potent and smooth. Wrap your frame around two or three of these, and winter's winds will become as the balmy breezes of summer.

6 tbsps. vodka
3 tbsps. advocaat
2 tbsps. heavy cream
1 tbsp. sugar

Crush 5 ice cubes and put all ingredients into blender. Whizz at high speed until smooth — about 15 seconds.

Did You Know . . .

. . . milkweed floss, which can be gathered in autumn fields and used to stuff the lining of a parka, is six times lighter than wool, and just as warm?

PATCHWORK QUILTS

One of the most decorative ways to stay warm in winter is to snuggle under a patchwork quilt. Patchwork quilts come to us from an era when fuel was only one of many things in short supply. Early pioneer women had to make whatever materials they had go as far as possible. Clothing and bedding were used until they fell apart, then the salvageable scraps were sewn together and used again. It is from these attempts at frugality that the very first "crazy quilts" were developed. These were eventually refined from random-sized and -shaped pieces sewn together to the beautiful and complex repetitive patterns sold at auctions and exhibited in museums today.

What Is a Quilt?

Quilts (from the Latin *cuilte* meaning a stuffed sack, mattress, or cushion) are made of three layers. The top layer is the decorative one, usually consisting of differently patterned cloth scraps sewn into a square design, which is in turn joined with other squares to create the quilt's pattern. This layer is sewn to a backing layer of plain material with batting or filler in between.

Utilitarian and Social

To our ancestors, quilts represented far more than merely a warm bed covering or blanket. Quilting bees provided a rare opportunity to combine social activity and utility in the days when leisure time was at a premium. Patchwork designs were given names with political, personal, and superstitious significance. A woman's collection of quilts was often a visual depiction of her own and her community's history. It is little wonder that these symbolically designed quilts were willed from generation to generation.

Make Your Own Heirloom

The renewed interest in American folk art has skyrocketed the price of these antique patchwork quilts. Rather than paying $150 or more for someone *else's* family tradition, why not create your own. With a little sewing acumen and a lot of patience you can make a traditional quilt. Long winter nights are perfect for creating an heirloom for *your* future generations.

QUILTING BEES

Lacking soap operas and bridge clubs, pioneer wives had to find ways to occupy their time when winter weather shut them indoors. The rigors of early American frontier life required that social functions serve some utilitarian purpose and quilting bees fit the bill. Women of the community would meet at a central location to sew a patchwork quilt for a bride-to-be or the reverend's wife. Local gossip could be exchanged while the work was being done. Later, the men would join them for dinner, and future husbands and wives could meet in one of the rare opportunities for social intercourse that their harsh existence afforded.

The Task

Oh, Winter, King of intimate delights,
Fire-side enjoyments, home-born happiness,
And all the comforts that the lowly roof
Of undisturbed retirement, and the hours
Of long uninterrupted ev'ning, know.

—William Cowper

RUG MAKING

A rug you make yourself is something you can love. Wiggle your toes in it, nestle in it with your favorite book. Your homemade magic carpet will be a source of pleasure for many winters to come.

For their combination of beauty and utility, wool rugs are unbeatable. A hooked or knotted rug weighs up to one pound per square foot; this insulating floor covering will hold down drafts and warm your feet. Even if you don't make a room-sized rug, a small one placed by a door, by a chair, or by your bed to step onto in the cold mornings will help provide warmth. Also, while making your rug, you can snuggle under it as you work.

With the new tools available, it's possible to fulfill your rug-design fantasies quickly and easily. It takes only three-quarters of an hour to speed-hook a square foot of rug. Imagine rug vignettes up and down the stairs, erotic rugs in the bedroom, a Picasso or Matisse design anywhere. Use your imagination! Art books are a great source. Many paintings, especially those with a solid color field, abstracts, and geometrics, make ideal rug design sources. Or you can be practical and use up all your scraps of yarn to make a "leftovers" rug of your own design.

Rug making is a form of adult play. It feels much as it did when you were coloring pictures as a child: you follow the outlines and fill in the color. You'll find that rug making is more fun and far less frustrating than your old watercolors and coloring book were. The wool won't dry out, and you won't lose your place if you stop for a while.

Some establishments (such as B. Rugged, 51 Spring Street, New York, NY 10012) will hook a rug for you if you send them the design.

KNITTING A MUFFLER

Even if you've just learned to knit, you'll find that a warm, woolly muffler is one of the easiest projects to tackle. There are no curves in the shape, and the length is merely a matter of preference. So all you have to do is get going with your basic stitches, which are diagramed here as reminders. Don't let all those tangled looking strands frighten you! With a little knowledge and a cold neck for motivation, you'll soon be turning out enough knitted goods to outfit your family for the winter.

Casting On

Your first step is to get the yarn onto the knitting needle. This is called casting on and is simply a series of knots. To begin, pull out a length of yarn. Figure one inch per stitch plus an extra five inches, so you will be able to hold the end as you work. 1) Starting on this strand, near the ball of yarn, make a slip knot. Slide the knitting needle through the second loop. 2) Pull the yarn ends and tighten. This is your first stitch. 3) To continue casting on, hold the knitting needle in your right hand, and loop the loose yarn strand around the thumb of your left hand. 4) Next,

BUNDLING

Our colonial ancestors knew that not all methods of keeping warm in winter had to be tediously practical. Rather than send a young man walking miles through the cold night, or burn fires they could ill afford, eighteenth- and nineteenth-century parents approved of a relatively harmless activity known as bundling. They allowed their daughters to lie abed, fully dressed, with their young beaux, which kept the couple warm as they courted all night.

Clergy would occasionally preach against the practice. It seems that the full-dress rule was sometimes bent — if not completely discarded — along with the clothes. Young men who transgressed were required to make "honest women" of the victims of their lack of self-control under pain of excommunication, but this was rare. More often, couples would court chastely until married, lying bundled against the cold.

If it seems ironic that the Puritans would bring such a potentially risqué practice to the New World, one must remember that it was their strict upbringing and beliefs that kept the potential from becoming the actual. With the decline of Puritanism came the decline of

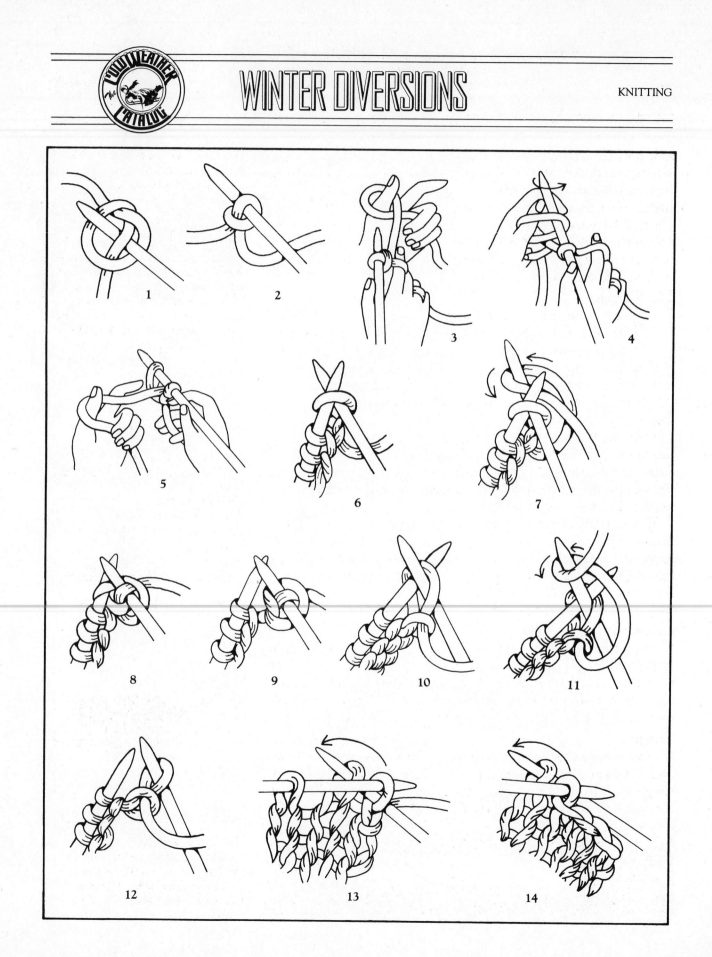

slide the needle along your thumb and through the loop of yarn wrapped around your thumb. With the ball end, wrap the yarn around the needle from underneath. 5) Flip this loop up and over the needle point, and tighten up on the short strand to secure. All of this sounds rather complicated, but once you've done it several times, you'll be able to cast on your entire row in a matter of moments. After you have cast on the number of stitches you need, do not use the loose end of the yarn. Trim it to 3 inches or so, so it won't get in your way.

The Stitches

You may choose to use a knit stitch throughout, which will result in a flat, herringbone effect on one side, and a nubby look on the reverse side. This is just fine, but using only one stitch can become rather boring after a while. To diversify the stitches slightly, make a ribbed muffler by alternating simple knit and purl stitches. If you decide to make this ribbed muffler, make sure you cast on a multiple of four so that there will be an even number of knit and purl stitches.

There are four steps to the knit stitch. 6) To begin, slide the empty needle through the right side of the first cast-on stitch. 7) Wrap the yarn strand around the needle point and draw the needle with the loop back through the first stitch. 8) Slide the first cast-on stitch to the top of the needle. 9) Drop the old stitch off.

The purl stitch has three steps, and is basically an "inside-out" knit stitch. 10) To begin, slide the empty needle through the first stitch, keeping the empty needle in front of the full one. 11) Wrap the yarn around the needle point. 12) Draw the needle back through, and drop the original stitch off. Then it's just knit two, purl two. You'll end up with an elastic, ribbed muffler that is bulky and warm.

Casting Off

Once your muffler is of the desired length, use the simple cast-off onto the empty needle. 13) Using the point of the full needle, lift the stitch on the right over the stitch on the left and drop off the right one. 14) Then continue by sliding the next stitch onto the needle. Lift the right stitch over it, drop it off, and continue in this way down the row.

Fringe

To make fringe for the ends, cut a few lengths of yarn about 4 inches long and fold them in half. Using a crochet hook, pull the folded end of one length through the first finished-off stitch and thread the loose ends through the resulting loop, pulling tight to anchor it. Continue down the row, spacing the fringe as desired.

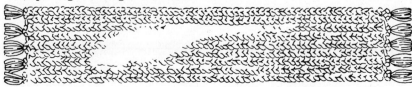

bundling, since the comparative moral laxity that followed caused an increasing number of accidents, making the risqué downright risky.

In 1869, Henry Reed Stiles, feeling the need to defend his birth state of Connecticut against charges of moral turpitude, wrote a history of bundling entitled, *Bundling: Its Origin, Progress and Decline in America.* This vastly entertaining book was first republished by the Book Collectors Association Incorporated in 1934 and more recently has been made available by Gale Research Company, Book Tower, Detroit, Michigan.

Nursery Rhyme

The north wind doth blow,
And we shall have snow
And what will poor robin do then,
Poor thing?
He'll sit in a barn,
And keep himself warm,
And hide his head under his wing,
Poor thing.

—*Anonymous*

Did You Know . . .

. . . sound carries great distances in extreme cold? At −60° Fahrenheit (−51° C.), the barking of dogs can be heard at a distance of 10 to 12 miles!

SAUNAS—DRY HEAT

In Finland, saunas (meaning baths) have been a community tradition for centuries. The log sauna lodge is a meeting place for men and women of the township who gather there to bake in temperatures of up to 250° Fahrenheit. After 20 minutes or so of this constant heat, participants use birch twigs to flick their skin, increasing circulation. After all of this good, clean fun, everyone finds a convenient icy pond or snowbank to plunge into before going home to a much deserved night's rest. If all of this sounds a little too invigorating for you, take heart. The sauna in the United States has been transformed into a restful, quiet pastime, a place in which to serenely cleanse the body and the mind.

The basic concept of the sauna is a simple one: an insulated room within a room, housing a controllable heat source. Most saunas have stones piled on or near this heating source to provide nonradiant heat, which is gentle and constant. The user can pour small amounts of water onto the stones to produce steam, adding diluted fragrances to enhance the experience. All you have to do is *relax*. Stretch out and let all the stress and tension of the day escape.

Most health clubs have sauna rooms available. However, if you decide that you cannot live without a sauna of your very own, there are kits available, which can provide you with your own private retreat. There are kits

Did You Know . . .

. . . the world's greatest fishing areas are in its coldest seas? Microscopic marine life, both animal and vegetable is at its richest—a veritable soup—in areas so cold that nothing grows on land. It's this soup of little stuff that the big fish and whales eat, and they don't seem to mind the cold in the least.

that show you how to turn an area the size of a closet into a snug little sauna for one, how to utilize a spare room as a family sauna. Kits include virtually everything you'll need, often right down to the stones. Many of the smaller models can be easily dismantled, so you can pack the sauna up and take it along when you move.

Sauna: Do's and Don't's

1. If you have doubts about the medical advisability of using a sauna, *do* check with your physician beforehand. Since the rise in temperature causes body temperature, heart and pulse rates to increase, it is definitely not recommended for the elderly or those with high blood pressure or diabetes.

2. *Do not* use your sauna directly after a heavy meal or at any time when you might fall asleep.

3. *Do not* drink any alcoholic beverages before, during, or immediately after using your sauna.

4. *Do* enjoy your sauna au naturel. *Do not* wear any jewelry or a wristwatch—they may heat up enough to cause burns.

5. To achieve the optimum effects, *do* alternate short periods in the sauna (10 to 15 minutes) with cool showers.

6. *Do not* allow the sauna to heat above 195 to 200° Fahrenheit (90-93°C.). Most people like 175 to 185° Fahrenheit (79-85°C).

7. *Do not* expect any magical weight-loss results from the use of a sauna. What you are losing is body water, which will be replaced.

8. If dry skin is a problem, *do* use a skin moisturizer before and after enjoying your sauna. Your skin will be super clean after a few moments in the sauna, allowing the moisturizer to sink in and do some good.

SAUNA DESIGNS

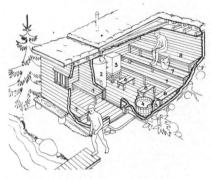

1. Dressing room. 2. Stove. 3. Hot-water tank. 4. Cold-water container. 5. and 6. Washing stools. 7. Lower platforms. 8. Upper platform.

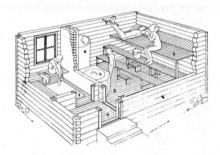

1. Hallway. 2. Dressing room. 3. Hot room. 4. Platform. 5. Hot-water supply. 6. Sauna stove. 7. Footrest.

Although the principle of basking in dry heat remains the same, designs for saunas vary tremendously. They may be anything from a spartan two-person sauna tucked away in a corner of a basement to the luxurious cabin-size types illustrated here. Both designs hail from Finland, where the sauna is an integral part of life. The sauna at top is meant to be part of a modern country home. The bottom design features headrests, footrests, and movable steps that can be pushed under the platform when not in use.

SCRIMSHAW

After providing warmth for your innards, that pot of Yankee bean soup can provide hours of fun in front of the fire by providing the raw materials for an art form developed by Yankee whalers. As anyone who has read *Moby Dick* can tell you, whalers spent much of their time at sea waiting for the whale sightings that would send the whole ship into a flurry of activity, culminating in the cleaning and storage of the catch. This combination of idle hours and ready materials gave birth to the art of carving whalebone and whale teeth, known as scrimshaw. The word comes from the British slang "scrimshander," meaning time waster.

Using Soup Bones

The once-plentiful whales that provided the bones and teeth for carving are now an endangered species, along with most other ivory-bearing animals. However, Yankee bean soup (or any soup for that matter) can provide soup bones as a substitute for the potential scrimshander. Soup bones are somewhat harder than ivory and more porous, so they require an extensive amount of preparation.

Did You Know . . .

Ice itself cannot cool anything below 32°, its own temperature? It is the melting of ice that absorbs heat from the things around it (144 btu's or 36,288 calories for each pound of ice that melts) and brings their temperature well below freezing while the ice stays at 32°.

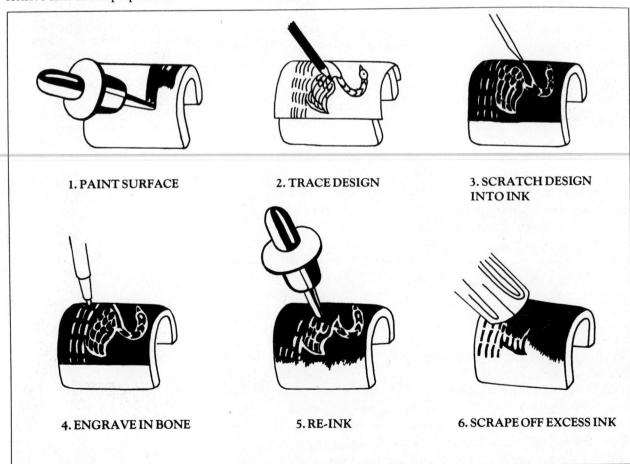

1. PAINT SURFACE

2. TRACE DESIGN

3. SCRATCH DESIGN INTO INK

4. ENGRAVE IN BONE

5. RE-INK

6. SCRAPE OFF EXCESS INK

Cleaning the Bones

Remove the meat from the outside and the marrow from the inside. A knife blade or spoon handle may be used to remove the marrow which, if saved, can be fed to your dog or cat.

Boil the bones for 1½ to 2 hours in a quart of water containing 1 teaspoon of alum and 1 tablespoon of baking soda. This will soften any fibrous material left inside and allow you to easily scrape it clean.

Rough-cut the bone to the shape desired using a hacksaw. Carefully study the bone so you can make the best use of its natural curves and shapes. Bone is extremely hard material so be sure to use a metal-cutting blade. File the rough edges down and sand the surface with gradually finer sandpaper. If you use a power sander, be sure to keep the surface cool by wetting it at intervals.

Treating with Paraffin

To prevent ink or dyes from bleeding during the engraving process, bones must be paraffin treated. Immerse the bones in liquid paraffin for five minutes, then remove them and scrape off any excess. After cooling for ten minutes, the bone will be ready for polishing and engraving.

Whale oil and sailor's wax were the traditional polish agents for whale's teeth, giving the finished product a dark honey color. Modern scrimshanders use bobbing compounds or tripoli (metal polishes) for the initial polishing and white diamond polish, jeweler's rouge, putty powder, or precipitated chalk for the final polishing.

Designing

The design you choose is entirely up to you. Beginners should probably start with a simple design, working up to more elaborate ones as they gain proficiency and experience. Marine symbols and scenes were favorites with sailors, as may be expected, but nature scenes, flags, monograms, and verses were also popular variations.

Draw your design on paper first, and then transfer it to the material to be carved by either tracing it over black carbon paper or painting the surface to be carved black and tracing the design onto it with white carbon paper. The second method has the advantage of allowing further design refinements to be made right on the object by scratching the ink with a pointed instrument.

Carving

Purists may want to attempt the actual carving with a jackknife, like the Yankee sailors did, but for the more practical minded, a carbide engraver, available at most craft and hobby stores, is best for working in bone. When carving, shavings will accumulate in the grooves and must be brushed or blown away. The deeper you carve the wider and blacker the line will be when inked. Lighter or darker shading is accomplished by closer or farther apart crosshatching or stippling.

Yankee Bean Soup

8 cups water
piece of ham, ham bone, or ¼ pound salt pork
1 cup Yankee beans
6 to 8 peppercorns
2 carrots
6 whole cloves
1 bay leaf
1 onion
6 ribs of celery
2 cloves of garlic

Prepare your vegetables in advance: dice the carrots, chop the celery, slice the onion, and mince the garlic. Boil the water and add the beans, meat, bay leaf, cloves, and peppercorns. Cook the beans slowly until they are soft. This should take between 2½ and 3 hours. (If you soak the beans the night before, it will cut down on the cooking time.) When the beans have softened, add the chopped vegetables and cook another 30 minutes. It is now time to remove the meat and chop it up. Strain through a sieve or in a blender. Put back the meat and season to taste. If the soup is too thick, it may be thinned with water or milk. Serves eight.

Inking

The final step is to cover the engraved design with black India ink and let it dry. Then, using the edge of a folded piece of cardboard, remove the excess ink, leaving a black design on a white background. Stubborn ink can be removed with fine sandpaper and the surface repolished. If you make a mistake, don't worry; a minor one can be corrected by resanding and recarving. Lines may still be added or deepened, just re-ink. If it's a complete mess, you can be glad it's only a soup bone and not an expensive piece of ivory.

The finished product may be a spoon, pendant, or earring, but whether it is decorative or utilitarian, a scrimshaw piece is a link with the folk art of America and a creative, fun way to spend a winter's eve.

HOW TO CURE PLANT BLAHS

Symptom	Cause	Cure
Tips of leaves are brown, wilting; bottom leaves are yellowish and falling fast.	Underwatering.	Give plant a good healthy drenching till water runs out of the pot; rewater according to the plant's requirements.
Leaves are turning yellow and curling under at edges.	Overheating.	Just move the plant to a spot that's cooler — that plant isn't sitting on a radiator, is it?
Leaves are turning brown and leathery or crinkly.	Air is too dry.	Increase humidity; mist leaves regularly.
Stems and lower leaves are dark and soft, rotting.	Overwatering.	Make sure drainage is not clogged; water plant less often.
Leaves become pale and seem to be growing abnormally long; new leaves are undersized.	Not enough light.	Move plant closer to sunlight or add artificial light.
Leaves are curling at edges, new leaves are undersized.	Too much light.	Move plant to a shadier spot.

YOU CAN FOOL MOTHER NATURE

If you play your cards right, you can have the brightest rainbow of flowers blooming in your home during the gloomiest part of winter. All that's necessary is a little planning and very little effort. Bulb flowers such as hyacinth, crocus, tulip, and narcissus, can be fooled into blooming any time you like; all you have to do is to provide them with an improvised winter and spring. The process is called forcing, and it's remarkably easy to do.

May in February

Forcing occurs over a period of about four months but requires less than an hour's actual work. October and early November are good times to select your bulbs; they will be blooming by the end of February, when you may really need some springlike cheer. It would be wise to check with your dealer to ensure that the specific variety you are interested in is good for forcing. Bulbs should cost only up to 65 cents each so you can afford to be lavish.

When you are ready to plant, select a container which is about twice as deep as the bulb is high and which has adequate drainage. Place the bulbs into the potting soil — close together for a densely colorful look — leaving the tip of the bulb exposed above the dirt.

Giving your bulbs the cold treatment is as easy as wrapping the pot

GREENHOUSES

Gardening need not end with the first frost. Greenhouses keep winter's cold out and let bright sunlight in. Depending on your budget and inclination, anything from a spice garden to a tropical rain forest can be cultivated under a greenhouse roof.

Types of Greenhouses

Well-designed greenhouses have narrow structural beams and wide panes that admit a maximum amount of light. A wealth of prefabricated structures are available to the winter gardener in all shapes and sizes. Made of wood or aluminum frames with glass sections, they are easily assembled with bolts and screws.

The many shapes of greenhouses available can cause some confusion to the prospective buyer. Each has its advantages and shortcomings.

LEAN-TOS: This style has gone in and out of favor with greenhouse gardeners over the years. A lean-to can be easily heated off your home's system, and the insulated wall that it shares with your house helps prevent heat loss. Recent fuel shortages have increased the value of these heat-retention properties.

FREE-STANDING MODELS: These are often span-roof houses that can be built away from the main house or connected to your home at one end. Their tentlike roofs admit more light than the lean-to's one-sided roof, but they cost more to heat. Free-standing greenhouses also come in circular, curved, and gazebo designs.

PLASTIC BUBBLES: Plastics loom large in the future of many products, and greenhouses are no exception. The increased durability of polyethylene sheets has led to their successful use, replacing glass, in commercial and domestic structures. Stretched over a tubular-steel

in paper and placing it in the refrigerator—be careful not to let the bulbs freeze. Place the pot on the lower shelf, and keep the soil moist.

In about three months, the shoots should be from 4 to 6 inches high, and roots will have developed. Now is the time for a gradual shift to springtime. Move the pot to a shady part of your home, and over the next couple of weeks, shift to a cool, light area. Once the bulbs are settled into their springtime environment, it will only be a matter of a few weeks until the blooming begins—all of which goes to prove: you *can* fool Mother Nature.

WINTER-BLOOMING PLANTS

Beautiful winter-blooming plants can provide your home with much needed brightness and color during the chilly, gray months. The following list will help you select from among the variety of plants which bloom during winter:

October-November
African violet
Geranium
Jasmine
Nasturtium (long cuttings)
Chrysanthemum (florist)
Wax begonia
Thanksgiving cactus

December
African violet
Geranium
Impatiens
Wax begonia
Sweet olive
Amaryllis, calla lily (white), French-Roman narcissus
Poinsettia
Christmas cactus (florist)

January
African violet
Begonia (many varieties)
Bouvardia

frame, sheets now may last as long as two years and are cheaper than glass.

The tubular structure is reduced to a minimum in the revolutionary plastic "bubble" houses. Electric fans are used to keep either the roof or the entire polyethylene structure inflated.

Where to Build

A greenhouse should be constructed where it will receive a maximum amount of sunlight. Morning sun is especially good for plants, making an eastern or southeastern exposure ideal. Some protection against strong winds provided by nearby trees or buildings is a good idea.

Firm Footing

A solid masonry foundation is essential to any greenhouse. Its below-ground depth will depend on the depth of your local frost line. A firm foundation will prevent heaving as the ground freezes and thaws. It will also keep a lean-to greenhouse from pulling away from the main house.

Heating

Any heating system that is good for people is good for plants. If your greenhouse is within 35 feet of your home's boiler or furnace, it is most practical to heat it by running pipes off the house system. In a hot-water or steam system, a separate pump is required for the greenhouse, controlled by its own thermostat. In a hot-air system, ducts and a separate fan are used in a similar manner. Only artificial gas is dangerous to plants—check with your gas company on this point.

If a separate heating system is required, an oil or gas burner is fine. Should electrical costs be low in your area, space heaters are the most accurate form of heating available (temperatures can be maintained to within one half of a degree).

Plants to Grow

Any plant that can be grown in nature can be grown in a greenhouse. This artificial environment allows the cultivation of flowers and foodstuffs out of their normal growing season. A greenhouse also gives the gardener a chance to grow plants that are not indigenous to his/her particular locale.

Imagine—tropical orchids, Asian camellias, or Brazilian passion flowers thriving in Connecticut. Or year-round access to Mandarin oranges, kumquats, or melons, fresh and only a few steps away. A greenhouse will allow you to set fresh tomatoes, cucumbers, peppers, and mushrooms on your table from January through December.

Books by the dozens are available to the would-be greenhouse gardener, offering advice and information on construction, heating, maintenance, and how to care for the plants you decide to grow.

Cyclamen
Geranium
Marica
Jasmine
Sweet olive
Forced branches: forsythia, honeysuckle bush

February-March
African violet
Azalea
Begonia (many varieties)
Blue sage
Geranium
Morning-glory (from seed)
Lily of the valley (forced pips)
Petunia
Miniature rose
Swedish ivy
Impatiens
Jasmine

With a little planning and care, you can maintain a continuous rainbow of blooming colors in your home throughout the winter season.

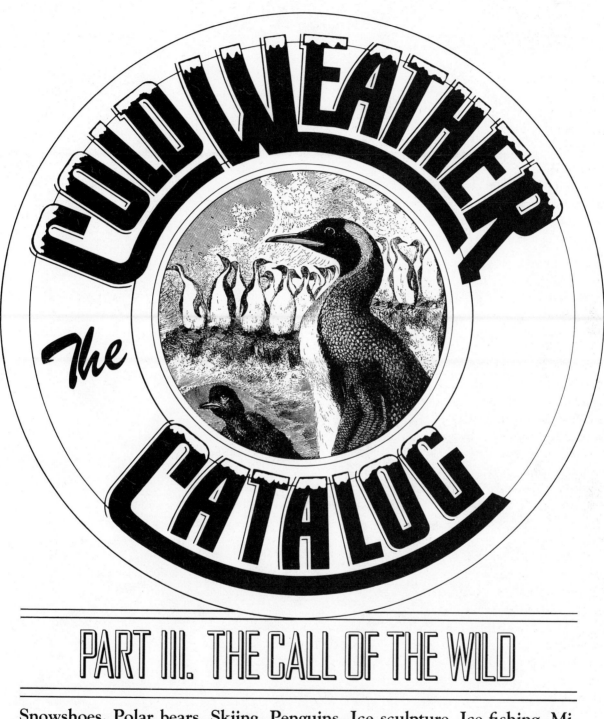

COLD WEATHER The CATALOG

PART III. THE CALL OF THE WILD

Snowshoes. Polar bears. Skiing. Penguins. Ice sculpture. Ice fishing. Migrating birds, hibernating beasts. The Northern Lights. Your own igloo. Wild food in the snow. Yeti. Bobsledding. Where is Rudolph now that we need him? (Perhaps he's outside.)

WHAT THE WILD THINGS DO

While we humans are closing up our summer homes and enjoying a few final weekends of Indian summer at the beach, the birds, beasts, and all other creatures that walk, crawl, fly, or slither about the earth are already preparing for winter. Many grow thicker coats; some stock their larders or build, find, or steal special winter quarters. Others avoid winter altogether by migrating or hibernating.

Hibernation

The incredible ability of animals to do all of the above is as amazing and mysterious to experts as it is to us. Many warm-blooded mammals, a few birds, some fish, various kinds of insects, and all cold-blooded creatures do it every year. They retire by early November, and don't wake up until April. But the dormancy of hibernation isn't just a long winter's nap. It's a deep, comalike stupor that in some creatures—such as the western poorwill bird, who when hibernating shows no heartbeat or respiration—more closely resembles death than sleep.

No one knows why the poorwill bird hibernates while others migrate, or exactly how any creature knows when it's time to retire to its hibernaculum. Most hibernating mammals are vegetarians who can't find enough to eat in the winter but are able to stuff themselves in the plentiful autumn months and survive on stored fat. Some eat until they're too gross to move around, then just drift off into slumber. Others apparently retire when they can no longer find food, but some creatures just can't seem to stay awake when the temperature drops

THE REINDEER

Every year Santa must go on a recruiting mission to northern Europe and Asia, where he can find replacements for any sled-pullers that have retired the previous year. Reindeer are members of the deer family, differing from their American cousins in that they have hairy muzzles, large, deeply cleft hoofs and in that both male and female have broad antlers.

Trained by Laplanders, these animals can travel 12 to 15 mph, drawing a loaded sled weighing up to 300 pounds.

below 50° Fahrenheit (10°C.) even if foraging conditions are still good.

The radical body changes, producing a dormant condition in which the animal actually spends nearly half its life, may occur gradually. For weeks, an animal may eat little, stay close to home, take lots of naps, and be rather bad-tempered—until it drops off. Then its metabolism slows down severely. Its body temperature may drop as low as the outdoor air. Respiration and heartbeat are reduced to a fraction of the normal rate.

If a hibernating animal is awakened roughly, it could die from shock. But under normal conditions, come spring, it will wake up weak, slow-moving, and slender, having lost as much as one third its body weight, but in excellent health. It gains back its strength as soon as it begins to eat regularly and will enjoy a longevity that researchers tentatively attribute to its annual winter sleep.

Medical scientists have already reproduced the conditions of hibernation in humans, and the possibilities have long been under study for the potential in space travel. Who knows, maybe one day we'll be able to do it. Meanwhile, here's how the *real* experts go about it:

Black Bear

During most of the year, the black bear sleeps outdoors and doesn't have any real home at all, but in September he chooses a winter den and stays nearby until the weather turns very cold, gaining as much as three pounds a day. A tidy bear will carefully clean out his chosen quarters, while a lazy one will just curl up in a thicket, or make himself cozy behind a fallen tree. His body temperature will stay high enough all winter to melt any snow that may fall on his coat or drift into his cave. Though he sleeps very soundly, he may wake up on a mild day, particularly if he was on the skinny side to begin with, and go outside for a bite to eat.

Raccoons and Skunks

Almost all animals that live in underground burrows hibernate. The woodchuck, who is the first creature to hole up each year, inhabits a spacious apartment, as far as five feet underground. He has at least five rooms, connected by tunnels, and keeps them meticulously clean. In the fall, when he has stuffed himself completely, he waddles into his grass-lined bedroom, seals the door with soil to keep out unexpected guests (such as the skunk, who may settle for sleeping in one of the chuck's other rooms), then curls up in a ball with eyes and mouth shut tight and his tail over his head.

Chipmunk

The chipmunk is one hibernator who doesn't lose weight over the winter, because he lives on stored food instead of stored fat. His

FOR THOSE WHO STICK AROUND

Nature does offer a little extra help to at least some of the creatures she hasn't programed to sleep or to go south.

The snowshoe hare turns from brown to white in the winter—which is why it's also known as the varying hare.

Weasels turn white if they live where it snows. If they don't, they stay brown all year.

The ruffed grouse or partridge develops snowshoes—comblike fringes along the sides of its feet. These are molted each spring.

In a swift burst of growth as cold weather arrives, fur-bearing animals develop thicker coats, the warmest of which, according to laboratory tests, goes to the wolf.

The red fox sprouts furry snowshoes to aid him in his long, lonely travels in search of food. When he's wandered too far to go home to sleep, he curls up on the ground, using his thick bushy tail as a warm blanket.

In addition to being able to store nuts, berries, seeds, and acorns, the red squirrel knows which mushrooms are poisonous, which are not, and the right time to gather them to save for a midwinter treat. His red coat pales a bit, and he grows extra tufts of fur that serve as earmuffs.

Snow itself is often a boon to chilly creatures. Millions of tiny air pockets in a snowbank eliminate the outward passage of the earth's heat and insulate against the cold, while providing ample air for breathing. In a blizzard, the cottontail rabbit will allow himself to be buried by drifting snow, and he assumes a drowsy sleep until the weather clears. The ruffed grouse will also dive into a snowbank to spend the coldest of winter nights.

family-style quarters include special chambers filled with nuts, acorns, and grains that usually overflow into the bedroom. Sometimes he piles his goodies so high he has to start his winter sleep up near the ceiling. He wakes up, of course, on the floor.

Snakes and Snails

Since the body heat of cold-blooded animals rises and falls with the temperature of the air, snakes, snails, frogs, turtles, and their various relatives must hibernate to keep from freezing. For tiny creatures like newts, toads, and salamanders, a pile of fallen leaves offers enough protection, but their larger relations have to plan ahead in order to beat the cold.

Turtles

The box turtle, like hibernating mammals, stuffs himself for weeks before going underground, but if he gets too fat, he's in real trouble: he can't fit back into his shell. He may be able to squeeze head and forelegs in, or tail and hindlegs, but to fit both ends in at once, he has to stop eating and rest long enough to lose weight. Several kinds of turtles hibernate underwater, including some that can only breathe on land. In their wintry dormancy they can live in water for as long as three months. Turtles can also be made to hibernate. Wholesale dealers keep them in winter storage, buried under mud and leaves, where they sleep soundly until dug up and delivered to pet shops.

Snakes

As the Indian summer draws to a close, snakes begin to gather on rocky hillsides, where they lie twined together, basking in the sun, until the temperature drops to around 50° Fahrenheit (10°C.). Then they crawl into crevices, or tunnel into the soil, some returning to regular dens where they get together. For maximum warmth, many kinds of snakes roll up in a ball to hibernate—sometimes hundreds of them to a ball.

Insects

Many insects die with the first frost, leaving egg and pupa to carry their kind through the winter. Not only can these embryonic forms survive the cold, they couldn't develop and hatch properly without it. But plenty of insects live through the winter in underground hibernation, and the more snow there is to keep the ground at a steady temperature, the better they survive. Ladybird beetles assemble by the thousands to crawl into their communal winter homes. Pill bugs, sow bugs, queen bees, and queen hornets hibernate beneath fallen logs. If you've ever wanted to study insect nests, now's the time to do it with impunity. But dormant, half-frozen insects will revive in the warmth of a room; so don't bring nests indoors.

TRACKING WILDLIFE

Our early American ancestors, and of course the Indians who preceded them, were expert trackers. The ability to identify a trail of animal prints along the forest floor often meant the difference between food and starvation. Today, this expertise is no longer a matter of survival, and it's fun to play nature detective, particularly with the assistance of a child, and following a track of prints through a fresh fall of light snow will eventually lead you to the home or hideout of the creature who made them.

It's easier to identify an animal by studying the whole track rather than a single set of footprints. The trail will also indicate the speed and gait at which it moved. A few general clues: when tracks of both forefeet and hindfeet are paired (you see two pairs of somewhat different prints in close succession) the animal was bounding, as cottontail rabbits, squirrels, mice, and weasels usually do. The front feet of all tree-climbing animals are usually paired when they jump. Animals that live on the ground tend to put one foot in front of the other except when bounding.

Here are the tracks of the ten creatures most likely to be seen in the winter—but the publishers make no guarantee that the markings you find will be as clear as these illustrations.

DEER MOUSE: The deer mouse is one of winter's most active mammals, and his prints are among those most commonly seen in snow. The straight line running between them is the track of his tail.

RACCOON: Unless you're feeding this fellow in your backyard, any 'coon prints you come upon are likely to be quite near his den. His legs are so short he can't get around in deep snow, and in winter he seldom ventures far from home. His long hind foot, with a well-marked heel and five comparatively short toes, leaves a print remarkably like that of a human child.

FIELD MOUSE: The field mouse is found as far north as the tundra beyond the tree line, and may be seen anywhere in the United States. His tail is short, at least for a mouse, and leaves no trail.

RED FOX: It could take days to follow the trail of this adventuresome fellow all the way back to his den; he ranges far and wide in search of food and doesn't necessarily go home to sleep. His trail *could* lead to the home of some smaller creature—or to evidence that the fox made a meal of it along the way. The amateur could mistake the fox's prints for those of a dog or a cat, but the paws are larger than a cat's, and the pads much smaller than those of a dog.

GRAY SQUIRREL: Squirrels usually travel by bounds, and the tracks of both forefeet and hindfeet are generally paired.

WHITETAIL DEER: Two or three inches of light snow make ideal

Wandering Through Winter

The snows of the north country being a winter-long succession of clean white pages on which are written, with paw prints and feather marks, a record of activity of wildlife.

—*Edward Way Teale*

conditions for deer tracking, and you may not have to go very far into the woods to find evidence of this shy creature. A hoofprint about three inches long is made by a full-grown buck. The doe's track is about half an inch smaller, and the fawn's only about an inch long.

COTTONTAIL RABBIT: A distance of 24 inches between groups of prints means you're on the trail of a slow-moving bunny. If Lewis Carroll's famous White Rabbit ("I'm late! I'm late!") had left prints, they would have been six to seven feet apart.

SKUNK: Like most fat, short-legged animals, the skunk waddles along, touching the ground with his whole foot. His tracks look a lot like a bear's, but in miniature.

WEASEL: This bold troublemaker may invade your camp, cabin, or farm. If there's been damage done, the weasel's bounding footprints may prove his guilt. He leaves two at each bound instead of four, placing his hind paws in the tracks made by his front paws.

BLACK BEAR: The tracks of this hibernator are seldom seen in snow, but in case you happen to be in his neighborhood early or late in the season, it's a good idea to be able to recognize them.

The Snow Storm

Announced by all the trumpets of the sky,
Arrives the snow, and driving o'er the fields,
Seems nowhere to alight: the whited air
Hides hills and woods, the river, and the heaven,
And veils the farm-house at the garden's end.
The sled and traveller stopped, the courier's feet
Delayed, all friends shut out, the housemates sit
Around the radiant fireplace, enclosed in a tumultuous privacy of storm.
—*Ralph Waldo Emerson*

HOW TO ATTRACT WILDLIFE TO YOUR BACKYARD

Winter is probably the easiest time to bring wildlife close to home. Even the most vulnerable forest creatures, ordinarily shy of proximity to humans, become more daring when food is scarce. But unless you live in an area with some dense trees and shrubs, you'll have to provide more than food. Wild animals need a sheltered place where they can quickly escape from dogs or natural predators, and newly built homes with infant plantings don't offer enough concealment.

Comfort—Not Luxury

Half a dozen discarded Christmas trees will provide adequate cover in the most barren landscape. The trees may be fastened securely against a fence, wall, or outbuilding to create a sort of lean-to, with the

branches trimmed on the inside to make more room. Such a structure will help make even wary pheasants and rabbits feel at home. A thin line of scratch feed will lure pheasants and quail to the larger supply under the evergreens. Rabbits will be attracted by the smell of apples, vege-

table peelings, and, if you want to get fancy, alfalfa hay.

Tricks You Can Learn

If you have an oak tree of any respectable size, chances are you've already got gray squirrels, but if you don't, they can be lured by ears of corn. Place the ears of corn in a wire basket lashed to a tree or post or impale them on a spike-pole feeder, easily constructed by driving a row of spikes into a piece of scrap lumber, which is then fastened between two supports. Don't use rope for hanging feeders, squirrels will

chew through just about anything but wire. After removing the corn from the cob, squirrels will eat only the germ. The remains of the kernel, which they drop to the ground, will attract birds and other animals, but you'll have to clean up the cobs—they won't get you anything but pack rats.

Night Visitors

The nocturnal mammals, often neglected, are among the most interesting and entertaining creatures you can attract. Flying squirrels (or tree squirrels), which might winter in a suitable birdhouse, love peanut butter smeared on tree limbs. Raccoons and opossums aren't as finicky. They'll eat commercial pet food, fish, meat, fruits, and most kinds of table scraps. Divide their meal into bits or the animals will use you as a take-out service and carry the food away en masse. Place it where you won't mind a little mess. Keep outdoor garbage cans tightly covered, or you'll have a big garbage area. Nocturnal visitors can be watched beneath a light with an indoor switch. Let them make first visits under cover of darkness. Once they've enjoyed a few meals at your expense, they'll get used to the light.

THE ABOMINABLE SNOWMAN

The abominable snowman of the Himalayas seems to make few personal appearances, but he's gotten almost as much publicity over the years as another mythical (?) creature: the Loch Ness monster. Where did this fierce ape-man get such an unusual name? Studies indicate that it is a poor translation of two Tibetan words—red bear—though believers in the existence of this cold-climate missing link become outraged when so mundane a creature as a bear is offered as the explanation of their terror.

Call Him Yeti

The abominable snowman, or yeti (another hard-to-translate term), seems to make his presence felt most often above the timberline in the higher peaks of Tibet, venturing into the forest for food (though it is also claimed that he dines on yaks and the occasional mountain climber). His white fur and cunning

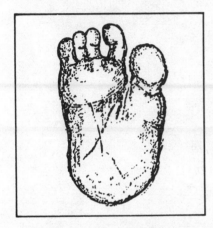

ways have not served to keep him completely invisible; Tibetans and Nepalese have pictured him in their art for hundreds of years, and in more recent times, western explorers have claimed sightings. In 1951, Eric Shipton's photographs of huge footprints started mountaineers searching in earnest (though skeptics say the prints could be those of other animals enlarged or distorted by snow). Sir Edmund Hillary, scaler of Mount Everest, went searching and returned with presupposed yeti scalps, which turned out to be the pelts of goatlike animals, woven by man.

The stories still come in: from the cold mountains of China, Russia, even from the California woods. The yeti is still not quite proven, still not quite a myth. He may be an ancient step in the evolutionary process, driven off to breed in the secrecy of the highest, coldest places on earth.

WINTER STARGAZING: USING A STAR MAP

A clear winter night affords one of the year's best opportunities to view the stars and constellations. Though winter is traditionally a time for indoor activities, a few minutes outdoors with a star map can provide you with a spectacular and unique light show.

Astronomers have created various types of star maps to help observers identify celestial bodies. The map included here shows the brighter stars that can be seen in the northern hemisphere, and although it's set up to resemble the view you would have if you looked straight up from the north pole, it can be used anywhere in the northern United States.

Using the Map

Here's how to use it. Suppose it's 9 P.M. on January 15. Find out which way is north and point the map, with January 15 at the top, in that direction. Locate the North Star as

your starting point, and then try to identify the other stars. Visualize the straight line on the map from the North Star to the Jan. 15 written at the top. This corresponds in the sky to a curve going from the North Star, up over your head, to stars behind you in the south. To identify those stars, just turn around and hold the map with the Jan. 15 date at the bottom.

If you can't be outside at exactly 9 P.M. you can still use the map. Hold it as if it were 9 P.M.; then turn it clockwise one month for every two hours before 9 P.M. or counterclockwise one month for every two hours after 9 P.M.

You can supplement the star map with one of the many available field guides to the skies that are designed for identifying the constellations. The patterns seen by the ancients may remain a puzzle, but once you learn the locations of the brighter winter stars, the pieces may begin to come together.

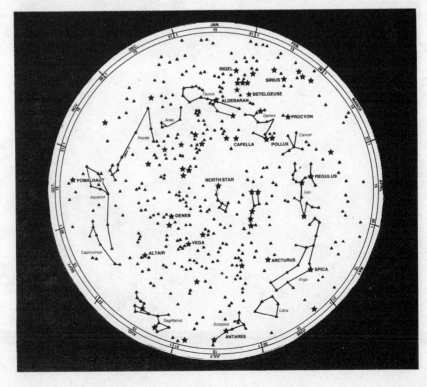

WINTER PHOTOGRAPHY

Many people put their cameras into cold storage during the winter, believing that the entire art of photography hibernates when the temperature drops. This idea, born at a time when most amateur photographers used only simple, nonadjustable cameras, is simply not true. With the introduction of modern cameras and film, almost any weather can be great for photography. In fact, as these pages show, some of the worst weather conditions have been the inspiration for magnificent photographs. With a little advance planning, you will be able to confront the glorious winter landscapes with the eye of the camera.

The Camera

It is necessary for your camera to function properly under normal conditions before venturing out into the cold. Most 35mm and roll-film cameras should be cleaned and adjusted periodically to ensure proper operation. Various types of cameras available today are suitable for use in cold weather, particularly if the exposure can be adjusted to prevailing light conditions. One of the biggest cold weather camera problems is batteries. Batteries lose much of their power in the cold, and this can result in a loss of exposure accuracy with light meters. In addition, cameras with electronic controls will stop working entirely. The solution to this problem is to carry a spare battery, keeping it in a pocket close to the body, and interchanging it often with the one in use. It should be noted that cameras of simpler design—rangefinder types—generally function better under these conditions than the more complex single-lens-reflex types.

Winter's Night Mulled Cider
Into a pot put 2 quarts of sweet cider, the peel (no white pith) of 1 lemon, one 3-inch stick of cinnamon, 6 whole cloves, ½ tsp. allspice. Heat to the boiling point. Let simmer 5 minutes and add ½ cup cognac. Strain the spices and serve hot in warmed mugs or glasses. On a cold winter's night, every extremity chuckles with the permeation from this brew.

A Few Words about Winterizing Your Camera

This involves taking your camera completely apart, removing all lubricants, and reassembling the camera using either special lubricants designed for use in extreme cold or using none at all. If the camera is then to be used under normal weather conditions, the process must be reversed. If all this sounds like a lot of work and expense to you, you are right; it is. Furthermore, a check with two major camera importers indicates that normal cameras, in good working condition, should function at temperatures down to 0° Fahrenheit (18°C.) without any special servicing at all. So the choice is yours; only you know what particular conditions your camera will be facing.

Film

Film becomes very brittle in cold weather, and may prove to be more of a problem than the camera itself. It is necessary to load the camera very carefully and to advance the film slowly to prevent it from breaking. Static electricity can also create problems in very cold, dry air. A static discharge will put chicken-feet marks on the film, rendering it useless. Again, the solution is to wind and rewind the film very slowly. Additionally, film speed and color can shift in cold weather. The best way to compensate for these fluctuations is to shoot plenty of film, varying the exposures. This should guarantee that at least some of the finished product is to your satisfaction.

Helpful Hints

When camera equipment goes from warm to cold (and vice versa), a problem with temperature adjustment may arise. Snow will melt on contact with the warm camera, and as the camera cools, will eventually turn into a crust of ice. Therefore, it is wise to store the camera in a cool place before going out of doors and to keep the camera covered while it becomes acclimatized to the cold. You can brush snow off the camera, but do not blow it off—your breath can melt the snow, which may then refreeze into ice. When bringing the equipment indoors, you may have a serious problem with condensation. If cold equipment is placed in a warm environment, it will sweat, leaving the camera dripping wet. To avoid this, put the camera into an airtight plastic bag—while you're still outside. Then, when the camera is brought indoors, the water will condense harmlessly on the outside of the plastic bag.

Exposure

There is no substitute for accurate focusing and correct exposure. However, this need not mean that the process must be repeated for every picture. For scenic pictures, for example, the camera will most likely be focused on the hyperfocal distance for the greatest possible depth of field. As long as the lighting conditions and subject matter don't change appreciably, the exposure should remain fairly constant.

Master Frost
The girl sat on the box, shivering with cold. Presently she heard Master Frost cracking the branches, jumping from tree to tree and coming nearer and nearer. "Are you warm, my beauty?
"Are you warm, fair maiden?"
"Warmth is from God, dear Frost, and the cold is from him too."
Then Frost had pity on her, and wrapped her up in rugs and furs.
—*Russian folk tale*

Travels of Baron Munchausen
What in the dark I had taken to be a stump of a little tree appearing above the snow, to which I had tied my horse,
proved to have been the weathercock of
the church steeple.
— *Rudolf Erich Raspe (1737-1794)*

Snow is such a good reflector of light that side- and backlighted subjects are well lighted on the shadow side. This effect reduces the need for change in exposure with lighting direction. The following table gives suggested adjustments to the basic exposure for a normal subject printed in the instruction sheet packaged with the film.

EXPOSURE CORRECTIONS FOR BRIGHT SUN ON SNOW
Adjustments from Normal Bright Sun Exposure

	Frontlighted	Sidelighted	Backlighted
Scenics	1 stop less	1 stop less	1 stop less
Medium distance, people	1 stop less	1 stop less	None
Close-ups of people	None	1/2 stop more	1 stop more

In the higher latitudes, the altitude of the sun is an important consideration. Normal exposure tables are based on a sun altitude of at least 30 degrees; if the sun is lower in the sky, an extra 1/2 to 1 stop more exposure should be given.

If you use an exposure meter to measure light reflected from sunlit snow, it will read high, perhaps off the scale entirely. It will indicate only half, or even a quarter, of the exposure actually required. Meters are fooled by snow because they are calibrated for the usual proportion and darkness of shadows, neither of which occur in snow scenes. The best procedure is to take the meter reading from the gray side of a KODAK Neutral Test Card. Use a lens opening 1/2 stop larger than the meter indicates as the basic setting for a frontlighted scene; then apply the adjustments given in the table above. Under overcast conditions, the meter reading from the Test Card can be used to calculate the exposure directly for subjects of average reflectance, without any adjustments.

(Exposure section and table reprinted from Kodak publication No. C-9.)

Glögg
A fine Swedish warmer

2 bottles dry red wine
¾ cup seedless raisins
¾ cup blanched almonds
1 piece stick cinnamon about 3 inches long
5 whole cardamoms, slightly crushed
6 cloves
1 small piece ginger root
1 pound sugar
zest of one orange (rind without the white)

Put the cinnamon, cardamoms, and ginger root into a cheesecloth bag. Into an enamel or stainless-steel pot, put the rest of the ingredients and the spice bag. Bring just to a simmer and remove from the fire. Let the mixture stand 3 to 4 hours. Reheat the Glögg to the simmering point, remove the spice bag, and serve the brew with a few raisins and almonds in each warmed mug or glass.

Weather Prophecies
If your cat sits with its tail toward the fire, very cold weather is on the way.

MAPLE SUGARING

The day the maple sap starts running heralds the end of the New England winter, and the coming of the New England spring. It's a time of harvest festival in sugarbush country, with spirits running as high as the sap, and adults and children alike gorging themselves on syrup-soaked snow, even though snow is no longer considered potable—sweetened or not—in these pollution-marred times. But tradition, and a certain innocence that goes with it, still reigns in New England, where the Indians discovered maple sugar longer ago than any of the Indians discovered by the Pilgrims could remember. Maple sugaring was industrialized by the Pilgrims themselves as early as 1723, and although tractors have generally replaced the yoked oxen that carried the pails of sap to the sugaring house until recent times, the traditional method of boiling down the sap over a wood fire is still considered best.

When?

A "run" may occur any time from mid-February to May 1, but trees can be tapped as early as January, provided the weather conditions are right. Any succession of days with temperatures that seesaw violently—freezing nights, about 20° Fahrenheit (−7°C.), followed by sunny days with a high around 45° Fahrenheit (7°C.)—may produce a run. The strongest flows are very brief, and a season may have only one run, a dozen, or no more than a series of drizzles, depending on the weather. The first run is said to produce the sweetest sap; sap collected late in the season may be bitter, and once the maple is in the leaf, no usable sap is produced. The appearance of large numbers of

A HARD DAY'S WORK

According to an old Indian legend, there was once a time when one could draw finished syrup directly from the tree. But some Calvinistic Indian—to coin an anachronism—feared this easy task would ruin the character of his people by making them lazy. So he climbed all the maple trees and poured water inside them, thus diluting the sap so that people would have to do a respectable day's work to boil it down and thicken it again.

Even Euell Gibbons, who was willing to go to lengths most of us would deem incredible to obtain and prepare wild food, thought this Indian went too far. If Gibbons says it's hard work, you'd better believe it.

Maple Syrup in the Snow

Put 1 quart of maple syrup into a saucepan large enough so it will not boil over. Cook the syrup until a candy thermometer registers between 230° and 232° Fahrenheit. Remove from the fire, and slowly pour the syrup out onto some clean snow. This will be a crispy tasting delight.

❄❋❄❉❅❄❄ ❄❋❄❉❄

WILD FOODS IN WINTER

According to the late Euell Gibbons, whose *Stalking The Wild Asparagus* is the definitive work on locating and preparing wild food, the following may be safely and

moth millers, small, tannish moths, is regarded as a sign that sugaring—and the last of winter—is almost over.

Where and How?

But you don't have to wait for a run to tap a maple tree. Just pick a warm, sunny day preceded by a very cold night, and be prepared to be patient. You don't necessarily have to be in New England, either. Maples can be tapped for sap sugars wherever the weather is right. Hard or rock maple is the true sugar tree with the sweetest yield, but most kinds of maples produce sugar, and some people insist that experts can't tell the finished products apart.

An enormous quantity of sap will drip from a single tree in a day during a run, but it takes a lot to make a gallon of finished syrup, and although collecting the sap is easy, boiling it down takes work. Maple sap is 97 percent water on the average, but its richness varies widely from tree to tree, year to year, even run to run. A yield of 3½ percent sugar is considered high.

The sap is collected through spigots (called spiles), which can be purchased in Vermont and other places where maple sugaring is popular. The spile is inserted in a ⅜-inch hole bored no deeper than 3 inches into the tree, about 3 to 4 feet above the ground. This doesn't damage the tree, but the hole, which takes four to five years to heal over, is never used twice. Most trees can take two taps at once, and large ones take many many more. Opinion varies widely regarding the best place to tap a tree, and in sugarbush country the question is endlessly debated. The south or sunny side of the tree is generally recommended. Buckets should be hung on the spiles at the same height above the ground, never one above the other, since sap flows up and down, not sideways.

Your spirits may flag somewhat once you get down to the business of boiling down the sap for syrup. Most of the work is just in watching it to make sure it doesn't scorch. In his *Stalking the Wild Asparagus* (McKay, 1962), the late Euell Gibbons recommends doing most of the cooking on an open wood fire, then bringing the almost-boiled syrup into the kitchen to finish it off on a gas or electric stove. If it's about to boil over, a few drops of cream, a little egg white, or a small lump of butter or salt pork, will, amazingly, quiet it down.

By the candy thermometer, the syrup is ready at about 219° Fahrenheit (103°C.). It will boil at a temperature 7° higher than whatever it takes to boil water at your altitude. It must be bottled while hot to ensure against fermentation. For sugar, let it reach 234° Fahrenheit (112°C.) then pour off immediately into buttered molds. The time-honored rule of thumb for finished syrup is to pour a little from a ladle. If it tends to thicken and stick along the edge, it's ready to remove from the pan.

palatably foraged during the coldest months of the year.

WINTER CRESS is best gathered between early December and March—the earlier the better, because it develops a bitter taste once the weather turns warm. Its dense, bright-green clusters grow when virtually nothing else does—in fallow fields, cultivated lands, or near streams and ditches in low, rich ground. Use it raw in salad, or cook as you would spinach.

CATTAILS were harvested by the Indians as a staple crop. The roots can be dug up all winter to produce a palatable white flour containing about as much protein as flour made from rice or corn.

ACORNS, the staff of life for many a primitive man, may be gathered anywhere the squirrels have left some, and can be roasted like chestnuts, boiled and dipped into clarified sugar following any French recipe (although it is a very difficult process) for *marrons glacés*, or ground into meal (a more complicated process) for various breads, muffins, and pancakes.

WILD APPLES, generally hard and bitter, are at their best when they've been softened and sweetened by frost. Just cut away the parts sampled by insects, and cook in any recipe that calls for apples.

The *JERUSALEM ARTICHOKE* is best spotted when in flower for foraging any time after the first frost. It's not an artichoke, however, but a sunflower, with lighter yellow petals than other kinds, and a yellow center instead of a brown one. The tuberous root is the part you eat—raw, pickled, or prepared like potatoes.

THE GREAT OUTDOORS

WHAT THE WILD THINGS DO: PART II

BIRDS

It may seem that birds have disappeared for the winter much earlier than they actually do, because they start preparing for the cold in late August. That's when they begin molting their worn summer feathers, and while they're growing new ones, they don't sing, fight, flap around, or do anything much besides eat. Once they've got their new plumage, they're ready to take on the cold, or to migrate to warmer winter quarters. They'll take off some time between Labor Day and December 1 but only the birds know how or why a particular date is chosen.

Daylight—the Key Factor

It doesn't seem to have much to do with the cold. Birds have exceptionally high body temperatures, and their features, when puffed out, provide good insulation. But birds need a lot of daylight to find the tremendous quantity of food they need to feed themselves and their families. A pair of wrens may feed their infants more than 1,000 times in one day. A single day's worms for a baby robin would stretch about 14 feet, laid end to end. It's generally believed that the timing of migration has something to do with shortened daylight hours, since the more daylight, the better fed the bird. Some species have worked things out so they have daylight 24 hours a day—by migrating between the Arctic and Antarctic as the seasons dictate: a mere 22,000-mile round trip.

Short Side Trips

Many birds, however, make relatively short migrations, often to places that could hardly be considered winter paradises of tropical plenty. For some birds, going south for the winter means heading for the coast of Maine. Wherever you live, as the weather turns cold, there will be birds arriving as well as leaving. But it's not always easy to know which are which. Chickadees and crows may move southward from your area in the fall only to be replaced by other chickadees and crows who summer further north. And individual birds of a migrating species may decide not to make the trip at all. So if you see a robin pecking around on the February ice, he hasn't returned to herald spring; he just never left.

Loyal to Their Homes

It may be that a bird is as carefree as a bird because he's equipped with some extraordinary mechanisms, scarcely understood by man, that tell him what to do and when to do it, where to go and how to get there. You won't catch a bird worrying over whether to go to Saint Petersburg this year because Miami's getting too crowded or wondering whether an early frost means it's time to leave. It's been

WHAT HAPPENED TO ALL THE BIRDS?

We understand very little about the annual migration of birds, but we're not doing so badly in view of the fact that it took centuries of bird watching for us to figure out just how all those birds manage to disappear when the cold sets in.

In 1768, Samuel Johnson wrote: "Swallows certainly sleep all winter. A number of them conglobulate together, by flying round and round, and then all in a heap throw themselves under the water and lie on the bed of the river."

The Great Transformation

Other people believed that hawks, arriving just as the cuckoos moved on, were actually cuckoos transformed for the duration of the winter. Birds seen silhouetted against the harvest moon were believed to be wintering on the lunar plains. Flocks of small birds gathering for flight along the Mediterranean shores were thought to be waiting for larger birds to carry them piggyback across the sea.

When the phenomenon of migration was finally discovered, many people believed that the birds made their annual flight of thousands of miles in a single night.

BIRD WATCHING

Held annually, the Christmas Bird Watching Count enlists over 1,000 teams from North America. The competition is to spot the most varieties of birds within a designated 175 square miles. A time limit of 24 hours is allotted to the contestants. The teams with the most consistent wins are from Freeport, Texas; Cocoa, Florida; and Santa Barbara, California. For information, contact: Robert Arbib, c/o American Birds, National Audubon Society, 950 3rd Ave., New York, N.Y. 10022

Did You Know . . .
the names Iceland and Greenland are misnomers? While it is no tropical rain forest, Iceland is covered by ice on only 13 percent of its land mass. The fact that it is an island, and a small one at that, causes a relatively mild range of temperatures.

Eric the Red gave Greenland its name in an effort to get settlers to leave Iceland and relocate on this new land mass he had discovered. The name notwithstanding, the world's largest island is covered on five sixths of its total land mass by glacial ice.

VISIT IN THE WINTER
Mattamuskeet, North Carolina features geese, swans, ducks, hiking, biking, fishing. Nearby camp: refuge headquarters.

Did You Know . . .
. . .the purest air in the world is found over the coldest places? The air with the fewest pollutants, and the greatest proportion of oxygen and nitrogen, may be inhaled in Antarctica.

established that the same individual bird may return year after year not only to the same winter resort but to the same identical nest, which he can single out while still high in flight. Young birds, migrating for the first time, set off alone for the family's winter quarters, without an adult to guide them, apparently knowing the exact route and destination in advance.

How do they do it? No one knows. One researcher gave up and started counting birds instead. During a full moon, he estimated that night-flying birds pass at the rate of 9,000 an hour during migration. If you want to take a look, the greatest number can be seen between 8 P.M. and midnight, and between 4 and 6 A.M.

FEEDING WILD BIRDS

Winter is a rough time for birds. Whether their preferred diet consists of insects, seeds, or berries, food is scarce, and any handouts you choose to offer will help. The latter part of winter (March/April) may seem like spring to you, but it's the time of most crucial food shortages for the birds. They've already consumed just about all the natural foods available—hibernating insects, frozen berries, seeds from dried, dead plants—and no insects or new seed-bearing crops have appeared yet.

It would seem that these hungry creatures shouldn't care whether you provide them with the elegant dining quarters of an expensive feeder or just scatter handfuls of seed on the snow, and to some extent that's true. But different kinds of feeding stations will attract different kinds of birds, and you'll need a good bird book to familiarize yourself with the wants and habits of the kinds of birds you'd like to attract—particularly if you plan to invest in an elaborate feeding station. If you want to keep it simple and just see who turns up, here are a few hints.

Guess Who's Coming to Dinner?

Small songbirds, mourning doves, and bluejays will be delighted to

EXTRA! EXTRA!
During April of 1968, the basin of the Lena River in Siberia was buried under a blanket of permafrost 4,920 feet deep. This is by far the deepest frost ever recorded.

eat whatever's on the ground. Vegetarian birds don't care for suet, but like stale bread, cookies, crackers, pretzels broken into small crumbs, cracked corn, nuts, and peanut butter. Birds such as the woodpecker, normally feeding on insects and fruits, will also be happy with the above. But suet is the preferred substitute for juicy worms and berries. Balls of suet stuck with seeds are available in many supermarkets, but you can make such a ball yourself, or just fill a mesh bag (the kind onions are sold in) with suet, seal the opening securely, and hang it from a tree.

Trees are the most aesthetic locations for hanging feeders, but if no appropriate limbs are available, use a clothesline, lamppost, trellis, fence—the birds don't really care. A plastic bowl (such as a small hanging planter) filled with sunflower seeds looks as good to the bird as a more elaborate hanging feeder. Half a coconut shell works well, too. Hanging feeders discourage greedy starlings, house sparrows, and several larger birds that dislike the swinging and swaying.

Large Dinner Parties

For the largest variety of birds, and to enable smaller, less aggressive birds to compete with the big, tough ones, feeders should be numerous, spaced fairly far apart, and should offer a variety of foods. Feeding trays fastened to a window will give you the best view if you're quiet and discreet enough not to frighten the birds away. A covered platform attached to a post keeps food dry, and the elevation offers the protection from dogs, cats, and other predators that ground-feeding does not. But be sure to attach feeders with material that can't be chewed through by squirrels. Even the heaviest rope won't do. Use wire.

If you want to buy or build a birdhouse, you should be aware that even in winter, birds are a lot more choosy about where they live than about what and where they eat. They may ignore a house custom-built for their carefully researched needs, and nest in a hollow stump or tree instead, or they may settle on the roof of your cozy birdhouse and refuse to go inside.

Be Careful

Bird feeding has become such a popular winter pastime that it was estimated that it was the basis of a 50-million-dollar industry in 1974, and the figures have probably risen considerably since then. But ironically, feeding wild birds is fooling around with Mother Nature, and no one knows exactly what the end result will be. Ornithologists do know, however, that the normal ranges and migration times of birds are being affected, and long-range changes in bird populations will probably occur. This could lead to the decreasing winter mortality of certain species, which in turn could threaten the extinction of others because of increased competition for food.

Did You Know . . .

. . . winter is longer in the southern hemisphere than in the northern hemisphere? Winter lasts approximately 93 days down south as opposed to 89 up north.

The Snow Queen

The windowpanes were often frosted right over, but then the children warmed up pennies on the stove, placed the heated coin on the frozen pane, and in this way made a splendid peephole.
—*Hans Christian Andersen*

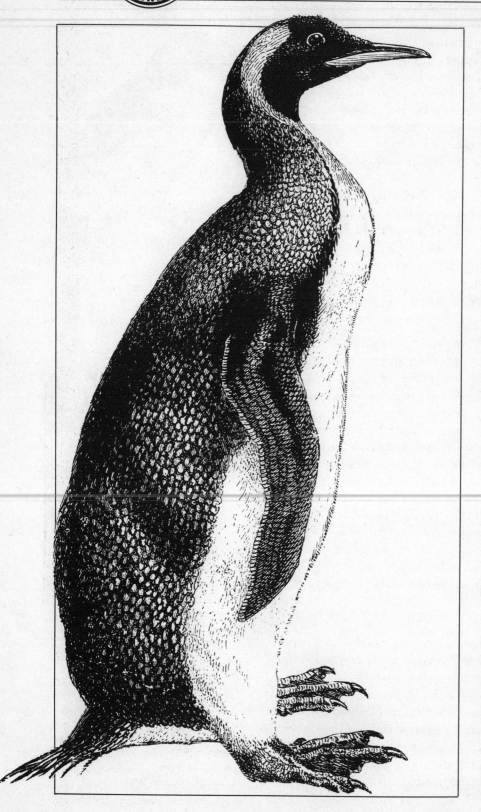

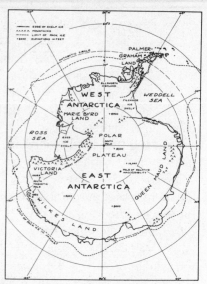

ANTARCTICA, THE COLDEST PLACE ON EARTH

If you think life becomes unbearable when the temperature drops to zero and the snow is piled so high you can't open your front door, remember, it could be worse. Imagine Antarctica—6 million square miles of icy wastes, the coldest place on earth. In winter, the temperature drops to −100° Fahrenheit (−73°C.), the coastal winds blow in hurricane gusts of 90 to 200 mph (try computing the wind-chill factor on that one!) and the sun doesn't show its face for six months.

Frozen Summer

Even in midsummer, when the sun never sets, there are few bright, sunny days. The weather is almost always bad; even when the blinding blizzards die down for a day or so, both land and sea are usually fog bound. On the icy shores, the temperature occasionally reaches its peak—32° Fahrenheit (0°C.), the freezing point. Not a tree or a flower grows on the entire continent— only the few mosses and lichens that can cling to rocks. All but about 100 square miles, mostly mountain peaks and rocks, are covered with

ANTARCTIC ANIMALS

Millions of years ago, when the ice age descended on what was probably a tropical Antarctic, the animals and birds either migrated or became extinct. While the south polar region is the summer home of numerous birds, whales, seals, and a rich variety of marine life, only the emperor penguin can endure the long, dark winter on land.

The Emperor Penguins

The emperor penguins arrive when the daylight hours are practically nonexistent, and the terns and summer-resident Adelie penguins have left the continental Antarctic for warmer places that are still so cold we won't even discuss them. From the ice-filled sea, these incredible creatures, three to five feet tall, in black dress suits and snowy vests, leap eight feet into the air, landing upright on the frozen shore. Scarcely pausing to look around, they march for miles, single file, to their rookeries. Individual penguins return to the same communities each year, where they crowd together by the thousands to mate, lay eggs, and raise their young in total darkness, at temperatures ranging between 40° and 100° Fahrenheit below zero (−40° to −73°C.).

No one knows why they travel to the coldest place on earth to conduct the most important business of their lives, but, protected by layers of blubber under an insulating coat of thickly packed feathers, they seem to manage very well. Each breeding female lays a single large, rough, pale-green egg that must incubate for two months without touching the ice for a second, lest the chick inside instantly freeze. It's nest is a cozy space between the adult's belly, tail, and feet, in which the egg can be carried across the ice as Mom goes about her business. However, communal day-care for both egg and chick prevails. The egg is carefully passed from one penguin to the other, with nonbreeding adults baby-sitting when Mom and Dad both want to go fishing for a meal.

The Wandering Albatross

The wandering albatross, the largest bird that flies, nests on the Antarctic island of South Georgia, a warm-sounding place that's about as toasty as the South Pole. It nests there when it isn't soaring around the South Pole at 60 to 100 mph, or making sailors nervous by hovering over their ships with its wings spread to their full 10- to 12-foot span. While pursuing these jolly activities, this legendary bird abandons its chick to the elements under the most desolate conditions imaginable. True, the two-month-old chick has plenty of stored blubber and a winter undercoat of black feathers under its down. But still, on the most exposed promontories of the headlands, rather than in a sheltered nest, the baby albatross is left to squat in total darkness for three months or more, alone, unprotected, and unfed. No wonder it goes around scaring sailors for the rest of it's life.

ice 8,000 to 14,000 feet (2 miles) thick.

Not a Vacation Spot
Though Antarctica has its summer and winter residents—including a few brave humans who man various scientific stations—not a single creature can take living on the continent 12 months of the year. Darkness starts to close down in February and lasts until August. Spring starts in September, summer in November. But ever since the first sailors set foot on Antarctica in 1820, men have been spending an occasional winter there. Admiral Richard E. Byrd, who claimed to love the place, treated himself to five dark months all alone in the interior in 1934, returning just in time for another somewhat less trying winter in the United States.

FAIRIE QUEEN
Lastly came Winter, clothed in all frieze,
Chattering his teeth for cold that did him chill,
Whilst on his hoary beard his breath did freeze,
And the dull drops, that from his purpled bill
As from a limbeck did adown distill.
—*Edmund Spenser*

CREATURES OF THE ARCTIC

While the Antarctic supports virtually no life in the winter, the Arctic, with an average temperature of −58° Fahrenheit (−50°C.) at its coldest spot, is temperate and populous by comparison. Among its year-round residents are nearly a million native humans who've lived there for thousands of years, most of them in Siberia. Living primitive, usually nomadic, tribal lives—some still preserving a stone-age culture—they are able to withstand hunger and fatigue at extremely low temperatures. Why they migrated to the Arctic, no one knows.

Most of the Arctic's nonhuman residents, including walrus, caribou, reindeer, many seals, and numerous kinds of birds, migrate below the tree line for the winter. But the heavy snowfall and strong winds that drive these creatures away help make life bearable for those who stay. High-blown snowdrifts provide warm shelter, and the winds blow high ground and hillsides clear, exposing lichens and other frozen plants. At least a dozen kinds of animals, from the 1,000-pound polar bear to the tiny lemming live year-round on the frozen Polar Sea, and on the even colder Arctic lands of northernmost Europe, Asia, and America.

The Polar Bear

This animal is the king of the Arctic, lives on the edge of pack ice,

TUNDRA

The low, damp plains surrounding the Arctic ocean in Northern Europe are called the tundra. Tundra is also the name of the peat moss that covers this land as well as large sections of Siberia and North America (Alaska). Minimal plant and animal life exist on this cold barren wasteland.

Permafrost

Except for a shallow surface layer that thaws in the spring, the earth under the tundra is permanently frozen to a great depth. This ground is called permafrost—a combination of earth, rock, and ice. About one fourth of the earth's land is permafrost, frozen the year round to depths of up to 3,000 feet. Mammoths and other prehistoric animals have been found preserved in permafrost.

and fishes in the open water between ice floes, where for unknown reasons, the sea doesn't freeze up entirely. He moves easily on both snow and ice, thanks to the hairs on the soles of his feet. He's also an excellent swimmer and his oily white coat helps him float, but he can't outswim the seal, his favorite dinner. Catching the seal unawares on land, however, is easy. The bear can see it a mile away across the ice, sneak up on it, and kill it with one blow. The female polar bear spends most of the winter in a cave she's made by digging deep in the snow and letting the wind blow great drifts over her. Her body heat melts enough of the snow to give her room in which to move around and give birth to two tiny cubs in the midwinter darkness. Occasionally, she'll have three, which the Eskimos say brings good luck to anyone who sees them.

The Arctic Fox

Unlike the polar bear, who adapts amazingly well to the warmer climates of our zoos, the arctic fox can't live much below the Arctic Circle. He ekes out a lonely and half-starved existence in the winter, wandering about in search of a lemming, hare, or ptarmigan, all of which have turned as white and invisible as he. He does better trailing the bear to scavenge his leftovers. During the warmth and **daylight** of summer, he may manage to put a few lemmings and birds

into cold storage under a rock, but he never saves enough to last the winter. In a snowstorm he burrows into a drift or lies down wherever he can find a sheltered spot, folding his bushy tail over his nose and face.

The Ringed Seal

This adaptable seal lives both under the ice and above it, spending much of his time catching and eating fish in the chilly sea. He makes small holes in the ice, which he uses for breathing every ten minutes or so, and a larger hole through which he can come out to stretch and rest.

The Ptarmigan and the Snowy Owl

These are the only birds that stick around for an arctic winter. The ptarmigan, a kind of grouse, grows a thick coat of white feathers, and long, hairlike feathers for snowshoes on its feet. Both birds find crevices between the rocks in which to hide from storms, and eat frozen berries and plants on windswept mountain slopes.

The Lemming

This poor animal may sooner or later become a meal for just about any creature of the Arctic, so it's no wonder he seldom leaves his burrow in winter, despite his camouflaging white fur. Even at home, where he lives on stored greenery and where he channels deeper into the snow to find roots, he's not entirely safe. His rooting channels are large enough to admit the ermine—his summer enemy, the weasel—in white winter disguise.

The Arctic Hare

This little fellow survives the winter on whatever frozen vegetables he can find on windswept hillsides. He's also able to sniff out live plants under the snow, and once he's dug them out, he'll eat leaf, bud, bark, twig, and root. He lives entirely out in the open, cuddling up with his fellows to keep warm.

The Musk Ox

Remarkable creature that he is, the musk ox can resist any temperature, high or low. His Latin name, *ovibós*, means sheep-cow, and that's exactly what he is—a sort of cow with a coat of wool nearly three feet long, sheeplike teeth, a cow's tongue, and heavy, curved tusks. He thrives on the dwarf willows and grasses of the tundra, pawing away at the snow to get at them, and manages well on the ice with the cutting edges of his large hoofs. The long-haired adults brave both enemies and storms out in the open, gathering in a circle, face outward, to protect the shorter-haired calves within. This habit has made them easy prey to hunters, however, and they are now almost extinct. They have no living relatives and are believed to be descended from a prehistoric animal.

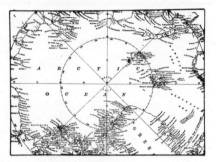

THE NORTH POLE

The top of the world is not a land mass, as the bottom of the world is, but is actually a vast expanse of ice moving on the surface of the Arctic Ocean at the whim of winds and currents. Because of the moderating influence of the sea beneath the packed ice, the North Pole is considerably warmer than land-based parts of the Arctic. Since it was first reached in 1909, the North Pole has been rapidly growing more accessible. Commerical airplanes fly over it regularly, and in 1958, the first atomic submarine slid under it. Contrary to earlier rumors, Santa Claus cannot be found there.

Is Santa a Laplander?

However, from all descriptions, Santa sounds much like a typical Laplander. The Lapps don't live quite at the North Pole, but in Arctic areas of Russia, Finland, Sweden, and Norway (there is not and never has been any such country as Lapland). Like Santa, the men wear jaunty, pointed caps with tassels hanging down, belted tunics (blue, not red), trousers, and curly-toed shoes made of reindeer skin. They usually do not grow over five feet tall, and their short legs tend to give their bodies a stout appearance. The nomadic Lapps are also known as the reindeer people, because for thousands of years, this half-wild, half-domesticated beast has provided them with all their food, clothing, and trading goods. Like Santa, the Lapps frequently travel on reindeer-drawn sledges.

REACHING THE POLES

For some people winter recreation means sitting cozily by a roaring fire, while reading about others who have risked cold, frostbite, and attempts to stand at the polar edges of our world.

Top of the World

What started as a search for new trade routes became, by the end of the nineteenth century, an all-out race to set a flag at the North Pole. But it wasn't until Admiral Robert E. Peary, a veteran of northern explorations, succeeded on his eighth attempt that a man could claim he had planted his frozen feet at the top of the world.

Peary was a clever fellow—his plan was to send small groups ahead to open up a trail through the snow, and then return to camp; each successive group was smaller, until on the last day, April 6, 1909, Peary and five assistants reached their goal . . . without hordes of fellow explorers along to share the glory. Later came the airplanes and research stations set up on drifting ice floes.

Go South, Young Men

The daring of Roald Amundsen and the hardships he endured would make those winter readers move their armchairs a few feet closer to the fire. But two years after Peary's victory in the north, Amundsen found the southernmost place on earth, 34 days before his competitor, Robert Scott. Scott's journey ended in disaster: blizzards and incredible cold cut off his return trip; he died trying to record his story with frozen fingers.

It was left to later explorers to chart the map. Admiral Richard Byrd's expeditions in the 1920s, 40s, and 50s noted a strange world of wonders: bays, islands, glaciers, underwater mountains, and secret plateaus. In 1957, the 12 nations

that participated in the International Geophysical Year were still making discoveries—but remember, armchair travelers, it was the brave men who first searched out the uncharted polar regions on foot who made it all possible.

AURORAS
(Northern and Southern Lights)

Countries such as Norway, Iceland, and Greenland would, at first, seem to be unlikely places for a winter visit, but their long nights during that season can provide a visual display that you would be hard pressed to find elsewhere north of the equator. The Aurora Borealis (or Northern Lights) is a natural wonder of the world and a visual experience that is well worth braving the northern cold.

Curtain of Light

This curtain of light is the subject of constant scientific research and the source of much of our knowledge about the composition of the Earth's upper atmosphere. Energized solar particles coming in a sort of wind during periods of intense activity on the surface of the sun collide with the earth's electronically volatile ionosphere to create the fantastic colors contained in the Aurora Borealis (Aurora Austalis in the southern hemisphere). These colors are determined by the particular

gases at that altitude: blue-green for nitrogen, red for oxygen at 250 km and green for oxygen at 130 km.

The Aurora (latin for dawn) hangs in a halo over the Earth around both poles. It may appear day or night, year round, mainly within 20 to 30 degrees of the geomagnetic poles, but the almost continual nights of northern Canada, Siberia, and the aforementioned countries provide the time of maximum visibility. Lesser displays are discernable as a glow on the horizon (air glow) occasionally causing people to report, erroneously, a neighboring town to be on fire.

Beauty Wins over All

This basically benign occurrence can cause power blackouts—when

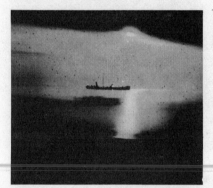

the highly charged air throws out of kilter the circuit-breakers in ground-level power plants—and can cause major interference in radio reception and transmission. These intermittent drawbacks pale, however, compared with the wonder of a natural phenomenon of rare and exceptional beauty. The opportunity to view these 1,000-mile-long by 500-mile-high sheets of color adds an enormous amount of credit to balance the debit side of visiting the northern climes in winter.

The Taming of the Shrew
Winter tames man, woman, and beast.   *—Shakespeare*

THE LAST RESORT

If you have the desire to contemplate the beauty of nature from atop the North American continent's highest mountain, rejoice! Camp Denali, located within view of Mount McKinley (all 20,320 feet of it) in the Alaskan interior, can offer you a comfortable jumping-off point for that climb to the heavens. Rustic, small, and very special, Camp Denali recently was awarded the Society of American Travel Writers *Connie* award, in recognition of its contribution to the preservation of the natural beauty of man's environment.

Everything but the Deer and the Antelope

If climbing up McKinley is a bit more than you're looking for, don't worry—the camp is nestled in one of the most spectacularly beautiful landscapes imaginable. Herds of caribou, moose, wolves, grizzlies, mountain sheep, and foxes are your neighbors, and above it all, the towering peaks of majestic Mount McKinley—truly a splendid place to get away from it all!

To obtain information, write during the summertime to: Camp Denali, c/o McKinley Park, AL 99755. During the balance of the year, direct inquiries to: Camp Denali, c/o Box D, College, AL 99701.

SNOW SCULPTURE—
YOUR MELTABLE MASTERPIECE

You may not find any examples of snow sculpture in your local museum, but this perishable art form is one of the most satisfying and creative ways to pass the winter. First, you'll have to get used to working with a substance that melts, tips over, and resists the artistic detailing possible with less seasonal material. If you have a yard full of wet, pliable snow (and a design in mind), a little advance planning can help you create your own masterpiece.

Mistakes Rarely Count

Carving snow has one big advantage—if you make a mistake, you can pack on more snow, let it freeze, and redo the art. It's no fun to work with bare hands on a cold day, so wear waterproof gloves for the basic building. (If you can stand it, take the gloves off to add the final details and flourishes.) A small hatchet, a hammer, and a chisel will

GLACIERS

Almost 10 percent of our planet is currently covered with glaciers—masses of ice that are so thick they last through the seasons, so huge they fill valleys and canyons.

The glaciers of Antarctica and Greenland make up large sections of those particularly chilly places. In fact, if Antarctica's central glacier were to melt, it would raise the world's sea level by 230 feet. (No need yet to pitch a tent on Mount Everest to stay dry. Its 7,500-foot-thick ice has remained fairly stable for ten million years.)

A Source of Fresh Water

Scientists are busy planning ways to tow huge chunks from Norway, Iceland, and Alaska, wherever the biggest glaciers have formed. They hope to melt them down and provide us with enough fresh water to quench everyone's thirst for a long time to come.

First Come . . .

Geologists have a field day, so to speak, studying the layers of rocks and fossils within glaciers. The preservative powers of ice have proven to be amazing: in the 1920s, residents of a town in Siberia discovered a perfectly lifelike Woolly Mammoth in their local glacier. Its meat had remained fresh for thousands of years. Before scientists could get there the populace ate it.

But you don't have to be a scientist, a fresh-water entrepreneur, or a ravenous citizen of frozen lands to appreciate glaciers.

come in handy when the snow starts freezing. Consider what size sculpture would be appropriate to the space you have to work in.

The Design

Draw a sketch, preferably to scale, of your design. It's easy to misjudge the dimensions of a snow sculpture when you're packing all the snow together. Many beginners misjudge the center of gravity in their first attempts, and the result is a Leaning Tower of Pisa effect—or total collapse. Keep most of the weight in your sculpture as low and central as possible. When you graduate to 40-foot-high snow lions and elephants, you might have to reinforce them on the inside with armatures, which are a kind of skeleton of wood and cable wire. But if you're doing some backyard work, and creating a snow sculpture that reaches only a few feet in height, snow alone should be all you need. Remember, though, that wet, packed snow can be quite heavy; don't let small children romp around near your creation.

Once you've checked over all the details of your completed sculpture, get out your camera and click away. If you don't, your masterpiece will be a fond memory come the first sunny day.

ICE SCULPTURE

Ice sculpture can be stunning but it requires planning and patience. Unlike snow, a block of ice will crack and split at the slightest incautious move. Also unlike snow, the possibilities and subtleties of design are practically limitless. Every time you add a detail to your sculpture, the reflected light will shift the color of the ice, creating beautiful visual dimensions. The results are well worth the extra care you must take.

Materials

Besides your own imagination, the tools you'll need are: steady hands; two chisels (one V-shaped, one flat); a ruler; a T square; a saw; a pair of goggles to protect your eyes from flying ice chips; and, of course, the ice. A 50-pound block, delivered by an ice dealer, is perfect. You don't want your sculpture to melt while you're working on it, so pick out a nice cool place to use as a studio. An outdoor shed or lean-to is fine. If there is an ice-packing plant or food-storage firm in your neighborhood, check to see if you can use a refrigeration area for a small fee. If you do, make sure that there is a two-way door to the area and that someone knows you are working within— you don't want to become an ice sculpture yourself.

Preparation

After deciding upon your design, make a blueprint drawing the same size as the finished sculpture. Include the block of ice in the drawing

BUILD YOUR OWN IGLOO

To an Eskimo, the word igloo means a home of any kind, but, to most non-Eskimos, the word means a round house made of carved snow blocks. If you want to build this familiar cold weather dome, you can do so in much the same way the Eskimos do it.

To build an igloo, first locate a spot with firm, compact snow left by a single snowfall. Layered snow tends to break apart. The Eskimos use a short, swordlike snow knife made of ivory to cut blocks. But you can use a large kitchen knife or a cake server to cut blocks about 3 feet long, 2 feet high, and 8 inches thick.

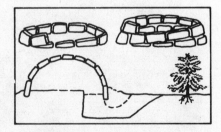

A tip to help you begin: Make the first few blocks wedge-shaped starting with one that looks like a doorstop and gradually adding height to each one until you have a 5-foot-high block. Arrange these blocks in a circle. Then place the first block of the second layer on top of the first wedge. Continue placing blocks in a circle and trim each so it fits snugly. Cut the top of each block to slant inward. This creates the final dome

so that you can visualize how much ice must be chipped away from each section. Next, get the ice block ready for carving. Smooth the sides with a chisel, and square it with a ruler and T square to prevent the block of ice from rocking while you are trying to make a delicate incision. Then, lightly sketch the outline of the design directly into the ice (sides and top), leaving extra space for the inevitable errors.

Carving

Ice is carved by chipping away *small* pieces. All your carving should be done in small areas, using one-step-at-a-time movements. Any attempt to slice off large ice chunks may shatter the block into enough fragments to keep your drinks chilled for a year. The V-shaped chisel is for your first cuts; switch to the flat chisel as you approach the sculpture's form. It is best to work in a spiral direction, moving around the block, to ensure consistency of size and perspective. Be sure to check the work every so often, from a distance of several feet, to make sure your masterpiece isn't developing odd bulges or lopsided features. Try to avoid touching the sculpture with your hands as you work; body heat can melt the ice. If that dreaded split or crack appears, it doesn't mean that your effort is ruined. Sprinkle salt over both sides of the break, and hold the pieces together for a few minutes (wear gloves). Pour water over the area, and let it refreeze.

The Masterpiece

Remember that ice sculpture is fragile, and must be handled with care. Know in advance where you intend to display the finished sculpture, and make sure the surface is flat and secure. Good luck, and happy carving.

shape. As you get to the top, slant the blocks even more. Use snow to fill in the spaces between blocks. This creates insulation.

Dig a tunnel as an entrance and you will have a shelf inside. It makes a good snow bed if you are tired from all that carving. If you want to see out of your igloo, make a block of solid ice and use it in place of one of the snow blocks as you are building the igloo. This serves as a window.

A large-sized igloo is about 15 feet wide and 12 feet high, and smaller domes can be added to serve as entrance tunnels. This cold weather shelter can be ideal for the winter wilderness or for any outdoor fun. But remember, Eskimos abandon theirs as the warmer weather comes. Start building early in the season while there is a chance to enjoy your igloo.

Did You Know ...

... a hardy medical volunteer had himself entombed, naked, in an ice igloo for 43 minutes? That's what is known as putting yourself on ice!

❄❄❄❄❄❄ ❄❄❄❄❄

A NEW ICE AGE
Winters have been getting longer, the ice in Antarctica seems to be expanding, warm-climate animals have been moving further south each year. Are we heading for another Ice Age?

A Little Ice Age
Scientists think we may be faced with what they call a Little Ice Age, which would mean that countries in the northern hemisphere would return to the kind of permanent winter that covered northern Europe from the 1600s to the 1850s.

Starting in the 1940s, researchers began noticing that polar air was spreading out across greater distances and that chemicals and pollution were blocking out sunlight. Small changes in temperature (a drop of one degree in a country that has remained fairly stable for years) tell scientists a great deal. Thousands of years ago, a climate of only 7.2° Fahrenheit less than our own was chilly enough to move huge icebergs as far south as Mexico City.

Only Ten More Warm Years?
The more alarmist of the forecasters believe that an ice age could come about in only ten years. Snow and ice could pile up, the air could become cooler, sunlight could be reflected off the earth and, once 12 or so inches of ice had formed over a large area, glaciers could begin to move. But other prophets say the process could take thousands of years, hopefully enough time for future technologists to come up with combative measures.

A Little Ice Age would be bad enough. Drought and famine would be common, dry regions would get drier, and wet regions soggier. A Great Ice Age is the more frightening prospect: whole portions of the world would be covered with ice. In the past 700,000 years there have been eight such ages—are we in an interglacial period, heading for the ninth?

ICEBERGS
Most icebergs originate near Antarctica and Greenland, homes of the world's hugest glaciers, and are, in fact, large chunks of glaciers that have broken off. A long icy current can keep the bergs cruising the seas for years, across great distances, and into shipping lanes. Warmer seas can melt icebergs, or they may freeze themselves onto land masses, but they've proven to be almost indestructible.

Just the Tip—
The cliché "just the tip of the iceberg" is firmly rooted in the fact that only one tenth of most icebergs is above water. Although that ratio stays fairly constant, the size of the ice mass can vary greatly: one that broke off Antarctica was reported to be 60 miles wide and 200 miles long. An iceberg of that size may be just the thing to force you to contemplate the power of nature as you look out from the deck of a luxury liner. Ships equipped with double-steel bottoms have sunk quickly on contact with such giants of ice. (The disaster of the Titanic is one of the most famous such collisions.)

It's not unusual for the Coast Guard to report 400 icebergs in a given year crossing the paths of freighters in the North Atlantic. It is careful checking with radar and other electronic equipment that has allowed ships to avoid meeting the fate of the Titanic in the well-traveled waters of the world.

EXTRA! EXTRA!
The largest iceberg ever recorded by man covered over 12,000 square miles. This icy titan was spotted near Scott Island in the South Pacific by members of the crew of the U.S.S. Glacier on November 12, 1956. At 208 miles by 60 miles, this enormous iceberg was larger than the country of Belguim.

THAT WAS NO SNOWBALL FIGHT, THAT WAS A REVOLUTION

Throwing snowballs at the wrong people and getting into trouble because of it is surely one of the great memories of childhood, but did you know that snowball-throwing shenanigans played an important part in American history?

Don't Fire!
In the years just before the American Revolution, the British soldiers quartered in Boston were under strict orders not to use their weapons unless they themselves came under actual gunfire. This order was quickly taken advantage of by the Bostonians, who pelted the Redcoats with snowballs, knowing the soldiers could not break ranks and retaliate.

Snowball Barrage
In March of 1770, with a good snowfall still on the ground, a crowd of angry Bostonians gathered in front of Murray's Barracks, commanded by one Captain Preston. The crowd began a snowball barrage directed at the sentries posted on the sidewalk. As feelings got stronger, the crowd started to wrap stones in the snowballs, some of which drew blood when they struck the faces of the soldiers. Captain Preston addressed the crowd, begging them to "Go quietly home and play at snowballs among yourselves if you wish to avoid bloodshed."

But Preston could not contain the situation, and his jittery troops finally fired on the crowd, killing six men. This was the *Boston Massacre,* a rallying point of the American Revolution.

The Snow Queen
There appeared a whole regiment of snowflakes, they were alive, they were the sentinels of the Snow Queen.
—*Hans Christian Andersen*

IN CASE YOU'RE ATTACKED—THE SNOW FORT

Here's a way for the kids to build their own outdoor snow fort. Most of the materials needed can be found around the house, and the only supervision that might be necessary is an occasional look to see that there are no injuries while the armies that defend and attack the fort are clobbering each other with snowballs.

The Basic Idea
This fort is made of snow blocks shaped with a makeshift push-out device.

You (or the kids) will need: a wooden box (open at both ends); a board slightly larger than the end of the box; an old broomstick with a flat piece of wood attached that can be pushed through the box (to use as a plunger).

Making the Block
To make a block, turn the box up and fill it with snow. Tamp it down firmly, making sure the board on a flat surface is beneath. When the block inside is well packed, push it out with the plunger. Spray the block with water to help freeze it solid. No soldier wants his ramparts to melt under his feet. Make as many blocks as you need. The dimensions of the fort are up to you.

For window spaces, make a few smaller blocks, and separate them.

As long as the snowballs don't fly a little too furiously, the kids should have a unique winter play-structure that will last all winter and that they have put together themselves.

THE $100,000 THAW
If you want the chance to win $100,000, start making plans to head up to the Tanana River in the town of Nenana, Alaska. If you are the lucky person to guess the exact day, hour, and minute the ice breaks up (or, failing this, the closest guesser), you can pocket over $100,000 in prize money.

Faster Than Watching the Grass Grow
This amazing contest started 50 years ago by helping the residents of this not very exciting community to get through the long, cold winters with something to get excited about. Nowadays, gamblers from all over the North American continent show up during April, each contributing a dollar. By mid-April, the banks of the Nenana are crowded with loiterers who stare into the center of the frozen lake, hoping to catch the first glimpse of the thaw. Often, the action holds off until mid-May, but spectators stick with it through the weeks of bitter cold. At the first sign of the thaw, cables move and a siren wails. If all this sounds like fun to you (and, in fact, it is for many), get an early start on next year's Nenana Ice Classic: start putting on your woollies now!

EVE OF ST. AGNES

St. Agnes' Eve—Ah, bitter chill it was!
The owl, for all his feathers, was a-cold;
The hare limped trembling through the frozen grass,
And silent was the flock in woolly fold.
—*Keats*

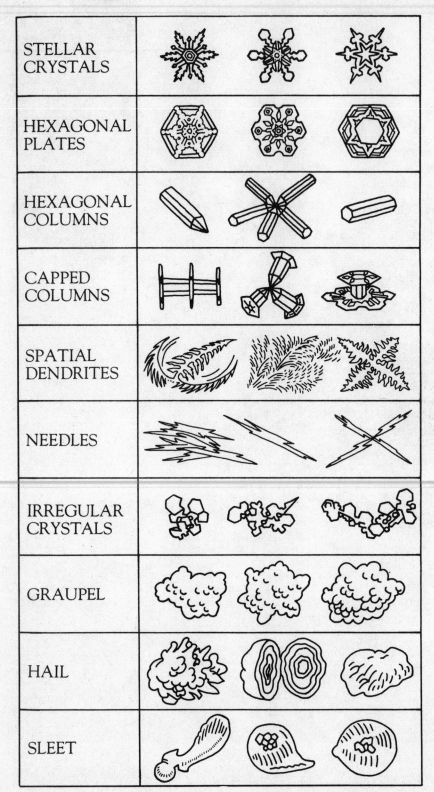

STELLAR CRYSTALS	
HEXAGONAL PLATES	
HEXAGONAL COLUMNS	
CAPPED COLUMNS	
SPATIAL DENDRITES	
NEEDLES	
IRREGULAR CRYSTALS	
GRAUPEL	
HAIL	
SLEET	

SNOW

Snow is, in fact, ice. Clouds often contain both water droplets and ice crystals. At temperatures between 5° Fahrenheit (−15°C.) and 15° Fahrenheit (−9°C.) the water droplets start to freeze onto the ice crystals, making them heavy enough to fall to the earth as snow.

Wet Flakes vs. Dry Flakes
Large wet snowflakes indicate that the crystals have passed through layers of warm moist air (though not warm enough to turn them into rain) on their way to the ground. These wet flakes tend to mat together, reaching sizes of up to one inch in diameter. A journey through cold dry air creates smaller drier flakes.

Once and for All, Are There Two Snowflakes Alike?
Consider this . . . your average snowflake contains 10^{18} molecules of water (that is 10x10x10, 18 times). Given the astronomical number of ways these molecules can be arranged, it is highly unlikely that, since the first snow fell on earth, any two snowflakes have ever been identical.

Looking at Snowflakes
If you are still unconvinced that no two are the same, you will just have to look for yourself. You will need a microscope, slides, and a spray can of clear lacquer.
1. Put the slides and the lacquer in the freezer.
2. When it starts to snow, quickly take them outside.
3. Handle the slide with a piece of cardboard so that it will not be warmed by your body heat.
4. Spray the slide with a thin coat of lacquer.
5. Leave the slide outdoors to collect snowflakes.
6. Still outdoors, but out of the snow, allow the slide to dry. Once dry you may bring in the slides and under the microscope inspect the fantastic variety of shapes.

ICE FISHING

"Gone fishing" ordinarily conjures up images of summer, motorboats, anglers lined up on a bridge, wading in the surf, or rowing on a lake. Possibly the most traditional image is the "ole fishin' hole" with barefoot boys in straw hats snoozing while awaiting a bite.

There is, however, another fishing hole that can make "gone fishing" a year-round term. It is a hole drilled through the icy covering of that lake or pond that yielded its bounty of fish last year. Ice fishing is probably as old as fishing itself and is still done with essentially the same techniques and equipment that were employed long ago by North American Indians and other peoples.

The Snow Queen

A few snowflakes were falling outside, and one of these, the biggest of them all, remained lying on the edge of one of the flower boxes. The snowflake grew larger and larger, till at last it became the figure of a woman dressed in the most delicate white gauze, which was made up of millions of tiny star-shaped flakes. She was a figure of ice—glaring, glittering ice.
—*Hans Christian Andersen*

Equipment

First, obviously, there must be a hole. A chisel attached to a long wood or aluminum pole and a bit of hard work will do the trick. Hand or power augers may be used as well. The hole itself should taper outward with smooth edges to avoid scraping or tangling the lines. A skimmer is then used to remove ice chips and slush.

While some fisherman use a shortened rod and reel, most do the actual fishing with either a tip-up or a jigging rod. A tip-up (or tilt) is either a rod of wood cross-braced over the hole or a pole cradled in a holder so that it bobs (up for bottom feeders, down for others) when the fish bites.

More active anglers prefer the jigging technique. A jigging rod is, if anything, easier to make than a tip-up. A 2-foot broom handle with a screw eye at one end and a cleat around which the line is wound is ideal. A 6-inch cleat will let you know that a foot of line is being dropped with each loop unraveled. Monofilament line is preferable to braided as it will not freeze—even better is fly line with a monofilament leader.

A favorite lure with ice fishermen is a lifelike wooden fish carved by Canadian Indians. Weighting the nose of a spoon will also provide a way to attract your potential dinner. Bait may consist of worms, larvae, frozen smelt, salted minnows. For larger catches live bait is best. Just remember, if you are going after a large fish you need a large hole.

Finding the Fish

This aspect of ice fishing may also involve little or no cost. "Find other ice fishers and fish there" sounds too simple to be true, but for the novice it makes sense. If money is no object you may want to investigate the Lawrence Lo-K-Tor, a sonar device used to locate fish right through the ice.

Safety

Once you have decided to "walk on water" in pursuit of fish, you should take some precautions against ending up in the water with them. One person requires a thickness of 1 inch of ice, a group in single file 2 inches, and a vehicle 7½ inches of ice or more. A rope and a compass are handy, and warm clothing, especially for the feet, is essential. A wind break of some kind can be built or rented and a thermos of any hot beverage can radiate the heat outward from the inside. Sunglasses for the glare and ice-creepers (rectangles of steel with downward prongs) attached to your boots can help assure maximum comfort in less than optimum climatic conditions.

There is no need to wait for summer to fill your frying pan. Ice fishing is inexpensive, fun, and best of all, you can catch as many fish as you like without worrying that they will spoil.

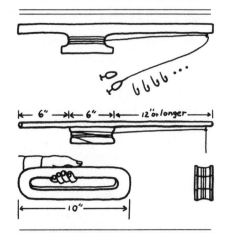

ST. STEPHAN

Horses, those faithful servants of man, have their own feast day on St. Stephan's Day (December 26). Their patron is usually portrayed wearing a wreath (Stephanos means wreath in Greek) and carrying a stone to symbolize his death by stoning. Horses' food is blessed on this day, and in Poland, a congregation will toss oats at their priest after Mass, simultaneously honoring their horses and reenacting Stephan's martyrdom.

Fertility Rite?

This tossing of food is thought by some to be more directly related to another Polish custom in which boys and girls throw walnuts at each other in a St. Stephan's Day fertility rite.

COOL IT

The cooling properties of ice have been known since 1000 B.C., when the Chinese used to cut and store it for refrigeration purposes. Insulated ice houses became commercially popular in the eighteenth century. In colder climates, ice was cut and put in these houses for use during the summer months when it was sold door to door. This ice, cut from local ponds and lakes, was also shipped to warmer climates.

SNOWSHOES

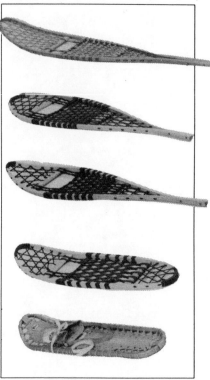

EXTRA! EXTRA!

Richard Lemay of Manchester, New Hampshire holds the world's record for fastest snowshoe travel. This hardy soul covered a snowy mile in 6 minutes, 24 seconds. Just try to match that feat this winter.

ST. BLAISE

One sore-throat remedy won't be found in any medical journals. For centuries, priests have been holding crossed candles against ailing throats and saying, "Through the intercession of St. Blaise, bishop and martyr, may the Lord free you from evils of the throat and any other evil." Blaise, before he was a bishop and martyr, was a physician; and according to legend, he miraculously cured a boy with a fishbone stuck in his throat. He was thus assured of his place in the community of saints.

The woods, under what hunters call the "hunter moon," are a thing of rare beauty. During this part of the winter season, the snow's depth can be well over a foot, making normal hiking difficult if not impossible. Only skis or snowshoes make this sort of terrain accessible—snowshoes being, by far, the easier of the two to master as well as being the superior vehicle for traversing densely wooded areas where great maneuverability is required.

What They're Made Of

A snowshoe operates by expanding the sole area that comes in contact with the snow's surface. The size of this area will vary according to the style of the shoe and should increase with the weight of the hiker and his pack. It consists of a frame and webbing, and in appearance, loosely resembles a tennis racket.

The frame is made of wood or more recently, aluminum. Hickory, white ash, and yellow birch are the preferred woods. Wood frames come in a confusing number of styles with such colorful names as teardrops, bear-paws, trappers, rangers, and cross-country. Others are named after states, Alaskans, Michigans, Maines, or even Indian tribes (Ojibwas).

The most common webbing materials are moose, horse, or cowhide for wood frames and synthetics such as vinyl or neoprene for the aluminum models. The spacing of the webbing depends on the type of snow in the area. Wide spacing is for heavy, wet snow so that the snow will not cling and accumulate, adding weight. Closer mesh is for fluffy, granular snow which falls at a lower temperature.

An important part of every snowshoe is the space in the webbing just forward of the cross member. This enables the foot to assume a natural walking motion, while allowing the tail of the shoe to drop, preventing the toe from digging into the snow. The foot rocks back and forth on the cross member, in and out of the space. Many snowshoes curve upward at the toe. This also helps the hiker avoid digging into the snow as the foot is set down.

Bindings are made from the same material as the webbing (natural or synthetic) and keep the shoe from twisting sideways. The bindings should be easy to tie in cold weather and, even more important, easy to untie in the event of a fall.

What to Wear with Them

Any high-top boot, shoe, or moccasin is suitable for wear with snowshoes. If using wood frames, moccasins are preferable—to minimize wear and tear on the natural leather webbing. Feet should be kept as warm as possible; so boots or shoes should be purchased a half size larger than normal to allow room for additional pairs of socks.

High Stepping

Walking in snowshoes presents fewer technical problems than either

SNOWSHOE SPORTS AND GAMES

Almost any outdoor sport or game played on foot can, theoretically, be played on snowshoes. Old standards, like baseball or tag, become hilarious comedies when the degree of difficulty is increased by snow and abnormal footgear, increasing the entertainment value without diminishing the competition. Such diversions can also be terrific training in the art of maneuvering snowshoes for the beginner and experienced user alike. There is no need to dread that first large snowfall in anticipation of weeks spent indoors. Break out the snowshoes and choose up sides. Some of the more common sports activities include:

Snowshoe Races
Rules for these parallel those for foot races. Four or more persons may team up for cross-country racing or "marching." Points are awarded for placing in heats, one point for first, two for second, three for third, and so on. The lowest score, after all heats, is declared the winner. Spotters (or checkers) are extremely important in winter long-distance events to provide immediate aid to fatigued or injured entrants. Speed events may include 110-, 220-, 440-, or 880-yard races, mile courses, or even, believe it or not, hurdles 24 inches high, 30 inches wide. For any and all competitive events, the snow must be packed

skis or skates. It merely requires stepping slightly higher, wider, and farther than when walking normally. This brings hitherto unused muscles into play, which, combined with the added weight of the shoe, can cause fatigue. With practice, one can soon avoid stepping on one's own shoes, and as new muscles develop, walking with snowshoes will rapidly become much easier than without them—in deep snow, that is. Beginners often use ski poles for better balance, especially when carrying packs. As you become more experienced, balance will improve, and soon one or both poles may be discarded. Veteran-users have been known to climb fences without removing their snowshoes.

Proper care of the shoe is essential for efficiency and safety. The webbing must be kept away from heat to avoid stretching. Natural leather webbing should be waterproofed with spar varnish as moisture will cause the webbing to loosen, rendering the shoes useless.

Prices for wood shoes may vary from $20 to as much as $50; aluminum frames cost even more. Cheaper all-plastic snowshoes have recently been marketed but are of debatable value. Used shoes may be purchased at considerable savings, but they should be carefully checked for cracked frames or torn and frayed webbing.

For the off-the-beaten-trackers and lovers of secluded, unspoiled places, snowshoes can provide an escape from the crowded ski slopes and can offer access to untapped hunting, fishing, and scenic areas.

firmly and evenly to provide equal degrees of difficulty for all.

The Compass Game
This involves laying out a circle 10 yards in diameter and marking the compass points with a mound of snow (north, south, east, west, northeast, southeast, northwest, and southwest). Eight players are assigned to the points with a ninth being the needle, or *it*. A referee calls on two points to switch places while the needle or *it* tries to beat them to either new location. If *it* sounds confusing, it is. This game sharpens a potential hiker's sense of direction, as well as his or her ability to maneuver on snowshoes.

Fox and Geese
This is a variation on the Compass Game. It uses the same circle, with the outside players or *geese* running from point to point, while the center player, or *fox*, attempts to catch them between points. The caught player becomes the fox and the game continues.

The Ring Game
This adds another twist to the uniqueness of snowshoe games. A long straight course is laid out, with the player's snowshoes placed 10 yards from the starting line. The contestants, carrying one ski pole, must race to their shoes, Le Mans style, put them on, and continue to a point midway down the course where they must pick up a ring, using only the ski pole held at the handle end. Racing to the end of the course, they must place the ring over a peg in the ground (the peg should be only slightly smaller than the ring) using only the ski pole, run back to where they donned their shoes, take them off, and be first back to the starting line. This game adds quick tying and untying of the bindings to the maneuverability problem, and in all fairness, bindings should be of similar style for all contestants.

ICEBOATING

If your idea of a good time is driving down a wet mountain road at 80 mph with no brakes, then iceboating should be right up your alley. Traveling at speeds approaching 120 mph over frozen lakes and bays, iceboat racers need the reflexes of a Grand Prix driver and the nerves of a lion tamer.

An Historical Note

When ice runners were first attached to the hulls of conventional sailboats in eighteenth-century Holland, their purpose was to carry cargo on the Baltic Sea and Dutch waterways. The Dutch brought this technique to the New World and by the midnineteenth century 50-foot iceboats carrying 600 square feet of sail were sailing up and down the Hudson River. These enormous tail-ruddered craft remained popular until the 1930s. In 1933, one Mr. Walter Beauvais switched the steering runner from the back to the front (stern to the bow in nautical terms) and built a 13-foot craft with 60 square feet of sail that he called the Beau-Skeeter. This boat became the model for the Class E Skeeter style iceboat of today, much faster than the larger Hudson River types and much less expensive as well.

WINTER WONDERLAND
Arkansas, Texas features whooping crane, a beach, biking, hiking, fishing. Nearby camp: Goose Island State Park, Port Lavaca Park.

English Bishop
Stud an orange thickly with whole cloves. Dip into cognac and dust well with brown sugar. Broil until the sugar caramelizes. Cut the orange into quarters and put the sections into a pot with one bottle of port wine. Simmer about 15 minutes. Add ½ cup warmed cognac. Remove the orange sections and serve in warmed mugs. This bishop is noted for taking care of chilly churches!

What It Is—And for Whom

An iceboat consists of: a hull that is 12 to 24 feet long and is made of wood, fiberglass, and fiberglass-covered wood; a crosspiece or runner plank of 8 to 20 feet in length with a 3-foot runner at each end; and one to three sails. The boat may carry one or two passengers and costs from $400 to $4000.

Since ideal conditions for the sport are extremely rare, iceboaters are a particularly dedicated breed of sportsman. The weather must be cold and windy but snowless. Areas such as the upper Midwest, New Jersey, and Connecticut are the most suitable climatically, with southern Wisconsin offering the maximum amount of sailing time (six to seven weeks). The ice must be hard packed and clean. Rapid temperature changes can cause ice to buckle and heave, and snowdrifts are dangerous obstacles to crafts traveling at 80 to 100 mph.

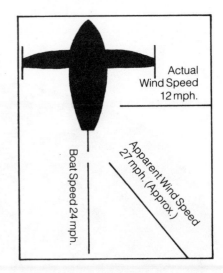

Actual Wind Speed 12 mph.

Boat Speed 24 mph.

Apparent Wind Speed 27 mph. (Approx.)

How They Go So Fast

The principles of iceboat propulsion are roughly the same as summertime sailing, with the added speed-increasing factor of minimum resistance. The actual wind velocity may be fairly constant and low (10 to 15 mph), but as the boat's forward speed increases, the relative motion of air past its sails combines with the actual wind to create an apparent wind velocity greater than either the boat's speed or the wind's. Combine this with the light weight (a two-year-old can push a 500-pound iceboat on smooth ice), and a 15-mph wind will propel these boats up to 60 mph or five times as fast as a conventional, summertime sailboat. One reason for the low resistance is three runners of heat-hardened spring steel. Unlike concave or flat-bottomed ice skates, these runners are sharpened to a razor edge to resist sideway slippage. This presents an extremely small area of actual contact between the ice and the boat.

The racing of these boats is organized by three major associations, the International Skeeter Association, the Northwest Ice Yachting Association, and the Eastern Ice Yachting Association, and is divided into classes according to sail size and design. The most popular class is the 12-foot DN—named for the Detroit News design competition held in the 30s. The DN carries 60 feet of sail, one passenger, and weighs 150 pounds.

Courses run from four to twenty miles and start with the skippers pushing their boats and hopping in (as opposed to conventional regattas that begin with a moving start). Even though the boats are all heading for the same turning point and finish line, the necessity of tacking across the wind would seem to make collisions inevitable. These are avoided, however, by an elaborate set of right-of-way rules in the *Constitution and Racing Rules of the National Iceboat Authority*.

Egg Nog (for 20)

1. Take 18 or 20 egg yolks; 15 tbsps. pulverized sugar; beat together, and grate into them 1 nutmeg; add 1 pt. best brandy or Jamaica rum, and 3 or 4 glasses fine sherry; beat to a froth whites of the eggs; whip all together, and add 5 pts. rich milk. A pleasant and nutritious drink; sherry wine may be substituted for the stronger liquors, should they be objected to.

2. Mix yolks 12 eggs; 2 qts. brandy; 1 pt. Santa Cruz rum; 2 gals. milk; 1½ pounds white sugar; beat well; put the whites of the eggs on the top for ornament, first beating them to a stiff froth. Serve cold.

ICE-SKATING—A BRIEF HOW-TO

Man is an ingenious creature, and we've devised many ways to propel ourselves about the earth, but no way is more visually pleasing than the graceful, gliding stride of the ice skater. It's one of the greatest joys of winter, and the basics are easier to learn than you think. In addition, ice-skating is one of the most accessible of sports.

For the Beginner

There is a special thrill to skating on the local pond, particularly if it's not too cold and maybe if there is a little light snow in the air, but this will pose some problems for the beginner. You'll have to contend with the uneven ice surface; sometimes ponds freeze smooth, sometimes they don't. Sticks and leaves may cling to the surface, or the ice may be deeply scarred by several days of heavy skating. And *someone* has to shovel the snow off that pond before you can skate. Furthermore, on a pond, beginners don't have the advantage of that wooden fence (the boards) that goes around an ice rink. The boards are a beginner's best friend because you can hang on there while you get your skating legs and work your way around the edges.

Indoor or Outdoor

Let's say you want to give it a try. All you'll need are a free afternoon, the price of admission to the indoor or outdoor rink in your neighborhood, a small fee to rent a pair of skates (all ice rinks have a decent supply of figure skates for rental), and some friends to come along with you—ice-skating is the most sociable of sports. Skaters of all degrees of proficiency spend at least as much time over hot chocolate or in chatting with each other in the center of the rink as they do in actual solitary skating.

You're at the rink and the fellow behind the counter is about to give you a pair of skates and take your shoes as collateral. Follow these hints about fit and you'll save yourself a lot of trouble: Ask for a skate a full or a half size *smaller* than your regular shoe size. This will ensure proper support and help keep your ankles from wobbling. Check to make sure your toes are absolutely free to wriggle about. Wear tights or only one pair of socks, and these of fairly thin weave. A couple of layers of socks won't keep your feet warm; they'll either make the skates too tight, cutting off the circulation and giving you really cold feet, or they'll get between you and the solid leather, robbing you of the support you'll need. Lace the boots with firm pressure, leaving them a little looser in the middle at the ankles so you'll have room to flex.

Walking Leads to Stroking

Now, presumably, you're on the ice, ankles a little wobbly, and you can hardly move about at all. How do you start? At this point, forget

BLADE ON ICE

The mechanics of blade on ice are simple. Since all your body weight is concentrated on such a small area of steel, this creates enough friction to melt the ice. It's this thin film of water that lubricates the blade as it slides and makes it seem effortless.

The blade is built along a rocking-chair curve from front to back, or "rockered" as skaters say, and it is the degree to which the blade is rockered that it is the essential difference between the three kinds of ice skates, hockey, figure, and speed. The less blade there is touching the ice at any given time, the easier it is to turn, curve, or alter direction. Figure skates have a medium rocker and are suitable for general skating.

WINTER WONDERLAND

Wichita Mts., Oklahoma features elk, buffalo, longhorn, hiking, biking, fishing, and camping.

From Hans Brinker

They are going to give a splendid prize to the best skater. A beautiful pair of silver skates—with straps and silver bells and buckles.
—*Mary Mapes Dodge*

all your fantasies of gliding about, and be content to just walk along in a cautious kind of shuffle. Once you get around the rink a couple of times in this manner all by yourself, maybe only stopping to hold onto the boards once or twice, then you're ready for the next step.

Begin your shuffling walk again. Then, once you've got some forward motion going, simply keep your skates parallel and coast for a bit. Then try coasting and picking first one foot then the other off the ice. This will be easier than you think, and, once you've gotten used to the audacious idea that you're not only on the ice, but fairly comfortable for a few seconds on only one foot, then you're ready to start stroking, which is the name given to the characteristic motion of the skater as he pushes off from one foot, then takes a long glide on the other. It's the basic action behind all kinds and styles of skating, and once you can get the knack of it, everything else is pure pleasure.

By the way, if you feel that you are about to fall, it would be wiser to simply stay loose and allow it to happen than to flail your arms wildly. Flailing might hurt others as well as yourself—and those blades on your feet are sharp.

ICE-SKATING DO'S AND DON'TS

1. Stay away from using the toe teeth of your figure skates when you're learning to stroke. Be sure to push off from the entire blade and to stroke almost perpendicular to it with the other foot. The toe teeth of figure skates are meant for specific jumps, spins, and stops demanded by certain figures and should not be used at all by beginners. Learn the basics first.

2. Don't feel you have to hold a youngster's hand and lead him around the ice while he learns. A kid can learn to skate much better if you leave him alone to discover his own balance and confidence. Some kids may spend the whole session going around the rink hanging onto the boards, but that's O.K. They'll step out on their own when they're ready.

3. Listen to the music while you're skating. The best ice skaters use a rhythmic stride that greatly enhances the beauty and pleasure of their motion. Listen for the beat, and try to follow it.

ICE HOCKEY

One of the most popular spectator sports every winter is a brand of organized mayhem known as ice hockey. While the object of the game is *not* to see how many of the opposing team can be put in the hospital, to the uninitiated observer, it may occasionally seem that way. Every season, in their mad rush to place the puck in the opponents' goal, National Hockey League players inflict and receive wounds requiring approximately 5,000 stitches to repair.

Hans Brinker, Move Over

It would be unfair, however, to assume that the participants of this sport are merely brutes engaging in semimortal combat and thus pandering to bloodthirsty fans. As anyone

who has so much as tried to stand on a pair of skates can tell you, skating requires skill, balance, and coordination. Hockey players not only stand, they walk, run, pass the puck, swing their sticks, and fight on those two thin metal blades. It is this last activity that has been questioned of late.

Violence = Winning + Business

One critic has remarked, "If they don't put an end to this sort of thing (fighting) we're going to have to print more tickets. . . ." Teams find that not only does physical violence help them win, it increases box-office business as well, which, in professional sports, is the true name of the game. One can also argue that since scoring is the most exciting part of any game, and since in hockey scores of 3 to 2, 2 to 1 and 1 to 0 are the rule rather than the exception, something else has to hold the spectators' interest for the 60 minutes of play. In this respect, teams have found that fans prefer the entertainment value of physical conflict over the appreciation of the finer points of playing technique.

Accidents Can Happen

Not all of hockey's violence is intentional. As one of the fastest sports in the world, it presents numerous opportunities for player to meet player, head on, at 30 mph, during the course of a game. In addition, goalies must attempt to block pucks traveling at speeds of 120 mph—hopefully not with their heads. Many pros have said that they have

sustained their most serious injuries as adolescents, when they were apt to take foolish chances in a game that requires constant awareness and split-second timing.

Perhaps tougher rules against un-

necessary roughness are the answer. Or stricter referees. Or a change in the play of the game to allow more scoring. But more likely, hockey will remain a winter ritual of trial by combat, and the fans will continue to want it that way. Just watch the flying gloves.

SNURFING U.S.A.

Let's go snurfing now, everybody's learning how—no, that's not a typographical error. If you're living in New Hampshire and your mind's in California, snurfing (skiing and surfing combined) may be just what you're looking for.

Using a laminated wooden board 4 feet long and 7 inches wide, the snurfer careens down the slopes in the upright surfing position, until he/she gets wiped out. There's an attachment for maneuverability, and applying wax to the ski surface can increase speed to dizzying swiftness.

Snurfboards are sold throughout the United States, and the cost is low (about $12). When you are proficient enough, you might want to enter the Annual National Snurfing Championships, held in Muskegon, Michigan, the birthplace of the snurfboard.

WINTER WONDERLAND

St. Marks, Florida features Canadian geese, eagles, ducks, alligators, historic sites, hiking, biking, fishing. Nearby camp: Newport Park Nat'l Forest.

Did You Know . . .

. . . water expands when it becomes ice? Even though an ice molecule has the same number of atoms as a water molecule, it is larger. The arrangement of the atoms in an ice molecule leaves more space between atoms than in a water molecule.

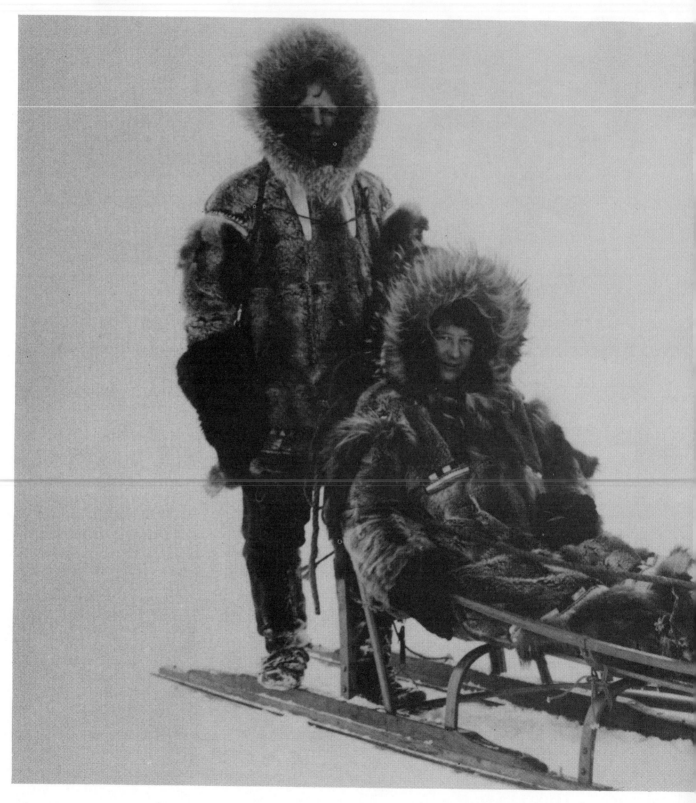

THE DOG SLED

What acts as vehicle, friend, blanket, companion, guide, and servant? Any Northerner could tell you: a sled dog. The Eskimo's reliance upon his canine companions has developed a special relationship between man and dog; a relationship built on trust, service, devotion, and love. To most Americans, dogs are man's best friends. To the northerner, a dog is often his *only* friend— and on those cold, barren, snowy plains, you couldn't ask for much better.

THREE TYPES OF SLEDDING

Tobogganing

Toboggans, as we usually think of them, are flat-bottomed wooden constructions with curled-up fronts. For normal recreational purposes they offer the advantage over runner sleds of not sinking into soft, wet snow. Competition toboggans resemble sleds, and are, in fact, often referred to as such.

Not for the Meek

The competition "luge" toboggan looks most like the wooden toboggan in that, while it uses runners, it is curled up at the front and is ridden in a combination sitting-reclining position similar to that used on the recreational variety (though the accent is more on the reclining). It also shares the limited steering capabilities of the toboggan since the runners are flexible, but fixed. Negotiating corners is accomplished by pushing in the outside runner while lifting the inner

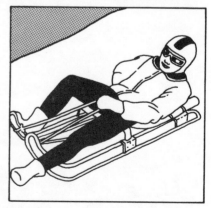

Don Juan
The English winter—ending in July,
To recommence in August.
—*Lord Byron*

one. Shifting one's weight properly plays a large part in avoiding spills at maximum speed. Traveling five inches off the ground at speeds of up to 80 mph makes lugeing an unlikely sport for people whose idea of excitement is going out on a cloudy day without an umbrella.

The Cresta Course

Because they were obviously not content with sliding down mountain roads at safe, enjoyable speeds, the Swiss built two artificial tracks in the town of Davos in 1879 and began to race. Around 1888 one Mr. McCormick found careening over a twisting, ice-covered course on his back too tame and proceeded to go head first down the Cresta Valley run near Saint Moritz, Switzerland—thus was born Cresta tobogganing. An even more sledlike vehicle, known as a skeleton, is used in this version of the sport, fortunately with more sledlike maneuverability. It consists of a platform that slides backward and forward on ball bearings attached to two 4-foot steel runners. The rider lies on his or her stomach and holds on (for dear life) to the runners.

A good rider will be traveling at 90 mph at the finish of the Cresta run, but only after passing through corners with such confidence-inspiring names as Scylla, Charybdis, Church Leap, and Cresta Leap. Helmets, goggles, knee and elbow pads, chin guards, and steel toe-rakes (for braking) make both Cresta and luge tobogganing safer than they sound and the skill of the participants makes serious accidents rare.

Bobsleds for Parties

For those who prefer company in their fun, there is bobsledding where two- or four-man crews are the rule. A bobsled uses two sets of runners—the front pair are turnable for steering by rope or steering by wheel. These sleds have brakes in the form of a steel rod that digs into the ice. The brake is used only in an emergency as it tears up the course; for the 20-foot-high banked curves, once again shifting weight becomes an important factor. Four-man crews must have the precision of a rowing team to avoid going over the top.

It is unusual for additional weight to be an advantage outside of contact sports (football, boxing) but in tobogganing and bobsledding it can mean additional momentum. Stocky builds take note: light-weight crews will often add lead weights to their sleds and a well-laden bobsled is potentially the sport's fastest vehicle, often exceeding speeds of 90 mph on the solid ice courses.

All three types of racing take extreme nerve and skill but less training than many other sports. So if you don't have time to become a championship skier but enjoy the thrill of competition and don't mind becoming an insurance risk, pack your bags and head for Lake Placid or Saint Moritz this winter.

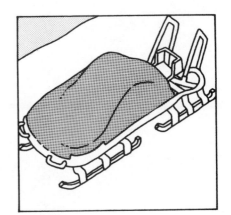

SLEDS

The word sled tends to conjure up images of belly flops down local hills; dragging your Flexible Flyer through one eighth inch of sparse powder, determined to make good used of the first snowfall of the season; careening down snowy streets, waiting till the last possible second to steer away from oncoming traffic; and other pleasant, albeit sometimes dangerous, childhood memories.

The original sled was in use long before the wheel was even a glimmer in mankind's eye. These ancient sleds were simply several logs bound together and were dragged along the ground carrying game over snow or grass.

Along about the Mesolithic period, Scandinavians hit upon the idea of fastening runners to these log platforms, thus developing the ancestor of the contemporary sled. It is believed that massive sleds with heavy runners were used in ancient

and racing-class categories.

Almost Anyone Can Play

If you have a driver's license and a four-wheel-drive vehicle, you qualify. The majority of entries are unmodified stock cars, which manage to finish the course in under 40 seconds. These racing enthusiasts cruise the course at about 20 mph, but speeds of up to 50 mph are reached by more daring drivers; so unless you have a natural ability for cornering and maneuvering a car, you're probably better off spending the winter toasting marshmallows.

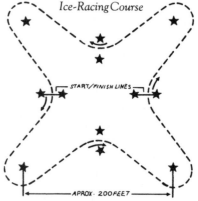

Ice-Racing Course

START/FINISH LINES

APROX. 200 FEET

Need More Excitement?

Those thrill-seekers who find this a rather sedate way to pass a chilly afternoon should try the cross-country competition. This rally invites competitors to drive from evening until dawn for three straight nights, covering up to 600 miles each night. Stretches of designated roads and trails are tackled at top speeds. The team with the best time and fewest penalties wins. You have to be quite an adventurer to assault the treacheries of the winding, narrow trails and the dark, frozen ground. To those who yearn for this kind of excitement, even the dangers will not chill their spirit.

Egypt to haul colossal statues to the building sites, but it is doubtful whether anyone got any particular joy out of that pastime.

Sleds for sport were introduced into the United States by the Pilgrims. Indians had previously devised the toboggan, a flat, runnerless sled; but they used it to transport game and supplies, not people. The Pilgrims used planks set on rigid wooden or iron runners to coast down the snowy New England hills. When they encountered a sharp twist in their path, they were in trouble, as sleds with steering mechanisms were not around until the 1890s.

So, the next time an overzealous sledder slams into your ankles, remember: that laughing blur that whizzes over you and on into the sunset is not merely a diminutive public menace; it's a piece of ongoing horizontal history.

CAR RALLIES AND ICE RACING—ONE WAY TO DUCK HEAVY TRAFFIC

Beginning in 1968, ice racing and car rallies have grown in appeal, and this surge in enthusiasm has been matched only by the elaboration of the sport. Recently, one winter daredevil's impulse has become institutionalized into an annual event complete with its own equipment

CROSS-COUNTRY SKIING (AND THOU BESIDE ME IN THE WILDERNESS?)

If you enjoy rambling about in the open winter countryside, cross-country skiing (also called Nordic skiing and ski touring), is probably just right for you. Wherever the snow leads—through forests, over frozen lakes, on winding country trails, uphill or downhill—the cross-country skier can follow. This method of traversing snowy terrain has been used for thousands of years, and the technique can become as natural as walking.

THE NATURALNESS OF WALKING

The increasing popularity of cross-country skiing (it is estimated that there are at least one million enthusiasts in the United States) reflects the fact that it is an entirely natural way to travel over the snow. What could be more natural than walking? With the incorporation of downhill skiing maneuvers, cross-country skiers have it made.

One Borrows from the Other

The first downhill skiers borrowed many of their turns and stops from the Nordic ski tourers. So it is only natural that, as new techniques in Alpine skiing developed, those suitable would be borrowed right back by the cross-countryites. It became apparent that cross-country techniques weren't quite enough for Alpine skiers—schussing down a steep slope might leave you embedded permanently in the banks below. Greater control of the ski was necessary for Alpine skiers, and so the development of Nordic and Alpine combined.

Skiers of the World Unite

Nowadays, with the advanced design of ski equipment, there is little reason for downhill and cross-country skiers to feud over the relative merits of their sport. It has become increasingly easy to cross over from one to the other; a few minor adjustments of equipment and attitude are just about all that's necessary. Skiers of the world can now unite to go pick on snowmobilers or some other nonskiing sportsmen.

✳︎✳︎✳︎✳︎✳︎✳︎✳︎ ✳︎✳︎✳︎✳︎✳︎

Weather Prophecies

Get down on all fours and check out the woolly-bear caterpillar this September. If the black markings on his back are wider than the brown ones, winter will arrive early and stay late.

147

The Technique

Although it would be unwise to attempt to fully explain cross-country technique here, a few basics will give you an idea of the simplicity of the method. The three fundamentals are precisely the same as for walking: rhythm, balance, and pace. Using ski poles for maneuverability and thrust, you simply kick off with one foot and glide on the other. Learning to feel comfortable wearing the special boots and skis is your first objective; afterwards, it's merely a question of mastering a few basic steps. The primary motion, however, is this step and glide, virtually identical to ice-skating strides. There are numerous books available that are excellent instruction guides. In addition, many areas have ski clubs that provide group instruction.

The Equipment

Cross-country skiing equipment is lighter, easier to get used to, and less expensive than downhill skiing equipment. You should be able to outfit yourself adequately for under $75, and with proper care, your equipment should last for years.

1. *BOOTS:* For the novice, a general touring boot is best. Cut to just above the ankle, these boots offer excellent mobility and support. Proper fit is extremely important. Be sure that you will be able to wear two pairs of socks comfortably. A handy method of judging proper fit is to unlace the boot, push your foot to the front of the boot, and check to see that there's enough space to insert your finger at the heel.

2. *SKIS:* Virtually any lightweight skis that are in good condition (smooth, with no cracks, splinters, or protrusions) are fine for cross-

ICE SHOWS

In 1864, Jackson Haines, an American ballet master living in Vienna, revolutionized the sport of ice-skating by combining it with the art of dance. Haines also performed stunts such as skating on stilts for the enjoyment of audiences and the enrichment of his reputation as the "Ice Master." The stunts and dances he initiated became the foundation on which all future ice shows were built.

Capades and Follies

Olympic star Sonja Henie turned pro in 1936 and made the ice show a profitable business venture through her worldwide reputation. Two Minnesota skaters, Oscar Johnson and Eddie Shipstead, followed her lead and built up a chain of ice carnivals that led to the famous Ice Capades and Ice Follies of today.

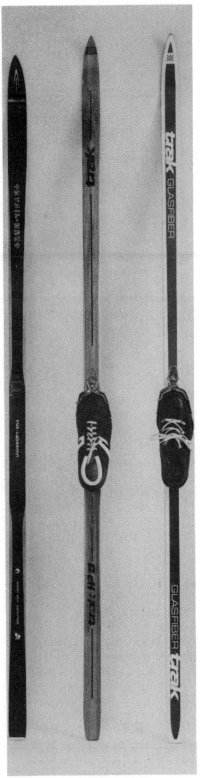

country skiing. The shorter the ski, the easier it will be to learn. However, as your competency increases, you will find that short skis limit maneuverability considerably. To judge the best ski length for you, stand the ski upright and stretch your arm towards the tip. If the top of the ski meets your wrist, the length is perfect. Also keep in mind that the thinner the ski, the swifter you'll glide over the snow.

3. *BINDINGS:* There are two main types of bindings available for ski touring: those with a toe clip, which clamps over a ridge on the boot, and those with a cable, which goes around the heel, forcing the boot toe into a set of toe irons. If you wear a large-sized boot, or intend to cover rough terrain, the latter is the preferable choice. If you are planning light touring or racing, the toe-clip model will allow you to lift your heel off the ski for greater mobility and speed.

4. *SKI POLES:* Ski poles should be lightweight and flexible (bamboo is ideal), should have angled points to guide into the snow, and, when set upright, should reach the middle of your shoulder.

5. *WAX:* The correct wax is essential. This ingredient is applied to the bottom of the ski and will stick to the snow for traction when you are going uphill and allow you to glide downhill. Most waxes have color-coded containers that correspond to different temperatures and terrains. Learning to select the appropriate wax by this method is far better than trial-and-error selection. Be sure to follow the manufacturer's application directions to the letter.

With the correct gear and preparation, you'll find cross-country skiing provides recreation, a test of skill, an adventure, and lots of fun. For young and old alike, this ancient means of transportation presents an opportunity for glorious winter travel.

sheet consists of two sets of four concentric circles marked out on the ice, 114 feet apart center to center. Four players are on each team, sliding two rocks apiece, and the winner of the game is the team with a rock closest to the center of the circles after all 16 rocks or stones have been delivered.

This, very basically, is the sport of curling. As in most other sports, the object of the game is simple to describe but the attendant rules, techniques, strategies, and esoteric terms could fill a book, and in fact have filled several.

The Art of Sweeping
One of the interesting techniques that evolved in the 200 or so years of curling's history is the art of sweeping. Team members use brooms to set the air in front of the moving stone in motion, thus creating less air resistance while also clearing the path of any small obstacles. In this manner, 15 feet or more may be added to the stones' distance.

If this sounds like fun to you and you are in good physical shape (stones weigh 40 pounds), you may want to contact a curling club this winter or form one of your own. As a sport it offers outdoor exercise at minimal expense. It is nonviolent and requires no skates, but rather a selfless team spirit and the arm and eye of a professional bowler. If, on the other hand, you have a phobia about falling through the ice, there is always Tossing the Caber.

Did You Know . . .
. . . biometeorologists believe that humans are most fertile when the temperature dips to 65°Fahrenheit (18°C.)? In addition, children conceived during the cooler months tend to be stronger, and fare slightly better on IQ tests, than children conceived during the warmer months.

CURLING
It is hardly surprising that the same Scottish race that invented Tossing the Caber (throwing small trees from place to place) would also originate a sport that involves grown men sliding rocks across frozen lakes (or lochs) while other men sweep the ice in front of the moving stone. What is surprising is that, as silly as it sounds in the description, the sport of curling is, in fact, a serious, technically involved activity played all over the world and with increasing popularity here in the U.S.A.

Down to Basics
Once skaters, fishers, boaters, and hockey players have been removed from your local pond (through peaceful negotiation, hopefully) you are ready to lay out a curling sheet, the rough equivalent of a bowling lane or shuffleboard court. The

DOWNHILL SKIING—NEW ON THE SLOPES

For the novice skier, the right school, teacher, and attitude are crucial. Learning to ski can be a frustrating, disappointing experience without these three factors. Overcrowded classes, indifferent instructors, and incomprehensible directions are often the reasons many abandon skiing lessons after their first attempt.

Picking the Right Resort

With the enormous popularity of downhill skiing, there are more than enough convenient ski resorts to choose from. Before you decide where you want to learn, do a little investigating.

Ask around. A friend's personal observations are worth more than all the travel brochures in print. Call the resort ahead of time to ask questions. You have a right to know what to expect. Speak to someone who actually participates in the ski instruction; the desk clerk who answers your call may never leave the lodge.

Be sure to determine these three factors:

1. Pupils are sorted into different classes by level of competence. Beginners and intermediate skiers should never be in the same class. Waiting for the beginner to catch on to fundamentals will bore and frustrate the more advanced skier. Beginners who realize that they are delaying the progress of others will feel guilty and embarrassed. These situations do not make for optimum learning conditions.

GLM

In 1966 SKI Magazine sponsored an experiment in ski instruction at Killington, Vermont. Beginning skiers were found to learn faster by starting on short skis and progressing, as they improved, to longer models. With the growth of the ski-rental industry, this Graduated Length Method (GLM) of instruction has become increasingly popular. Students begin by renting short skis (3-5 feet) and graduate to the longer lengths. When they are ready for the six-footers they can then buy a permanent pair of their own. Rental fees are often included in the price of a GLM course.

Weather Prophecies

The higher the hornet builds its nest, the deeper the snowfall to be expected.

2. Classes are kept relatively small. Ten to twelve students per class will assure that every member gets a chance to practice the exercises with the instructor. Some classes are so large that each participant is lucky if he/she can squeeze in five minutes of in-class practice per two-hour session. It is absolutely necessary that your first skiing maneuvers be practiced under the guidance of your instructor; so be sure that this is possible. For this reason, it is wise to avoid the resorts at Christmas and Easter when crowds are huge and instructors are overworked.

3. Students and teachers are assigned by common language. This sounds too obvious to be mentioned, but many students have found themselves with perfectly competent instructors who were completely fluent—in Swiss, Austrian, or French, but not English. Likewise, many instructors have had to try to communicate with students vacationing at the slopes from foreign lands. Obviously, this slows things up for all concerned.

IF YOU THINK IT'S COLD OUT—

If you have a particularly strong faith in the powers of science and a love of cold climates that is so intense you would consider spending hundreds of years immobile in an overgrown thermos set at minus 310 degrees, maybe you should investigate cryonics. To put it simply, and as unmorbidly as possible, cryonics is the new science of freezing the bodies of the recently deceased in the hope that future doctors will find a cure for what ended the preservee's life and thaw him out, restoring him to a new life, at room temperature.

Only Patients?

Freezing has been used for some time to preserve organs and blood, and surgeons have used the technique to perform operations on localized parts of the body. However, the majority of doctors are not quite ready to accept the claims of organizations like Trans Time, Inc. and the New York Cryonics Society, who believe that all cadavers carefully preserved in liquid nitrogen will one day be considered only as patients. Proponents of cryonics say that if a recently deceased person has his body temperature slowly lowered to the point where cells can be preserved safely with a kind of body antifreeze substance (and no earthquake or fire interrupts the icy slumber of the deceased), there is no reason why the people of the future cannot thaw out the sleeper with a minimum of damage.

Something to Ponder

A cryocapsule and the cost of maintaining it for only one year run about $7,000. You have to make detailed plans for insurance and trust funds if you want to make certain that future generations will bother to take a look at your capsule (what about inflation in 500 years?) and that an

Finding the Right Teacher

When all is said and done, without the right teacher, nothing else really matters. To help you judge your instructor, look for or avoid the qualities described in the narrow columns below. Armed with this knowledge, you should be able to determine the best resort and instructor for you. Your own attitude, however, plays a large part in the success of your instruction. Learning anything new can be ego deflating and embarrassing. Be assured that you will fall down plenty of times in full view of others, that other classmates will catch on to certain steps before you will, and that the whole prospect may seem impossibly complex at times.

The Good Teacher	The Bad Teacher
Will work on one ski movement at a time and praise you when you get that right. He knows that skiing is 60 percent confidence.	Will always be finding fault.
Will lead his group down the slope doing the movement he expects them to do. He will always make it look simple.	Will do parallel turns when he is leading down a beginner's group. He will always be showing how good he is.
Will be prepared to check your equipment. Perhaps he will carry a screwdriver for adjusting ill-set bindings (in some countries teachers are officially discouraged because of the legal risk).	Will let a lightweight beginner ski on 200 cm skis, or even worse, will overtighten bindings to keep beginners on their skis.
Will keep rotating the order in which the group skis so that the poorer skiers get a chance to ski behind him.	Will let the weaker skiers be the tail-enders—learning little and feeling worse and worse.
Will vary the runs and the routines and keep you in the sunshine so that skiing is fun.	Will spend a week on the same things—and never learn anybody's name.

Reprinted from *We Learned to Ski*, by Brian Jackman and Mark Ottaway, St. Martin's Press, Inc., New York.

unpaid guardian doesn't get annoyed and leave you by a particularly hot stove. There are more philosophically troubling questions—what if evolution has so changed future men that the thawed-out specimen from the twentieth century becomes a walking, talking curio, a kind of futuristic version of the caveman, who can't adjust to a new world? And what if doctors eventually find cures for diseases that afflict living people but still can't revive someone who has actually died from one, no matter how well frozen he is? It's worth thinking about—if you are still capable, that is, of meditation at minus 310 degrees.

WINTER CAMPING

If you intend to do any winter camping, there are two terms which you should understand fully: winter and camping. If you think of winter camping as sitting before a blazing fire, toasting marshmallows while one or two stray snowflakes drift gracefully to the ground, think again. Winter camping calls for an adventuring spirit and some specialized equipment—if you are improperly prepared, the trip may be more an ordeal than the beautiful, if challenging, experience it can be when undertaken correctly.

Why Camp in Winter?

Winter opens up areas of back country which are never explored during the warmer seasons. Difficult terrain becomes smoothed by snow, brooks develop exquisitely wrought ice-bridges, otherwise monotonous landscapes become glorious winter scenes. The skies are clear and the stars shine brilliantly. The air is clean and seems to sparkle—all of nature is new and invitingly fresh.

Getting Ready

To comfortably enjoy all that winter camping has to offer, a certain familiarity with basic camping techniques is desirable. If you are a

L.L. BEAN, INC.

With 60 years' experience, L.L. Bean maintains a well-deserved reputation for good traditional outdoor equipment. The store has an exceptional line of cold weather garments including shirts, hats, underwear, snowshoes, and windbreakers. L. L. Bean is particularly cherished by hearty woodsmen, campers, and hunters. Several name brand varieties of equipment are available. The stock is enumerated in a free, 120-page catalog.

WINTER WONDERLAND

Valentine, Nebraska features waterfowl, prairie chickens, biking, hiking, fishing. Nearby camp: Big Alkali Area.

❄✻❀☀❋ ❀✻❀❋❀✻❀☀❀

complete novice, you should try to make a few preparatory camping trips during the autumn, when conditions are kinder, so that the experience of roughing it outdoors will not overwhelm you during a winter trip.

Equipment

When you are ready to purchase your cold weather camping gear, bring along a friend who has camped in the area you are planning to visit. Obviously, advice from an experienced camper is the most valuable consumer guide you can use. In any event, there are certain items that will be necessary no matter where you plan to set up camp:

SLEEPING BAG: A down-filled sleeping bag is the best buy for winter camping. A 3-inch loft (thickness) will provide comfort in temperatures well below zero. There are mummy bags available; these have a drawstring around the opening which enables you to securely fasten the blanket around your neck and shoulders. This type is ideal and will guarantee maximum coverage and warmth.

HIKER'S STOVES: It's a good idea to bring along two single-burner stoves if you are planning a prolonged camping trip. If one should fail, you won't be reduced to eating frozen soup. Gasoline- or naphtha-fired stoves are excellent for very cold climates—for more moderate weather, butane may be a better fuel. Check with your dealer to find out the proper model for your needs, and make sure you understand how to operate the stove before you leave the store.

TENT: Nylon tents that are specifically designed for winter or mountain climbing are the best choice. Nylon tents are lightweight and easily pitched—requiring less hardware and effort than bulkier varieties. In addition, they are designed to withstand heavy winds, and the sloped sides allow snow to slide off quickly.

FOOD: With the increased popularity of camping, many new freeze-dried foods are available. Most are packaged compactly for easy storage and are easily prepared. Remember to include plenty of high-calorie foods; you'll be burning more energy than usual.

CLOTHING: Plan your camping wardrobe carefully; to a large extent your comfort depends upon your selection. Thermal underwear, hooded sweatshirts, several wool shirts, good warm socks and mittens, head and ear protection, and waterproof boots should all be included. An excellent checklist of cold weather camping clothes can be found in *The Boy Scout's Field Manual,* available at your local library.

FIRST-AID KIT: Some sort of first-aid kit is essential no matter what the season. Prepackaged kits are available at most camping-gear stores.

✳❋✳❊✳❀❀ ❋✳❋❄✳❋✳❊ ❀❀❅❈ ❁❃◎◉ ❋❀❄❋

EDDIE BAUER
This is the top-line, high-quality merchandise emporium. Eddie Bauer has a long-standing reputation based on the variety and quality of its stock. Bauer caters to most outdoor recreational needs: hunting, fishing, and camping. There is an especially complete selection of down garments. Items are outlined in a free, 144-page color catalog.

SNOW BLINDNESS
Bright sun combined with the glare of white snow can cause a temporary loss of sight known as snow blindness. Caution should be exercised whenever long periods of time are spent outdoors in the snow as even dull sunlight can cause it. The best protection is a good pair of sunglasses or shaded goggles.

Symptoms and Treatment
If your eyes feel gritty, turn red, and cause you pain after long exposure to sun and snow, get indoors and close your eyes. Mineral oil will dispel the grittiness but eyes should remain covered until the redness and pain have completely gone away.

This is the absolute minimal amount of equipment you'll need. In fact, depending upon the duration of your stay and the site of your proposed trip, you may need as many as a dozen additional items. Your camping-gear salesperson can offer valuable suggestions; an Ensolite pad to lay your sleeping bag on, snowshoes, canteens, fishing equipment—all may be practical additions to this basic list.

Camping Hints

Now that you've assembled your equipment and familiarized yourself thoroughly with the operation and maintenance of each item, a few helpful hints are in order.

1. Familiarize yourself with your campsite. Carefully study maps of the area, making sure that you learn the precise locations of forest ranger/game-warden/sheriff stations. Map out several alternate routes, and check with the local weather authorities before starting out to be sure that weather conditions will be favorable.

2. Select your tent site long before dark. It always takes longer than you think it will to set up your tent, and it gets dark very early in the winter. It's uncomfortable to be struggling with several yards of nylon and rope in chilly darkness.

3. Be sure to pitch your tent on solidly packed snow. Many an inexperienced camper has failed to do this only to find himself suddenly falling through the tent floor with the tent collapsing on top of him. This is extremely funny to watch, but not much fun to experience.

4. Whenever possible, cook outdoors rather than in your tent. This is safer, because of the danger of fire and of asphyxiation, and you will be able to keep a better fire going in the open than when it is confined in your tent. In addition, if you cook inside your tent, steam may arise to the ceiling and freeze there. If this happens, you may wake up in the middle of the night to find a nice little blizzard raging inside your tent.

5. Make sure that your clothes are as dry as possible—*never* allow clothing to become excessively damp (a wonderful way to develop frostbite or hypothermia—subnormal body temperature). Pay special attention to socks, boots, and gloves—hands and feet need particular care. If your clothing does become wet, let the water freeze and beat off the ice crystals.

All of this may sound off-putting, but all the measures you take will ensure that you have a rewarding camping experience. There are many excellent books and magazines available which can give you detailed information on winter camping. The aforementioned *Boy Scout's Manual* is one of the best all-around guides available. The Sierra Club, described elsewhere in this section, offers literature, as do many state parks and camping-equipment manufacturers.

Cream of Mushroom Soup with Cognac

A hot mushroom soup laced with Cognac is a great frost antidote.

Wipe clean and slice 1 pound of mushrooms. Finely chop 1 medium onion. Sauté these gently with 2 tbsps. butter for about 3 minutes. Make a roux of 4 tbsps. flour and 4 tbsps. butter. Into this put 1½ tbsps. curry powder. Blend well. Now add 1 cup chicken stock (can be made with bouillon cube) and 1 cup milk. Put mushroom mixture into blender. Pureé until sooth. Add to the stock mix. Pour in 2 tbsps. of cognac and salt and pepper to taste. Simmer for about 10 minutes. Serves four.

FEDERAL RECREATION SYMBOLS

The above symbols have been adopted by United States recreational areas to help foreign travelers and children familiarize themselves with the different activities offered on the nation's public lands.

The changeover from word signs to these pictorial guides is in progress, although the change is not in full use as yet. A knowledge of the different symbols used should prove helpful to the winter vacationer.

PADDLE, ANYONE?

Platform tennis, also called paddle, was developed over 50 years ago as a winter tennis alternative. With the increased popularity of tennis in recent years, paddle will undoubtedly be enjoying a resurgence of interest as well.

Platform tennis is played on an aluminum (or occasionally wooden) court, roughly one third the size of the traditional tennis court. The racquet is made of perforated wood and has a short handle, and the ball is larger and spongier than the regular tennis ball. The entire court is elevated (so that snow can be brushed off) and encircled with a wire fence. This fence comes into play during the game; several wire shots (bouncing the ball off the wire) are integral parts of the sport. With this and one or two other minor variations, platform tennis is much the same as traditional tennis. Anyone with reasonable skill and dexterity should find the game easy to learn and enjoy. Playing in the great outdoors during the brisk winter weather is exhilarating. Many devotees find that they can play paddle longer with less fatigue than warm-weather tennis. In addition, there is something to be said for enjoying this sport in the naturally beautiful winter landscape.

DRIVING (AND PUTTING) THROUGH THE SNOW

Anyone who would get up at four in the morning to stand ankle deep in frozen dew to smack a little ball around with a stick must be really devoted to the game of golf. Sooner or later golfers were bound to come up with some way of extending their fun through the winter. The result is the Lake George Polar Ice Cap Open.

Goodbye, Sand Traps

Held annually every February since 1970, this frigid nine-hole event is a testimonial to the persistence of the average golf fiend. Of course, winter golfing has its advantages: no chance of sunburn, no pesky insects to contend with, and sand traps are but an unpleasant memory.

Be advised, however. Unless you

have the constitution of a walrus, you might find yourself just a bit uncomfortable. Temperatures tend to hover at the zero-degree mark at tourney time. Of course, this didn't stop the 150-plus players who doggedly stuck it out in 1970, although the wind-chill factor made the temperature on the green a brisk −33° Fahrenheit (−36°C.).

If you're determined to spend this February on the links, write to the Chamber of Commerce, Lake George, New York 12845 for information on the great Lake George Polar Ice Cap Open.

POLAR BEAR CLUB

Would-be water sprites need not be sidetracked by winter weather. There are a growing number of swimmers who participate in outdoor ocean swimming in the coldest weather under the auspices of the local Polar Bear Club.

DO'S AND DON'TS FOR SNOWMOBILERS

Ski-type runners and sleds have been used for winter transportation since the dawn of recorded history. It is, therefore, not surprising that, sooner or later, someone would attempt to motorize them. In 1928, someone succeeded, and so was born the first crude snowmobile, a toboggan powered by an outboard motor.

Since 1928, snowmobiling as winter recreational activity has grown by leaps and bounds. Increased leisure time, harsher winter weather, and the mobility of the sport have all contributed to its popularity. Snowmobiles have opened up new vistas in winter sports and camping. Hitherto inaccessible areas have become winter playgrounds for the avid snowmobiler, and parks and resorts are welcoming this new potential patronage with open arms.

Just More Pollution?

Not all reaction to the growth of snowmobiling has been positive, however. Environmentalists and wildlife watchers have decried the

SNOWMOBILE

A new form of transportation—a new outlet for the competitive instinct? It seems as soon as someone makes something that goes, someone wants to make it go faster—and snowmobilers are no exception. Snowmobile races are run on prepared courses or cross country and competitors are constantly trying to improve the speed and maneuverability of their machines.

WINTER WONDERLAND

Squaw Creek, Missouri features snow geese, eagles, deer, hiking, biking. Nearby camp: Big Lake State Park.

introduction of yet another form of pollution. With the growth of the sport, new areas have been plagued with littering, tree damage, and wildlife harassment. To make this sport an unsullied pleasure, conservationists and snowmobile manufacturers have joined together to come up with a code of ethics for snowmobilers. Careful observance of these rules will make this winter sport enjoyable for participants and agreeable to area residents.

Code of Ethics for Snowmobilers

1. Be a good sportsman. Don't give the entire sport and all its participants a bad name by your own unsportsmanlike conduct.

2. Never litter trails and camping areas.

3. Never damage living trees, shrubs, or other natural features.

4. Respect other people's property and rights.

5. Lend a helping hand to anyone in distress.

6. Make your vehicle available to assist search-and-rescue parties.

7. Never interfere with hikers, skiers, snowshoers, ice fishers, or other winter sportsmen. Respect their rights to enjoy recreational facilities in their own way.

8. Obey all federal, state, and local laws that pertain to the operation of your snowmobile. Be sure to inform local officials when you are going to be using public lands.

9. Never harass wildlife. Avoid any areas that are posted for the protection or feeding of wildlife.

10. Stay on marked trails that are open to snowmobiles.

SAFETY TIPS FOR SNOWMOBILES

Unlike hikers or skiers, the snowmobiler spends long periods of time in the winter cold without expending the energy required to keep up the body temperature. This fact combined with the wind-chill factor created by the moving vehicle makes extremely warm clothing essential. Wearing layers of cotton and wool clothing, topped off with a down-filled parka, warm, waterproofed shoes, and woolly mittens and cap will enable the snowmobiler to enjoy the sport in comfort.

Speed Demons—Take Heed

In addition, the far-ranging, high-speed capabilities of these vehicles make elaborate safety precautions a must. Helmet and goggles are absolutely necessary, and every snowmobiler should be well versed in winter woods survival.

No one would think of setting out on an extended winter car trip without first checking that his or her car was in good working condition. Snowmobilers, who are apt to find themselves in more isolated areas than those traveling by car, would be well advised to do the same. Proper snowmobile maintenance, and pretrip check-ups will help reduce the risks of breakdowns and malfunctions far from help and home.

BUYING A SNOWMOBILE?

Snowmobiles have come a long way since an inventive sportsman first fastened an outboard motor to a toboggan back in 1928. If you're in the market for a snowmobile, a little fundamental knowledge will prove useful.

Modern snowmobiles consist of a metal-framed chassis with a pair of skis attached to the front. A two-cycle or rotary engine powers a track which rotates, bulldozer fashion, propelling the machine through the snow. Steering is accomplished with handlebars, which manipulate the front skis. The driver sits on a bench seat, protected by cowling and a windshield.

More than 50 companies now offer these vehicles at prices ranging from $500 to $2,000 and more. Purchasing a snowmobile is much like buying a car; they are available both new and used from dealers, and the mechanically unschooled buyer would be wise to have his/her potential purchase (used) thoroughly examined by a professional mechanic.

Nothing to Sneeze At

The ancient Greek philosopher, Aristotle, developed the theory (possibly during an attack of hay fever) that a sneeze was divine in origin, and a sure sign of sanity and sagacity. In parts of Greece the belief that an idiot cannot sneeze still prevails. Hippocrates, the Greek "Father of Medicine," had very distinct thoughts about sneezes. They would cure hiccups, rouse lethargic women, and snap anyone out of catatonia.

The Snow Queen

The walls of the palace were built of drifting snow, and the windows and doors of cutting winds. The rooms were just as the blizzards had made them and all were lit by the Northern Lights.

—*Hans Christian Andersen*

WINTER OLYMPICS

Chamoix in the French Alps hosted the first official Winter Olympics in 1924. Figure skating and hockey had been included in the 1908 and 1920 summer version (presumably indoors), but it took some prodding from speed skaters and skiers to get the committee in Paris to organize a separate meet for winter sports. What began with only 13 events has grown to a massive operation including over 30 forms of competition.

It is interesting to compare the winning times of 1924 with more recent achievements to see the results of advanced equipment and training methods.

THEN AND NOW

Event	Distance	Time*	
		1924	1972
Cross-Country Skiing	50 kilometers	3:44:32.0	2:43:14.7
Speed Skating	500 meters	44.0	39.4
	5,000 meters	8:39.0	7:23.6
	10,000 meters	18:04.8	14:01.3
4-Man Bobsled		5:45.54	4:43.0

*All winning times = hours:minutes:seconds.tenths

WINTER JOGGING

Dedicated joggers need not despair when winter sets in. With the proper clothing, jogging can be a year-round pursuit. Although it is unwise to jog when the ground is unnavigable due to heavy snow and ice accumulation, the cold itself need not hinder your exercising routine. Investing in the following cold weather jogging wardrobe should enable you to hit the road in any but the most severe arctic conditions:

1. Wool fishnet underwear
2. Wool or cotton turtleneck shirt
3. Wool- or fleece-lined cotton sweatshirt with a hood
4. Lightweight windbreaker
5. Wool or nylon warm-up pants
6. One pair of cotton socks worn under one pair of wool socks
7. Waterproofed running shoes
8. Leather or woolen mittens
9. Ski mask that covers head and face

Keep in mind that it is dangerous to allow perspiration to saturate clothing. Be sure to taper off your activity as your body perspires, so that the moisture will be able to evaporate. Remember too, that you must not lounge around in your jogging gear after your run is complete; this is asking for chills and trouble.

VISIT IN THE WINTER

Carolina Sand Hills, South Carolina features waterfowl, turkeys, deer, doves, hiking, biking, fishing. Nearby camp: Camden resorts.

Mulled Beer

On cold days days draw 2 qts. beer in a bucket, and stir with a red-hot poker until warm.

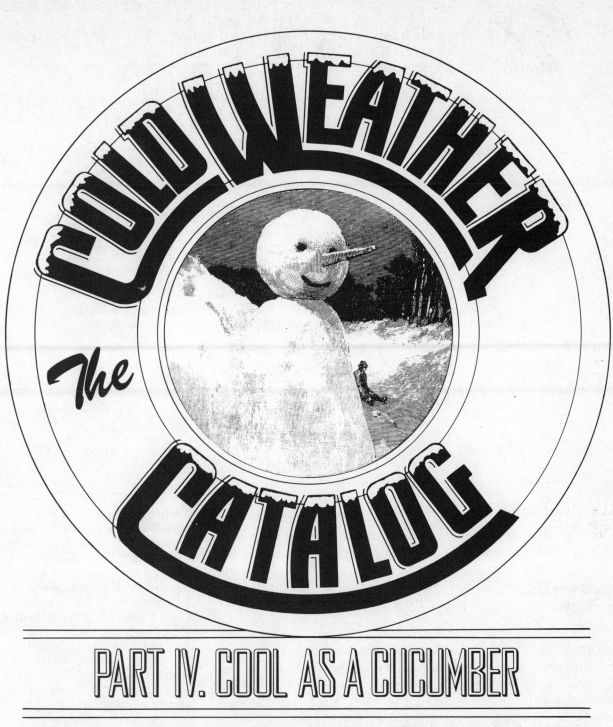

COLD WEATHER
The CATALOG

PART IV. COOL AS A CUCUMBER

Air too dry? Clothes too wet? Room too drafty? Thermostat broken? Car won't start? Car won't stop? Skin too chapped? Need a fur coat? A new blanket? A parka? <u>Now's</u> the time to get ready.

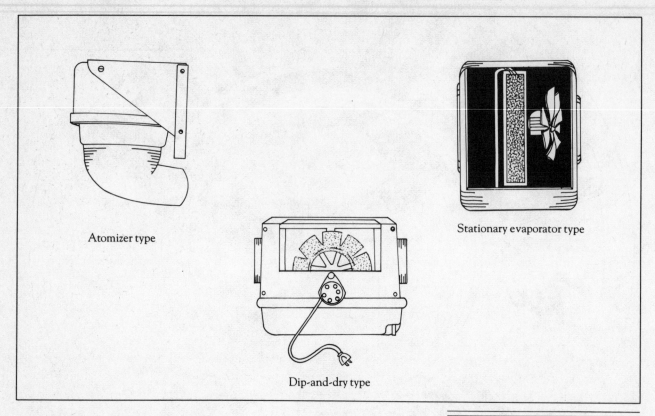

Atomizer type

Stationary evaporator type

Dip-and-dry type

HUMIDIFIERS

If your throat feels like sandpaper, your grandmother's love seat suddenly develops creaking joints, and your plants are going down for the count, you need a humidifier. Humidifiers will put more moisture into the air, thereby making winter a little more comfortable for everyone (and everything) in the home.

Built-In Models

If you live in a house with forced-air heating, you can have the most effective system: a built-in humidifier that connects with your furnace and water supply. With this type, warm, moist air is carried through the ducts and distributed evenly throughout your entire home. The most satisfactory of the built-in models are electrically powered units, which evaporate water from moist padding. Other power models either force air through a fine waterfall or spray water directly into the ductwork. These are not recommended, since they can cause damage to the furnace and may distribute mineral dust throughout your home.

Portables

Portables can be used with any kind of existing heating system, require no permanent hookup to furnace or plumbing, and are mounted on casters so they can be rolled where needed.

Nothing to Sneeze At

In the West Indies, it is believed that if you sneeze, it means that someone is saying nasty things about you. (Of course, if you sneeze all over someone, this would be entirely logical.)

In rural areas of the American south, it is thought that if you sneeze while eating, you will hear of a death. (If you sneeze your meal all over your dining companions, the death may be your own.)

In Germany, it is considered unlucky to sneeze while putting on your shoes (well, you could fall over while balancing on one foot), but sneezing during an argument lends veracity to your position.

Frost at Midnight

And ice, mast-high, came floating by,
As green as emerald.
—*Coleridge*

Your portable humidifier will probably "drink" a lot, and let you know when it's ready for a refill (a light will go on and the machine will automatically cut off). Refilling three times a day may be necessary in cold weather; so keep your eye on the water level and a watering can handy.

Maintenance

Depending upon the hardness of your water and the speed with which mineral deposits form, you'll have to clean the humidifier anywhere from once a week to once a season. For your own convenience, avoid purchasing a model that requires disassembly or removal of heavy components in order to properly clean the humidifier. Always clean and empty the reservoir at the end of the winter. In fact, you should drain the humidifier during any spell of unseasonably mild weather. By doing this, you can avoid slimy deposits and disagreeable odors.

PORTABLE ELECTRIC HEATERS

Next to a loving friend, a portable electric heater may be a wise second choice for low-cost, energy-saving warmth. This is particularly true for apartment dwellers who have no real control over the

THERMOMETERS

There are two basic types of household thermometers. The glass column style contains a liquid, usually mercury, that expands and contracts within the glass tube as the temperature varies. This is the familiar style that is used (without the mounting piece) to take your body temperature. The dial thermometer contains a coil made of two different metals that press against each other. As the temperature changes, the pressure of the metals changes. This is registered on a dial in degrees.

Indoor-Outdoor Variety

If you'd like to be able to ascertain the temperature both indoors and out simultaneously, you can purchase a handy version of the glass column thermometer. This model comes in two parts: one device that is mounted on an indoor wall, and a sensor bulb that is hung on the porch or garage. The liquid is forced through a length of thin tubing from the outside sensor bulb to the indoor thermometer. Twin columns on the indoor unit enable you to read both temperatures. Hopefully, they won't be the same on a wintry day.

thermostat setting. Most models are small, upright, and weigh between 7 and 12 pounds, making them as conveniently mobile as an old-fashioned portable typewriter.

Electric heaters work by reflecting heat out (that's the principle of radiation—most models have a shiny reflector that beams the heat outwards in a straight line) or reflecting heat up (that's the convection—most models include a fan for this purpose). In either case, the air that is warmed by the heating element rises and circulates within the room.

If Concentrated, Spot-Heating is Wanted

When you're showering, dressing, or shaving in an icy bathroom or watching the late movie on television, fast, direct heat is what you want. Radiation heaters are best for these situations; properly positioned, they provide quick, directed heat. Baseboard models, which have low, horizontal housings, are less conspicuous than other styles. However, because of their construction, they may prove to be the least satisfactory choice for quick warm-ups; the heat tends to stay down around the floor for a while. In addition, these models have no fan to help convection take place, which increases the time necessary for these models to heat a room.

If You Want to be Warm All Over

Cold hands may mean a warm heart, but they also mean that your heater isn't putting out sufficient vertical heat. Placing the heater on a chair won't help; this will merely result in warm hands and cold feet. Horizontal (wall-to-wall) heat is necessary along with vertical (floor-to-ceiling) heat to ensure that the entire room area is properly heated. For this purpose, a radiation-convection combination unit or a convection-only heater will do the job.

Things to Look For

1. Many newer electric heaters have a thermostat that adjusts the electrical current so that the room is maintained at a specific temperature. Before purchasing such a model, however, check to see that the control allows for reasonably narrow variations in temperature. A model that allows for variations of six degrees or more may not be suitable for individual comfort—there is quite a difference between 62° Fahrenheit (17°C.) and 68° Fahrenheit (20°C.).

2. Be sure to check that the handles are positioned in such a way that the heater can be lifted without hands coming into the "line of fire." Be sure that the handles are properly insulated so that the risk of accidental burns is decreased.

3. Since portable heaters are usually put on the floor, top-mounted controls are generally more convenient than those placed on the side or front. In addition, top placement of controls means you are less likely to expose your fingers to heat when making adjustments.

Dial Thermometer

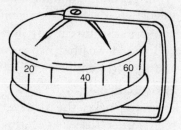

How to Buy and Test One
When purchasing a thermometer, pick one that registers near the same temperature reading as the other models on display. It's unlikely that all of them are defective. At home, you can check the accuracy of a thermometer by plunging it into a bowl of ice water and swirling it around for a few minutes. If it registers 32° F. or close to it, it's pretty reliable.

It's a comedy standard to show a character trying to read a thermometer by holding it over a match—you probably don't have to be reminded to keep thermometers away from excessive heat sources.

Little Italy
3 oz. hot espresso
1 tbsp. Sambuca Romana
1 strip of lemon peel

Twist the peel over a demitasse cup and drop it in. Add espresso and Sambuca.

Radiant Heater

Combination Heater and Fan

Radiant Heater

Convection Heater

Once You've Made Your Selection

Finding the temperature setting that suits you best is not as simple as it sounds. A good method is to set the control on the highest setting. Then, when you're warm, turn the thermostat down slowly until the heater cycles off (you'll either hear the fan go off, see the heating element fade, or see the indicator light go out). Now set the machine on the low setting (or 1,000 watts).

The floor area 6 to 12 inches in front of the heater will warm up considerably. It is a sound precautionary measure to check this floor space periodically while the heater is in operation. If the floor feels quite hot to the touch, turn the unit off for a few moments, or move it to another area.

Finally, it should be noted that most portable electric heaters make some noise when operating. Admittedly, it's not in the same class as a supersonic take-off, but you should be aware of this in advance. Most people would agree, however, that a little noise is a small price to pay for this form of economical, convenient heat.

Some companies manufacture radiant heaters cleverly disguised as pictures to hang on the wall.

KEEPING THE HEAT UP AND YOUR BILLS DOWN

These days, everyone spends a great deal of time talking about high fuel costs. But, since no one seems to be doing anything about them, it's up to you to try to keep your own fuel bills down.

Additional Steps

Major insulation work is covered fully elsewhere in this catalog. Here are additional steps that you can take to avoid mortgaging your home to pay the heating bills this winter:

1. Probably the most highly publicized economy measure is setting the thermostat on 68° Fahrenheit (20°C.) by day and 60°Fahrenheit (16°C.) by night. This small effort will save you up to 15 percent annually on fuel bills—nothing to sneeze at these days. If you have radiators, putting metal sheets behind them will recycle the heat by reflecting it back into the room.

2. If you've ever sat by a supposedly tightly shut door or window and felt a stiff nor'easter blowing about your head and shoulders, you realize the importance of storm doors and windows. This precaution prevents substantial amounts of cold air from penetrating your home.

3. Any areas that do not have to be heated should be sealed off as completely as possible. There is little point in heating your closets, cupboards, garage, or chimney. Keep doors shut, and when not in use, keep the fireplace damper closed. Conversely, it will defeat your purpose to cover baseboard heat outlets, hot-air registers, or heat ducts with rugs, draperies, or furniture simply because they are not decorator approved. The point is to keep warm economically—wait until springtime to be featured in the latest interior decoration magazine. Keep all heating sources free of obstacles and let them do their job.

4. During the daytime, open shades and curtains of windows that get direct sunlight. Why not let Mother Nature pitch in whenever possible? You should close them at night to keep the accumulated heat in.

5. To save on hot water, take showers instead of baths. To save further, make sure that you repair any leaky faucets. This is literally money down the drain, and a washer or two (for repair) is a very small investment indeed. Whenever possible, use cold water in your washing machine. There are plenty of reliable cold-water detergents available today: use them. In addition, running washing machines, clothes dryers, and dishwashers with only full loads will help cut costs as well.

The above should help you to set fire to your gas and electricity bills. The huge, roaring blaze that results will probably last all winter.

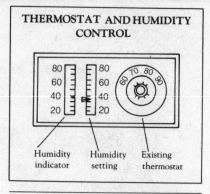

THERMOSTAT AND HUMIDITY CONTROL

Humidity indicator — Humidity setting — Existing thermostat

THERMOSTATS

A thermostat controls the flow of fuel to the furnace by measuring the room's temperature. As the temperature drops, a piece of metal or bulb of mercury within the thermostat tilts into position, completing an electrical circuit. Result: on comes the heat. Making sure it is functioning properly will mean a savings in fuel costs.

Wait Until Evening

To set your thermostat efficiently, wait until the house is fairly cool (evening is a good time). Then set the dial at 60° Fahrenheit (16°C.). When the burners are on, make the minor adjustments to arrive at your personal comfort level. You can mark the setting with a pen for next time.

A Willful Furnace?

If you find that your furnace clicks off despite freezing cold temperatures, this doesn't necessarily mean it has developed a will of its own. Too many appliances in operation throughout the house or a shaft of sunlight falling directly on the gauge may cause the thermostat to register a deceptively high reading, resulting in the automatic shut-off of the furnace. A piece of aluminum foil around the thermostat will reflect the sun's rays away from the gauge, and shutting off unnecessary appliances will allow the thermostat to operate efficiently while conserving energy throughout the home.

INSULATION

Why?

Black gold has never been a more appropriate name for oil than in these days of spiraling fuel costs. In colder sections of the country, the cost of keeping the family dwelling comfortably heated can put a severe crimp in the budget, requiring outlays of cash that would have seemed absurd five years ago.

It becomes, then, more important than ever to see that this highly prized heat remains indoors where it belongs. To this end, insulation can be an investment that will easily pay for itself in a few years.

The goal is to allow as little heat as possible to pass through walls, windows, floors, ceilings, and doors. The basic materials used in the construction of these parts of the house offer some resistance as does the air trapped between the inner and outer walls. This resistance, however, is not enough to keep a home comfortably heated at a reasonable price. Special materials are available that prevent the passage of heat from the living areas of a house to the unused storage spaces and outside air. Proper use of these insulating materials can result in saving hundreds of dollars in fuel costs—without sacrificing comfort.

Using a Timer

A timer, or clock thermostat, will enable you to set temperatures in advance. If you know you'll be up at 8 A.M., you can set the timer for an hour or so earlier, giving the furnace a chance to crank up without having to operate full blast all night. Conversely, you can set the timer for a lower temperature before you turn in for the night. However, setting the timer to reduce heat by more than eight degrees will cause your furnace to do double duty to reheat the home the following morning. This may cause you to lose out on fuel savings.

The simple thermostat unit costs about $30; the clock thermostat may run up to $100 including installation. Either one is a sound investment in comfort and fuel economy.

COAL

As far back as 3,000 years ago the Welsh used coal to fuel their funeral pyres. Early recorded mentions of this energy source include the Bible and Aristotle.

A Pollutant?

It was the Industrial Revolution that brought on the widespread use of coal. Until the 1700s, its inefficient burning characteristics (i.e., thick black smoke) had led people to believe that it filled the air with poisons. These early environmentalists were finally overcome by commercial and industrial interests. The railroads in particular became a major coal consumer, both directly, for steam engines, and indirectly, through stimulating the iron and steel industries, themselves major consumers. As recently as 20 years ago, coal was being widely used to heat homes in the United States. Now coal furnaces have been almost entirely replaced by the cleaner gas, oil, and electric systems.

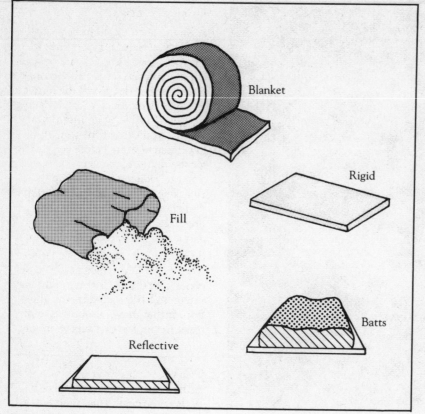

Blanket

Rigid

Fill

Reflective

Batts

What?

Insulation comes in five basic types—flexible, reflective, rigid, fill, and foam.

Flexible

This commonly used type of insulation is available in blankets or bats (short strips). Blankets come in 40-foot rolls that may be 1 inch to 3 inches thick and widths that correspond to the standard spacing of building studs (boards)—16 inches, 24 inches, and 48 inches (irregular widths are also available). Bats come in similar widths, thicknesses up to 6 inches and lengths of 38 to 48 inches.

Both blankets and bats are most often made of fiberglass but also come in mineral-wool and cellulose-fiber or wood-fiber varieties.

Flexible insulation is low-cost, lightweight, and available with vapor barriers on one side. It is best used in new construction, as it requires access to building studs that may be covered by walls in finished sections of the house. Bats are particularly good when working in tight spaces since their shorter precut lengths make them easy to handle.

Reflective

Just as cooking foil reflects the oven's heat on your roast, aluminum foil may be used as insulation to reflect heat back into your house.

THE LANGUAGE OF INSULATION

Conduction

All materials conduct heat—that is, allow heat energy to pass through. Insulating materials should be poor conductors so that heat will not escape.

BTU (British thermal unit)

The amount of heat energy required to raise the temperature of one pound of water 1° Fahrenheit.

The K Factor

The K factor of a material is a measure of its conduction properties— that is, the number of BTUs per hour passing through a wall that is 1 degree cooler on one side than it is on the other side. Insulation should have as low a K rating as possible.

The R Rating

Insulating materials are often given an R rating. This is a measure of the material's *resistance* to heat transfer per inch, i.e. 3 inches of a material rated at R-4 would have a rating of R-12. The higher the R rating, the better.

Vapor Barriers

Water vapor from cooking, bathing, or laundry will pass through most building materials, condensing when it strikes a cold outer wall. This condensation can damage paint and the structure of the house itself. Asphalted paper, aluminum foil, or polyethylene sheets are applied towards the inner, heated wall, floor, or ceiling to provide a vapor barrier.

Some Comparative R-Ratings
Blanket type (mineral fiber)
Width: 15 inches or 23 inches
Thickness: 2 inches - 2¾ = R-7
3 inches - 4 inches = R-11
5 inches - 7 inches = R-19
Blown or poured type (per inch of thickness)
Mineral fiber = R-2.5
Cellulose fiber = R-3.6

Foil (or any other specially treated reflective surface) should be used as the sole insulating material only if facing an air space. When used directly behind an interior wall, reflective insulation is most often combined with some type of blanket or batting insulation.

Rigid

Sold in sheets, like plywood, this type of insulation acts as a sound barrier as well as a heat barrier. It also adds structural strength to walls, ceilings and floors. Modern technology offers fiberglass, polystyrene, and urethane boards to replace the older processed-wood and mineral-fiber varieties. Plastic boards are fire and vapor resistant as well as being strong and lightweight. They are easily cut to size and applied with adhesive.

Fill

Loose fill is sold in bags and used mostly for floors. It can be used in new construction, but its main advantage is that it can be blown into existing walls and floors without having to first tear them apart. It is made of fiberglass, polystyrene beads, cork granules, cotton or mineral wool, and provides a tight fit around pipes and wiring.

Foam

This is the most recent innovation in home insulation. Polyurethane foam offers the structural strength of rigid insulation combined with the sprayability of fill. Spraying insulation, whether foam or fill, is

Vermiculite = R-5
Urethane foam = R-5
Rigid type (per inch of thickness)
Polystyrene boards = R-4 or 5

I SCREAM, YOU SCREAM,

As Nero watched Rome burn he may have stopped fiddling long enough to eat one of the first ice-cream cones.

A Chinese Delicacy
It is recorded that Nero occasionally enjoyed a mixture of snow and fruit juice, but it was Marco Polo who introduced the first frozen dessert made with milk. He discovered this Chinese dish during one of his trips to Cathay and it soon became known as a "dish fit for a king." Royalty of the Middle Ages took this phrase quite literally and tried in vain to keep the recipe to themselves. By the eighteenth century, however, the ice-cream parlor was in existence in New York and the rest, as they say, is history.

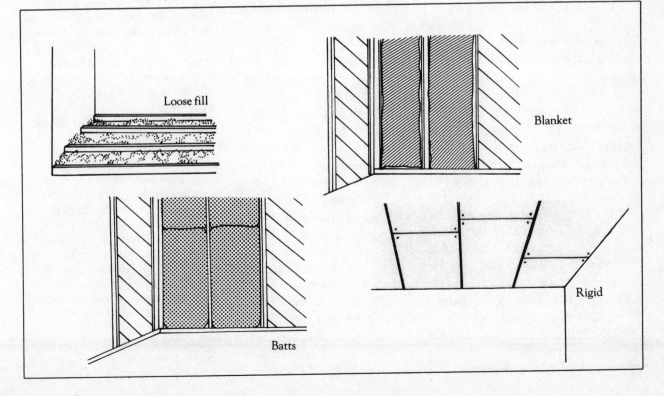

Loose fill

Blanket

Batts

Rigid

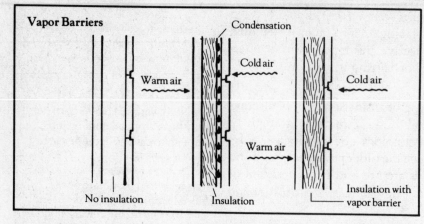

Vapor Barriers

Condensation

Warm air

Cold air

Cold air

Warm air

No insulation

Insulation

Insulation with vapor barrier

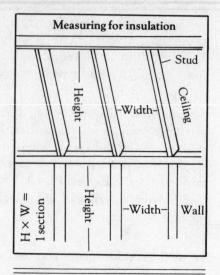

Measuring for insulation

Stud

Height

—Width—

Ceiling

$H \times W$ = 1 section

Height

—Width—

Wall

not a do-it-yourself job. Suppliers can arrange for professional installation and should be consulted about the vapor and fire-resistant qualities of any plastic insulation materials. Be sure to check local building codes as some types of foam insulation are banned in certain areas.

Where?

For maximum efficiency in heating your home, any and all walls, floors, or ceilings that separate a heated space from an unheated space (outdoors qualifies as an unheated space during the winter months) should be fully insulated.

This is easily accomplished when building a new home or adding a wing to an old one. Adding insulation to an existing structure is a little more complicated.

Check the ceilings first as most heat is lost there. If you can spare an inch or two of ceiling height, rigid insulation may be added right onto the existing ceiling, then painted or covered. If your ceiling was originally insulated with loose fill, the fill may have settled, reducing its effectiveness. More fill can be added or you can lay batting over the original fill.

You may want to turn an uninsulated summerhouse into a year-round dwelling. There is no need to tear the walls down to the frame in order to insulate. The removal of a few boards will allow loose fill or foam to be blown in, giving a tight seal around pipes and wiring.

If you use your basement for anything but storage it should be insulated to 2 feet below ground level. Proper insulation will help eliminate dampness, making it a livable space. An unused basement or one used only for storage should be sealed off from the heated portions of the house by insulating the ceiling (with a vapor barrier facing the upstairs floor) and weather-stripping the connecting door.

Closets should be checked to see if they abut an unheated space and unused attics should have their stairwells as well as their floors properly insulated from the rest of the house.

INSULATING YOUR ATTIC

We all know that heat rises, but does your house's heat rise up to the roof and keep on going? If your attic floor and ceiling are uninsulated it will do just that.

Do-It-Yourself

Insulating your attic is a comparatively easy do-it-yourself project that will pay off in reduced fuel costs and added living space for your home. Insulation material, safety goggles, a ruler, large scissors, a staple gun, and a marking crayon are all the tools you will need.

How Much?

To determine how much insulation you will need, first measure the distance between the wall studs and ceiling studs (rafters). The standard widths are 16 or 24 inches. Next, measure the height of each section. Multiply the width by the height to determine the square footage. For example, 24 inches (width) by 10 feet (height) equals approximately 20 square feet. Finally multiply this result by the number of sections. Be generous in your measuring, and add 10 percent of your total to make sure you have enough.

What Kind?

Blanket-type fiberglass insulation is best and inexpensive. Whether you

buy 40-foot rolls or precut bats, they will probably come in compressed bales. Store the insulation in a dry place and bring the bales up to the attic one at a time, as needed, since once opened they will expand to many times their original size.

Installation

Installing the insulation yourself is simple. Just cut it to size. (Be generous, since it is better to force fit than to leave space.) Friction will hold the pieces in place while you staple them fast. Insulation can be stuffed into small spaces where friction alone will hold it securely.

Some Hints

1. If the type of insulation you choose has a vapor barrier, make sure that all seams overlap. If not, a separate barrier must be installed.
2. Do not cover electrical sockets or ventilation ports.
3. Starting with large straight areas will help you get the feel of the project; then move on to the more difficult odd spaces.
4. Be sure to wear goggles, and keep your body covered against falling dust and fiberglass splinters.

Once insulated, your attic may be finished at any time as an additional room, and you will rest assured that the heat you buy is the heat you get.

A HINT FROM NATURE

A careful look at your roof after a snowfall will provide you with plenty of clues as to the trouble spots in your attic insulation. The pattern of melting is determined in large part by heat leaking through poorly insulated sections of your roof. Big patches of black roof showing through the snow on a freezing, cloudy day mean that you are paying to heat a portion of your house inhabited solely by birds and the occasional squirrel.

WEATHER STRIPPING

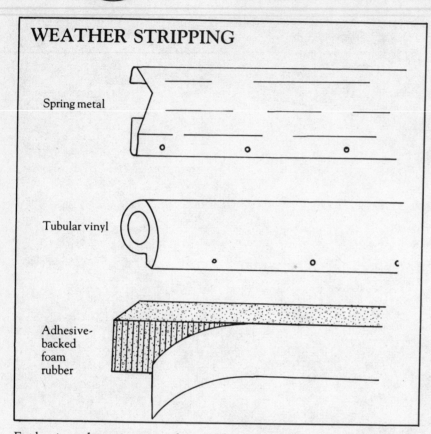

Spring metal

Tubular vinyl

Adhesive-backed foam rubber

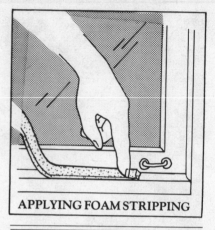

APPLYING FOAM STRIPPING

Fuel prices show no sign of going down, so any method of reducing home fuel consumption must be welcomed with open arms. To provide heat efficiently is only part of the battle. This heat must be kept from escaping (insofar as possible), and the main avenues of exit are windows and doors. In old residences especially, settling of frames can create gaps that will afford easy entrance for cold air and exit for your dearly bought heat. One method of sealing the chinks in your home's armor is weather-stripping, that is, using strips of various materials to ensure airtightness around doors and windows.

To check for leaks, a hand-held hair dryer of the blower variety should be directed around the inside and outside perimeters of both doors and windows. A helper is needed on the other side to feel for drafts and mark the spots where air is coming through. You are now ready to start weather-stripping.

When your door hums a tune every time the wind blows, there is something amiss about its weather stripping. If the door's current weather stripping is a springy metal strip all around the jamb, you may be able to fix minor leaks by bending out the metal flap.

A new door or badly worn weather stripping requires starting from scratch. Of the many types available, the adhesive-backed foam strip is the easiest to use. It comes in rolls, can be cut to size with scissors, and

WINDOWS AND DOORS

Weather stripping and caulking will help prevent hot air from from escaping *around* windows and doors, but what about *through* them?

Windows

Check your windows—if your house is more than 25 years old there is a good chance that the windows were made with a single pane of glass. This type of window has an R rating of only .88 as opposed to R-13 for a well-insulated wall. You can cut your heat losses 50 percent by replacing these old windows with new thermopane windows. Thermopane windows have two plates of glass mounted in a single frame with an air space between them. Recently, manufacturers have been filling this space with inert gas, cutting heat transference another 20 percent.

If you are not in the mood to replace all your single-pane windows, or you already have doubled glazed (thermopane) windows, you may want to add storm windows. In combination with single-pane windows, the effect is even better than thermopane windows—due to the greater air space. Added to thermopane windows, the triple glazing effect can cut heat losses by as much as two thirds.

It is important that both inner windows and storm windows are forms a tight seal when pressed against the door jamb. One type of spring-metal weather stripping is not much harder to use. Just cut to size with a tin snips or heavy-duty scissors, and nail it to the jamb so that the door compresses the metal flange when it closes. The more complex J-strip style forms the tightest seal through a set of interlocking aluminum strips. This type is impossible to use, however, on warped doors and requires cutting grooves in both the door and the jamb and is best installed by a professional carpenter.

Once we have sealed the door on three sides, we can proceed to the threshold. Aluminum channels with vinyl inserts are the most popular means of ensuring airtightness against winter winds and cold. These may be screwed either to the floor or to the bottom of the door itself, depending on the type purchased. If carpeting makes installing this type of threshold impractical, a flap-type sealer that raises itself to clear the rug may be used.

All weather stripping should be measured carefully and should fit snugly. After installation, check once again with the hair blower for leaks.

Windows
1. Accessibility: if the weather stripping needs to be installed on the outside of the house, the windows must be reached by ladder, fire escape, or some other means.
2. Number: though windows are smaller than doors there are usually more of them. If you plan to start from scratch on all the windows in the house, you should consider buying weather stripping in bulk, especially if you are going to use the same type as on your doors.

Both spring-metal and foam-type weather stripping are usable on windows as well as doors. Felt was one of the first weather-stripping

properly weather-stripped. An improper seal is indicated by sweating on the glass. If it occurs on the inside glass, it means that the storm window is allowing cold air to leak into the air space. If the storm window sweats, it means the inner window's weather stripping needs attention.

Plastic film, available in rolls, provides a cheap temporary method of preventing heat loss through your windows. Stapled to screens or an outside wall, this easy-to-use material makes a suitable storm window. Just cut the film to size, leaving enough of a margin so that you can roll back the edges a few times for additional strength. Vinyl film is transparent and durable but is more expensive than the plastic variety.

Doors
There is no way to avoid a certain amount of heat loss through your doorways during entry and egress, but storm doors can provide that all-important air space when doors are shut. In addition, a strong spring or hydraulic closing mechanism will help ensure that the door stays open only as long as is necessary and then shuts itself tight.

Derby Toddy
bourbon
sugar
hot coffee
vanilla extract
cinnamon sticks
butter
Add 2 drops of vanilla extract and a shot of bourbon to a cup of coffee. Add sugar to taste and garnish with a cinnamon stick. Float a pat of butter on the top.

WINTER WONDERLAND
Agassiz, Minnesota features moose, waterfowl, auto tours, hiking, biking. Nearby camp: at city parks.

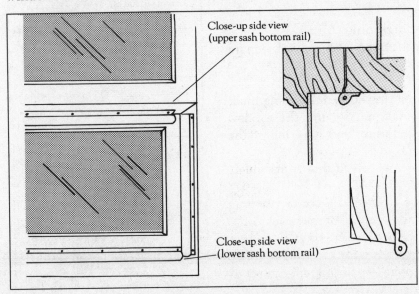

Close-up side view
(upper sash bottom rail)

Close-up side view
(lower sash bottom rail)

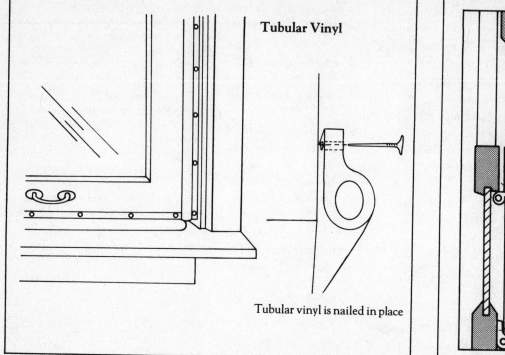

Tubular Vinyl

Tubular vinyl is nailed in place

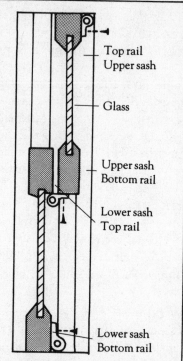

Top rail
Upper sash

Glass

Upper sash
Bottom rail

Lower sash
Top rail

Lower sash
Bottom rail

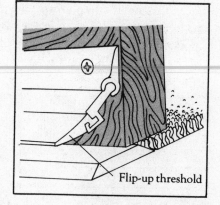

Flip-up threshold

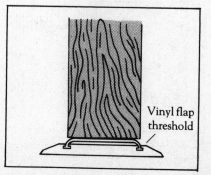

Vinyl flap
threshold

materials and with the modern addition of aluminum casing is still available and effective. Jalousie, casement, or hinge-type windows that you plan to seal off for the winter can be made airtight with transparent vinyl tape.

The vinyl tubular type of weather stripping is easily installed, long lasting, and effective. It is available in rolls and is quickly cut to the required lengths using household scissors.

Installing Vinyl Tubular Weather Stripping

1. Cut the required lengths—one for the upper sash top rail, one for the upper sash bottom rail, one for the lower sash bottom rail, and two for the parting strips.

2. Nail the stripping to the vertical parting strips first, using brads placed 2 inches apart. The tubing should press against the window sash, but not hard enough to impede raising and lowering of the window.

3. Attach a strip to the lower sash bottom rail so that it fits snugly against the sill when the window is down.

4. To the bottom rail of the upper sash, attach a piece of stripping with the tubular part lightly pressing the upper rail of the lower sash.

5. The final strip should be nailed to the upper sash's top rail, pressed firmly against the window's yoke.

Do not paint this type of weather stripping—painting will cause it to lose flexibility and diminish its sealing effectiveness.

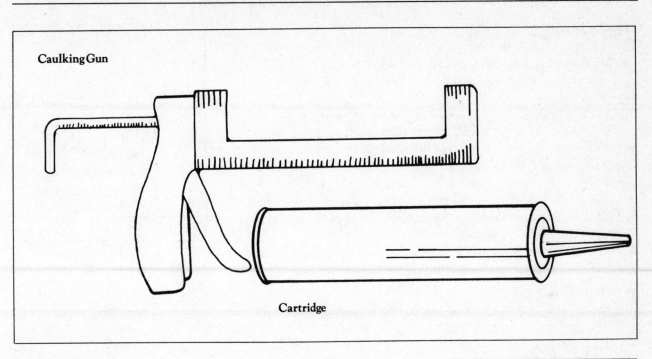

Caulking Gun

Cartridge

CAULKING

As buildings settle, cracks and spaces almost inevitably start to appear. It can happen anywhere that two parts of the house are joined, and the result can be higher fuel bills due to heat loss. Caulking compounds are used to close these gaps and keep heat from escaping. Caulking also improves the appearance of your house and prevents water, insects, and dirt from causing damage. Caulking may come in bulk or rope form, but more often it is sold in cartridges and applied with a caulking gun.

Caulking Compounds Come in Five Types

1. Oil based—this type is most common possibly because it is the least expensive. It will bond to masonry, wood, and metal but it is not as long lasting as some of the other types. If you decide on oil-based caulking compounds you will have to wait 24 hours before painting, and you'll need solvents and thinners for cleaning.

2. Latex based—latex cleans with soap and water and will adhere to most surfaces. Because it dries so quickly, this type of caulk can be painted almost immediately.

3. Butyl-rubber caulk—this type is best for metal-to-masonry joints. It is long lasting but requires solvents for clean-up.

4. Polyvinyl acetate—this is better for indoor work, and it sticks to anything, including paint. However, it dries hard and brittle and lacks the flexibility of some of the other types.

5. Silicone—even though this lasts longest of all the caulks, it is rarely used for large jobs because it is relatively expensive.

Coffee Con Amore
½ ounce triple sec
1½ ounces brandy
hot coffee (brewed)
sugar
whipped cream
finely ground coffee (granules)

Mix brandy, triple sec, and coffee in a mug and add sugar to taste. Top with whipped cream and garnish with coffee grounds.

How to Apply

1. Clean the area to be caulked—scrape or peel away the old caulking; then remove any other dirt, dust, or oil and let dry.

2. If an extremely large crack has to be filled, use oakum in combination with the caulk to fill the space.

3. Cut the cartridge spout at an angle—close enough to the tube to provide a bead that will overlap both sides of the gap.

4. Caulking flows best during warm weather; so try to take care of the trouble spots before the weather gets too cold. If the caulk is too runny, put it in the refrigerator for a little while; if it is not flowing freely enough, it may require some warming next to a heat source.

5. Hold the gun at a 45-degree angle to the crack and slant it in the direction you are working.

6. When you stop, crank the L-shaped rod back from the cartridge to prevent the caulking compound from oozing out.

Where to Caulk

In general, caulk anywhere that two parts of the house are joined—especially when different materials meet (i.e. where metal pipes meet wooden walls): where the roof meets the chimney; roof flashings; between window frames and walls; where the siding meets at the corners; between doors and siding; where the plumbing goes through the walls; where steps and porches join the house; between the walls and the foundation.

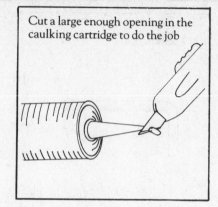

Cut a large enough opening in the caulking cartridge to do the job

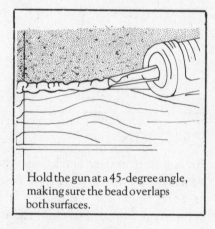

Hold the gun at a 45-degree angle, making sure the bead overlaps both surfaces.

SOLAR HEATING

The sun is the one source of energy which, as yet, remains unaffected by rising prices, profiteering, and shortage scares. As fuel supplies dwindle, it is becoming increasingly practical to harness the sun's energy for home heating.

How It Works

The process of solar heating a home is complicated, but the basic principles involved are not. Glass collectors backed with black, heat-absorbing material are placed on the roof. Water is pumped through this material and carries the absorbed heat down to a furnacelike storage tank in the basement. Air is blown through this heated water (sometimes through a mound of stones piled around the storage tank) into the ductwork, which circulates this warm air through the house. As the water cools, it is pumped back up to the roof, where the process is repeated. This is the basic solar heating cycle: from the roof to the basement and back up again.

And When It's Cloudy?

One frequently asked question about solar heating is what happens

HOT-WATER BOTTLES—AN OLD ENERGY SOURCE

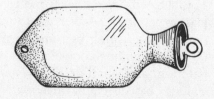

Do you sometimes feel that modern life is a bit more complicated than is necessary? Come winter, are you confused by the welter of electric blankets, heaters, thermostats, and central-heating units? Do all the brands of cold capsules, time capsules, four-way pills and inhalers give you a headache? Does it require a

HOW A SOLAR HEATING SYSTEM WORKS

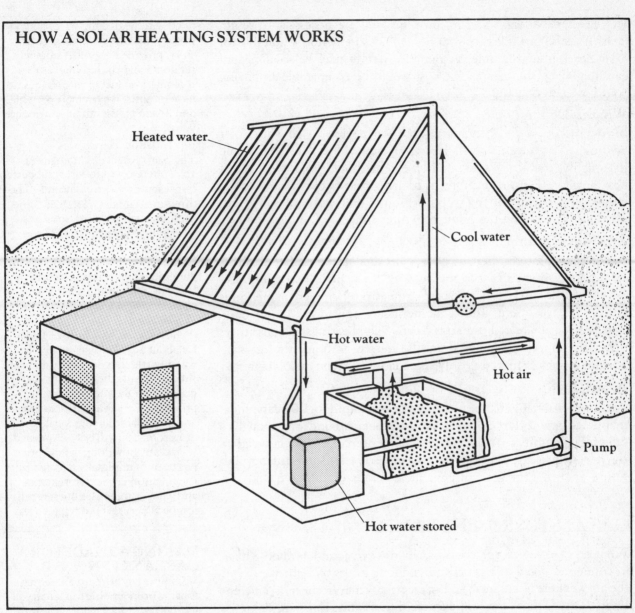

Heated water

Cool water

Hot water

Hot air

Pump

Hot water stored

when the sun simply isn't there. Does an overcast day reduce the inhabitants to huddling under blankets for warmth? In fact, a system of heat traps and adequate insulation will retain accumulated heat on cool, cloudy days, and when night falls, heat-collecting panels on the roof will continue to radiate stored warmth. For those who live in particularly cold climates, conventional gas, oil, or electric heating systems may be needed to supplement solar heating.

Before You Run Out to Buy Your System

Your house will need many additional features before it can efficiently take advantage of the sun's heating power: insulated shut-

rent strike to obtain heat for what used to be an apartment but now feels like a frozen-meat locker?

Stay Where You Are

Before you let oil prices force you to sell your house and move to Key West, take heed. Your great-grandparents, grandparents, and probably your parents had an inexpensive, natural way to stay warm and recover from winter's illness. Their trusty hot-water bottle (or bag),

ters, concrete floors, water-filled drums—all are necessary to retain heat. It is also possible that your home may simply not be suitable for solar heating at this time. A rambling estate may be solar heated eventually, but right now, the cost would be comparable to buying your own oil company.

What to Do First

If your home is fairly compact, and you decide to go with solar heating, a few measures will ensure efficiency. Insulate your home thoroughly; the attic, walls, and basement should hold every bit of heat possible. Planting evergreens on the north and east sides of the house, and deciduous trees on the south and west sides will cut wind chill and open the home to winter sun.

Too Much Trouble?

Planting trees? Setting glass collectors on the roof? All of this may seem like too much work for a little fuel economy. Although installation of solar-heating equipment at present is costly, improvements and refinements are constantly being made that will, ultimately, bring costs down. Solar heating still constitutes a healthy monthly savings from the outset. A home that eats up $60 per month in fuel costs only $7 per month to heat by solar energy.

Be Advised

Although solar-heated homes have been around for 20 years, most manufacturers of the equipment have not been around long enough to offer full guarantees. You may find that maintenance is not covered on the necessary parts. The solar-heating industry is still in its infancy, but future energy shortages will push its development along quickly.

GAS AND KEROSENE LAMPS

What do Paul Revere, cowboys on a cattle drive, and a caboose have in common? You'd be right if you said long hours of night work, but the answer here is lanterns. Today, electricity may be the most efficient light source, but the old-fashioned gas and kerosene lanterns still have their charm.

The kerosene lamp (or lantern, when referring to the portable type) remains an old reliable. If you live in an area where electrical power vanishes during winter blizzards and windstorms, it's an essential back-up tool. A gas or kerosene lamp may not be as bright as a 100-watt bulb, but it's easy to operate, lasts years, and runs on inexpensive fuel.

The Kerosene Lamp

These haven't changed much over the years. Except for a little rust, the older models are virtually identical to the newer ones: the same

filled with heated tap water and thrust under the covers or nightshirt, provided fast relief from winter's cold and colds. Now, as then, it requires no fuel or repairs, has no moving parts, is extremely portable, and it won't wear out or electrocute you.

No Inflation Here!

The Sears Roebuck catalogue of 1897 offered two Goodyear rubber hot-water bottles for 75 cents. The three-quart model was 80 cents and the four-quart economy size was a whopping 85 cents. By 1927 the prices ranged from $1.19 to $1.98. One could also purchase an aluminum model complete with a holder for filling and a felt bag to prevent scalding when placed next to the body.

Now for the big surprise. Today, for about $3.50, you can buy a hot-water bottle that does not differ significantly from the one your great-grandfather took to bed. It will probably be guaranteed for two years and is available at your local drugstore. You will be hard-pressed to find any other item whose price has been so minimally affected by the inflation of the passing years, and whose simple usefulness recalls a less bewildering if not happier era.

MAKING A SHADE FOR A GAS LANTERN

A gasoline lantern can be a tremendous aid on a camping trip, but if you give it even a quick glance, the intense light can make you see stars. Few stores will have ever heard of a shade for a gasoline lantern, but never fear—by following these directions, you can make your own. The shade is light and easily packed, quickly attached and detached, and won't interfere with ventilation.

To make the shade, use a set of metal shears to cut an 8- to 10-inch diameter disk from a sheet of aluminum (available at hardware stores).

In the center of the disk, cut a hole large enough to fit the lamp through. Next slit the disk from the edge to the center. Then bend one edge of the slit up and one edge down so that they interlock when they are pulled together.

Set over the lantern and presto— no more glare.

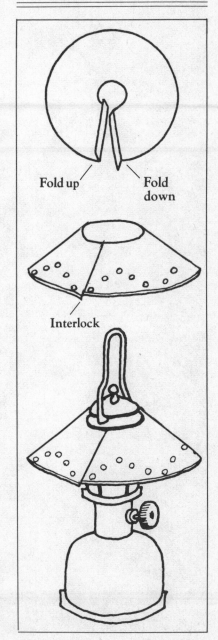

Fold up   Fold down

Interlock

kerosene, the same cotton wick in the glass tube, which you adjust by turning a little wheel. And it's still a great bargain; you can pick one up in a hardware store for about $5. Once you realize that you can get up to nine hours of continuous light from one and a half pints of kerosene, the economical aspects of this light source are undeniable.

The Gas Lamp
Gas lamps are larger and produce brighter light than kerosene-fueled lamps. Those charming streetlights in nineteenth-century prints ran on gas until Thomas Edison changed all that. They have no wick; the gas (not the automotive kind) flows from the base of the lantern through a small opening where it burns after mixing with air. One quart of gas will furnish eight hours of light bright enough to illuminate the fine print on your camping map or canned goods.

The Advantages
The great thing about gas or kerosene lanterns is their portability. Outdoors, they can be hung from trees, fences, or poles; indoors, they can be set up practically anywhere, as long as there are no flammable materials nearby.

Those living in isolated country areas should not be the only ones to own these reliable, portable light sources. Anyone who does any winter driving would be wise to invest in a lantern to keep in the car's trunk. This light can be seen for miles if your car becomes stuck or is disabled.

Safety Tips
Avoid spilling any fuel when filling the lamp and always use a long match or twig to light the wick (keep your hands as far from the flame as possible). Be sure to purchase the correct fuel for your lantern, and always follow the manufacturer's directions for operating the specific lantern model.

PLANT PROTECTION—OUTDOORS

Outdoor trees and shrubs suffer during the winter cold. Taking a few precautionary steps enables your leafy friends to survive the season.

What Winter Can Do

Most hardy plants should be able to survive a normal winter, but severe cold can affect all growing things. Even if you live in a generally mild area, sudden cold snaps can be a big problem. Frost is a major culprit, often responsible for killing young plants, so special care must be taken. In addition, frost and ice can damage buds, which will result in fewer spring flowers. High winds can snap tender branches, and heavy ice and snow accumulation can stunt or deform otherwise healthy plants.

What Can Be Done

If you live in an area that is subject to high winds, erecting some sort of windbreak for your garden will help reduce the chance of wind whip. Wind whip can result in your garden being blown halfway into the next county and should be reckoned with. Rosebushes and other flowery shrubs with slender branches should be tied together to help resist wind gusts.

Remember that frost, snow, and ice accumulate most heavily at low spots. If you have any plants which are "downhill," they will be most affected by these winter problems. Fastening a burlap (not plastic) wrap around the base of these plants will protect them somewhat. Lashing the base trunk of shrubs to a secure stake will give them something to hold onto during the assault.

Other Methods

Another protective device is a wire-mesh cylinder placed around the lower part of the plant. Fill this cylinder with straw or leaves to keep the base of the plant well insulated. Burlap screens will also help to cut the wind while blocking frost and ice penetration.

There are various commercial products designed for winter tree and shrub protection. These coat the leaves and stems and prevent excessive moisture loss due to high winds and dry, cold air.

All in all, you should be able to take the precautionary measures necessary during one afternoon. Making sure that your trees and shrubs are safe and secure this winter will help guarantee that they will repay you by blooming this spring.

WINTER: START TO FINISH

The evolution of our Western calendar through religious and agricultural influences has given us a winter that begins on December 21 and ends on March 20.

Start

The path the Earth takes as it revolves around the sun results in a constantly changing angle between the sun's rays and the horizon at noon. On June 21 the sun is directly overhead at midday. Every day thereafter it is slightly lower on the horizon at the same time of day, until on December 22 it reaches its lowest point. We then have the shortest day of the year.

Finish

Winter ends on March 20, the day before the vernal equinox. On March 21 the sun is at a halfway point on its climb back up, and day and night are of equal lengths (equinox means equal night).

PET PROTECTION

Drafts

Dogs and cats grow their own fur coats every winter (lucky beasts) and so are in little danger of cold weather. However, they *are* susceptible to colds from drafts, much like their masters. Pet coats and sweaters offer some protection, and vitamins will help keep their resistance up.

Salt

Rock salt, used to melt sidewalk and road ice, is highly corrosive and can burn pets' feet. Boots are available for dogs and cats to protect sensitive paws.

Radiators

Exposure to the drying heat of a radiator is bad for an animal's coat. Applying lanolin oil or feeding the pet wheat germ or glycerol will help keep the fur healthy and prevent drying out.

HOW TO MAKE SURE YOU GET STARTED

One of the worst things about winter driving is the nagging question, "Will the car start in the morning?" Well, the answer should be yes, if you've really prepared your car for the task.

Tune, Check, and Flush

A car in good running condition is always easier to start and more economical to run, and winterizing your car means doing a lot more than putting in some antifreeze. Before the winter gets bad, have your car tuned up. A tune-up means adjusting points, plugs, timing, and carburetor. Also make sure the automatic choke is working correctly. Check your electrical system thoroughly—battery, alternator, and voltage regulator. Flush out your cooling system and change coolant yearly. The optimum mix is between 50-50 percent and 70-30 percent antifreeze to water, depending on the temperature in your area. The commercial antifreeze container gives clear, detailed instructions.

Avoid an Oil Crisis

Paying proper attention to your oil is one of the most important things you can do to ensure prompt starting. Engine oil gets substantially thicker as the temperature drops, making it harder for engine parts coated with that oil to turn. Frozen water droplets in the oil

STARTING SEQUENCE

Every car has its own special quirks and its own preferred method for starting, but here are a few general tips that should help you get going on cold days.

1. According to the AAA, most cars will start more easily if you observe the following procedure: first push the gas pedal all the way to floor—just once—and release it fully; then hold the pedal halfway down while turning the key. Release the pedal completely once the engine starts.

2. When turning the engine over. hold the key in the start position for ten seconds, no more. Don't run the battery down. If the car won't start, wait a minute or so and allow the battery to recharge itself.

3. If the engine starts, then dies, try pumping the pedal lightly to keep it running.

4. Even if your car seems to be one that needs more gas to get going,

184

make the situation worse, as do built-up dirt and sludge. So change your oil every 3,000 miles in winter, and switch to a thinner grade. Try a 5W-20, 10W-40, or one of the new synthetic oils such as Mobile I, according to your auto manufacturer's recommendations for temperatures in your area. Synthetic oil is used in the Arctic, and has proved excellent in cold so severe that conventional oil turns to jelly.

Different Methods

There's not much more you can do by way of preventive maintenance for winter starting, but in areas where the temperature hangs around 0° Fahrenheit (−18°C.) and below for much of the winter, many people follow one or more of the procedures below.

Electric Heater

Almost everyone who lives north of Massachusetts has a plug-in cooling system heater, and in legendary frostlands like North Dakota and Montana, electric outlets are provided at curbside so that motorists will be able to restart after dallying in town. The electric engine heater is a simple heating-coil device that attaches to the lower radiator hose and keeps coolant and engine comfortably warm all night, giving you the equivalent of a warmed-up car when it's time to start in the morning, and usually ensuring immediate hot air from the interior heater. Electric engine heaters must be fully insulated before use, and mustn't be plugged in unless the cooling system is filled.

Dipstick or Blanket

Plug-in dipsticks are available to preheat engine oil and block, and a 100-watt light bulb or an infrared heating lamp left on overnight in the engine compartment can make the difference between starting the next morning and just sitting there fuming. Many people swear that just throwing a blanket over the engine overnight works just as well. The new space blankets, made of super-insulating metallic fiber and available cheaply at Army-Navy stores are as good as those marketed specifically for automotive use selling at a much higher price.

Trickle Charger

Some people cover their batteries as well, or even bring them indoors for the night, but the latter can be messy and dangerous. A method just as effective to avoid the need for a jump-start is the overnight use of a one- or two-ampere drop or trickle charger, which costs under $10 and is designed to work so slowly that it's impossible to overcharge the battery, no matter how long the charger remains connected. There are quicker, high-output chargers, too, but the slow ones are much better for your battery. Definitely not recommended: the

don't pump the pedal more than three or four times before turning the key. And don't pump the pedal at all while the engine is turning over. If you do, you may flood the motor and make getting started much more difficult.

5. If you can smell gasoline from inside the car, you've definitely flooded the engine. Wait three or four minutes; then try starting the car again, this time with the accelerator pedal fully depressed.

Winter Frost

5 oz. rum
16 oz. iced coffee
1 oz. chocolate-mint liqueur
4 teaspoons orange syrup
mint sprigs

Mix the ingredients in a pitcher. Pour into glasses and add ice; garnish with mint sprigs. Serves 4.

pour-in "miracle rejuvenators," which can completely ruin a battery in a single application.

If You Still Can't Get Going

You mean you've done all or most of the above and you still can't get out of the driveway? What's gone wrong? Frankly, severely cold weather can cause so many mechanical problems—to say nothing of those that may not have to do with the weather at all—that we can only mention a few of the most likely possibilities.

1. Your gas line is frozen. This may not make itself apparent until you try to accelerate and don't. Try adding one or two cans of dry gas to your tank, wait 15 minutes, and then, hopefully, drive off contentedly. This problem is less likely to occur if the tank is full or nearly full, but if you live in a climate that's damp as well as cold, you should have some dry gas in the tank all the time. Add a 12-ounce can every second or third tankful.

2. Your fuel is too cold to vaporize and ignite inside the engine. Starting fluid (actually liquid ether under pressure) will help. Remove the air-cleaner top, push the choke plate open, and squirt a dose of ether into the carburetor throat. One or two short squirts will do. More can be dangerous. It may take a second application to get the engine to do more than kick over once and die. Use only where ventilation is good.

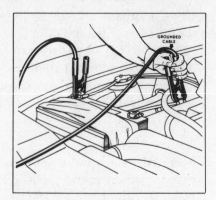

THE SAFE WAY TO JUMP A BATTERY

The safe way to jump a battery is to first connect the jumper cable from the positive post of the donor (charged) battery to the positive post of jumped (presumably dead) battery. Then connect the negative post of the donor battery to the frame—*not* the battery—of the jumped car. Locate the clamp as far from the battery as the cable will allow it to go. This method ensures that any sparks that might fly when

3. Your choke plate is stuck. It has to be fully closed for the engine to start in the coldest weather. Remove the air-cleaner top and look into the carburetor to check. If the plate is stuck open, you can usually free it with your fingers. Have someone hold down the accelerator pedal while you're doing this. If it doesn't work, you can probably get the engine started by holding your flattened hand over the carburetor barrel and having someone start the engine for you. **4.** Your fan belt or alternator belt has cracked and slipped. Then again, maybe the shift lever, accelerator linkage, clutch pedal, or emergency brake handle is frozen stuck. It helps to lubricate pedal, cable, and shift rod linkages with a low-temperature-rated, antifreeze-based lubricant before winter hits. It's definitely worth planning ahead.

SAVING FUEL IN WINTER

When your car's automatic choke is engaged, the engine is using two to three times as much fuel as it would otherwise. A choke that works correctly—which automatic chokes seldom do—is usually set to stay closed for four or five minutes after your engine starts up, but except in extreme cold, you don't really need it for more than the first 20 or 30 seconds. Converting your choke to manual operation gives you control; a kit makes this a job that can be accomplished in an hour or two using simple hand tools. But once you've made the switch, don't forget and drive around with the choke closed. That's why Detroit gave us all automatic chokes in the first place.

Choke Lubricant

A simpler way to avoid fuel waste from a sticking choke is to use choke lubricant. A few well-directed squirts around the top of the carburetor should free the stuck choke and keep it working properly for several weeks. It's easy to tell if the choke plate is stuck open: it will probably prevent you from starting the car one cold morning. If the plate is stuck closed, the engine will race while idling, sputter on acceleration, and gasoline mileage will drop noticeably. In extreme cases, the tail pipe will emit clouds of black smoke—unburned fuel—and your neighbors will complain audibly.

Idling Equals Waste

Another winter gas waster is the acquired habit of warming up the engine. Most modern cars utilize engine air preheaters and special carburetor circuits so that you can drive off 20 to 30 seconds after starting. Letting the motor run longer not only wastes gas but can actually encourage gas line freeze-up. In general, if you're going to be standing in one place for a minute or more, it's more economical to shut down the engine and restart it than it is to let it idle.

you make the final connection will occur far from the potentially explosive battery.

Test Before You Jump
A live battery produces hydrogen gas, and a spark set off nearby can ignite the gas and cause the battery to explode. Rare, but it happens. So be careful, just in case your battery isn't as dead as you think it is. You should carry your own jumper cables—and not the bargain kind. Buy only the cables with thin strands of braided copper wire and heavy-duty spring clamps. These will carry much more current and retain good flexibility in sub-zero weather, when you'll most likely be using them. At $10 to $18, they're worth it.

Cider Grog

apple cider (heated)
rum
butter
cinnamon sticks

Fill a mug with hot apple cider. Add a shot of rum. Top with a pat of butter and garnish with a cinnamon stick.

SLEIGH RIDING

"Jingle bells, jingle bells. . ." In old New England, winter was often heralded by the sound of sleigh bells. Sleigh rides were organized, townsfolk meeting at an agreed-upon location to begin a procession of gaily decorated sleighs that would culminate at a tavern or dance hall. The procession was governed by strict rules, separating old from young and single from married folks. Fines were levied for fast, reckless, or drunken driving but the occasion was by no means solemn. After much cavorting and carousing at the party, the procession would begin again, taking the merrymakers home in the same order in which they had arrived.

WINTER DRIVING TECHNIQUE

Driving on snow and ice is difficult and demanding work. It's hazardous not only because of unpredictable and often dangerous road conditions, but also because of the number of unskilled motorists and unprepared automobiles out on the slippery roads. This is especially true in warm-cold border states and in tourist areas where large numbers of good-weather drivers may be testing their winter driving skills for the first time.

Extra Thinking Needed

Even if the going seems smooth, you should remain alert for the unexpected at all times. This goes for safe driving in any weather, but on dry pavement you can usually handle an emergency by jamming on the brakes, whereas in snow, that response is likely to send your car into an uncontrollable skid. To avoid the need for sudden braking, you must learn to anticipate your own actions and those of other

GAUGING WINTER ROAD CONDITIONS

Expect the worst of road conditions in winter, particularly on longer trips, because where there's snow or ice, there's no way to predict how rough or smooth the driving will be. Highways that appear to be plowed clear are likely to have poorly plowed patches where the road surface is irregular, and parts of most roads become at least temporarily drifted over, after plowing, with snow blown by the wind. Local variations in road-work budgets, efficiency, and environmental restrictions on the use of road salt can

drivers further in advance than you would ordinarily. And observe the following safety rules.

1. *Don't do anything sudden.* Steering, acceleration, and braking should all be accomplished gradually, easily, and smoothly. Any sudden change in direction or rate of motion—rapid acceleration as well as sudden braking—can send you into a skid.

2. *Expect the worst of road conditions.* If you see one patch of ice, assume there will be more. Expect heavily traveled areas to be polished smooth by traffic. Approach every bridge with extra caution. And whatever kind of road surface you're traveling, remember, conditions are likely to change mile by mile.

3. *Keep your speed down.*

4. *Never tailgate.* Leave twice as much following distance between yourself and the car ahead of you as you would ordinarily.

5. *Make sure you've got good visibility.* Clear *all* windows before starting out, and make sure the entire body of the car is free of snow accumulation. Snow will dislodge as you drive and slide or fly around, obscuring your view. And snow that lodges around taillight surfaces can make it difficult for other drivers to see your brake, turn, or warning light signals.

6. *Take longer and more frequent breaks.* Make sure you're relaxed and alert. But don't do your relaxing behind the wheel.

7. *Stay off the brakes as much as you can* when road surfaces are slippery.

How to Stop Without Skidding

Manual-shift cars are recommended if you do even a moderate amount of winter driving. A properly executed downshift makes it easier to come to a smooth halt on a slippery road. Get into the habit of releasing the clutch slowly but steadily after shifting, and accelerating slightly before the clutch engages, to keep the wheels moving at nearly constant speed. Then you can gently come off the accelerator and let the lower gear slow the car down. Use the brakes only to come to a full stop.

If you have an automatic transmission, or if you are making an emergency maneuver and don't have time to downshift, pump the brakes in short smooth strokes while holding the wheel lightly, letting the tires find their own path of least resistance (see How to Skid, below). If you have a choice, do your braking where the road is straight. If it's icy, try and wait for a relatively clear spot; *then* hit the brakes, jabbing at them first to test traction, then coming down hard and steady once you find you're getting a good grip.

If You Have to Go Into A Skid

Let's say you're coming down a hill and around a curve on a two-lane road, and suddenly find yourself approaching a car that's fishtailed

make for a patchwork of road conditions, and a clear road may turn into a toboggan run of snow and ice as soon as you cross a county or town line.

Bridges

Highway bridges tend to be the most hazardous areas for driving. We all know that bridge surfaces freeze before the rest of the roadway does, because bridge paving isn't insulated by contact with the ground. Bridges are especially dangerous at night, when melted snow from the plowed-up banks along the edge often refreezes. Bridges are frequently located on curves and/or where the land dips, so you may find yourself approaching a bridge at an increased rate of speed. If you have to slow down, do your braking before you reach the bridge, and always remember that it may be icy even if the road you've been traveling isn't.

The Hierarchy of Snow Removal

Interstate highways are usually the first roads to be plowed out after a storm and generally receive the closest care, because they're usually main arteries and, in ski country, economically vital for tourist travel. But just like local streets and roads, interstate highways are the responsibility of local road crews, and clearance efficiency can vary. Danger spots are at entrances and especially exits, where the plows don't pass as often or at as efficient a rate of speed.

Major state highways are next to be cleared out, followed by local roads that are on school bus routes. Back roads not used by school buses are the last to be plowed, and some of these are classed as trails, which don't get plowed at all.

Back Roads

If your itinerary includes any amount of back road driving, or if you're thinking of doing some winter camping where you last

SKIDS
If your car starts to skid, turn the wheels in the same direction as the skid and take your foot off the gas. Don't brake!

pitched tent during the summer, it's wise to check ahead with the state police or the town's road manager to make sure you can actually get there in winter. The status of back roads is likely to change from year to year, and most road maps are printed too far in advance to be reliable.

WINTERIZING YOUR BICYCLE

If you are ready to put your trusty bicycle into cold storage for the winter, these steps will ensure that you'll still have a functional bike come springtime:

1. Thoroughly lubricate all bearings and moving parts.
2. Deflate the tires.
3. Check spokes; tighten loose ones and replace broken ones.
4. All spokes and chrome parts should be wiped with a cloth dipped in Vaseline or other petroleum jelly.
5. To preserve the leather, rub saddle soap into the seat.
6. If possible, store the bicycle by hanging it from the ceiling. If this is not possible, store it upside down so that it rests on the handlebars and seat. Protect the wheels from dust by placing a cloth over them.
7. Store the bicycle in a cool, dry place.

out and come to a complete stop in the middle of the roadway. You downshift, decelerate, then pump the brakes lightly, but the road is too slippery, and you, too, start to skid.

How do you get yourself out of the skid, regain control of the car, and—hopefully—steer around the obstacle? You've probably heard the old winter saw that runs, "Steer in the direction of the skid."

Here's How You Do It

1. Turn the wheels gently in the direction that the rear wheels have taken. This will bring the front end of the car back in line with the rear. In other words, when your rear end swings out to the right, the nose of your car will swerve to the left, and you must turn your wheels to the right. If the rear end swings to the left (front is to the right), turn the wheel to the left to pull out of the skid.
2. Once you've corrected the steering and regained some control of the car, ease off the accelerator gradually, at the same time turning the wheel gently to balance out any over-compensating you may have done.
3. After making the steering corrections, you may pump the brakes gently to slow the car down.

Most people will automatically react to a skid by steering as described above, but unfortunately most people jam on the brakes at

the same time. *Never jam on the brakes.* And don't oversteer.

If your vehicle is equipped with front-wheel drive, it is less likely to skid. If it does, follow this procedure: if a manual-shift car begins to skid during acceleration and the front wheels begin to plow, ease off the accelerator and release the clutch. Rather than trying to steer away from the skid, simply hold the wheel steady as it was before the car began to slide. If the rear wheels let go, follow the same procedure, but steer into the skid as with a rear-wheel-drive car.

If You Have to Crash

If your choices are skidding into a car blocking your path, or sliding out into the opposing lane, look for a third alternative: head into a snowbank, or off the right side of the road—provided, of course, there's no steep drop, deep culvert, or solid obstacle there.

At low speed—the way you should be driving on these slippery roads anyway—you can usually grit your teeth, brace yourself against the steering wheel (you're wearing your seat belt, of course), and plow right into a snowbank without damaging your car or yourself. If it has been snowing hard enough to put you into a skid, chances are there will also be enough plowed-up snow alongside the road to bring you to a reasonably gentle halt.

WHAT TO CARRY FOR WINTER DRIVING

To travel safely on unpredictable winter roads and to get where you're going with the minimum of delay and inconvenience, be prepared to handle as many potential problems as possible without outside help. This doesn't mean you have to equip yourself like an arctic explorer cruising around on the tundra, but we do suggest you carry the following items in your trunk at all times.

1. A scraper-brush combination to ensure good visibility, preferably with a long handle for better leverage.

2. A can of spray-on windshield de-icer or bottle of rubbing alcohol, which works just as well.

3. A sturdy shovel for digging out of snowbanks and applying sand.

4. A can of *Liquid Chain* for emergency traction.

5. Battery jumper cables to get yourself or someone else started when the battery won't.

6. A 12-foot length of metal chain, cable, or heavy rope so a helpful passerby can pull you out of a snowbank if all else fails.

7. A 50-pound bag of sand covered with a plastic wrapper to keep moisture from getting in and freezing the sand uselessly solid. Place the sand bag in the center of the trunk to aid traction on the rear wheels. Plastic traction mats can be substituted for sand, but if you do use the mats, place two cement blocks in the

CORROSION AND RUST PROOFING

Road salt, that life-saving substance that makes slippery winter roads navigable, will probably start corroding your new car after only two or three winters, and if the car lives long enough, rust may finally do the car in altogether, even though it's still mechanically sound.

Invitations to Rust

The typical car has a predisposition to rust virtually built into its design, with oddly shaped pockets under the body and behind the fenders where salt and water are easily trapped. Fender wells (the area around headlights and taillights) rocker panels, and under-trunk surfaces are especially vulnerable.

Factory undercoating offers little real protection against increasingly heavy applications of road salt and the vagaries of automobile design. The undercoating is formulated to harden to a rigid surface that doesn't flex with the car, and it begins to chip and fall off almost immediately. In the industry, this undercoating is regarded as sound-deadening only and not as rust protection at all. Dealer-applied undercoating is even less effective. It's one of those price-increasing options warned against by consumer groups.

The Best Method

Perhaps the best method of rust protection is the commercial technique of heavily coating and filling all surfaces and cavities with a flexible, petroleum-paraffin-based solvent. But the widely heralded five-year, money-back guarantee proclaimed by the better-known rust-proofers, like Ziebart and Tuffcote, actually applies only to new cars given the treatment at an average price of $145. This policy points up a basic truth about rust: once it starts, it can't be stopped. Only by cutting away the affected area and welding in new sections of metal can the disease be cured. The commercial rust-proofing technique will, however, slow down the rusting process and in some cases can extend the useful life of the car by several years.

A Good Washing

If you don't want to make the investment in commercial rust-proofing, the best thing you can do for your car is to wash it clean of road salt as often as possible and immediately after any long journey on heavily salted roads. It's a good idea to take the car through a commercial wash at least twice as often in winter as in summer months. And at the beginning of the season, wash the underbody of the car clean, brush off any flaky rust or dirt, and apply a can of spray-on undercoating (about $3 in most auto-supply stores) to the vulnerable areas listed above (wear goggles).

Proper care of its underbody will add years of life to your vehicle, and keep it water- and airtight for as long as it runs.

trunk to substitute for the weight increase and traction improvement the sand bags would provide. This additional weight load in the rear of a small front-wheel-drive car is a very important aid in stability for winter driving.

8. A spare can of gasoline de-icer (dry gas).
9. A can of starting fluid.
10. Set of strap-on tire chains.
11. Can of carburetor/choke lubricant.

JEEP

For negotiating snow-covered roads and rough terrain, nothing beats a four-wheel-drive jeep. With power going to both the front and rear axles, two wheels can be on a slippery surface and still leave you two wheels that will pull or push you to safety.

General-purpose Vehicle

Originally developed by the armed forces (jeep is a slang contraction of general-purpose vehicle), jeeps are currently available to civilians who desire a no-frills, workhorse-type machine. Attachments can be purchased that will allow owners to plow snowy driveways, dig post holes, and with the addition of a power winch, pull themselves out of icy ruts and ditches.

ROAD HANDLER - ICE - SNOW - RADIAL.   SPEC.

SNOW TIRES AND CHAINS

The ideal winter tire would provide super traction in any and all of the wide range of road conditions a driver is likely to encounter—snow, ice, thaw, refreeze, rain—sometimes all in one day. Sounds impossible? It is. Ordinary snow tires do provide increased traction under some of the above conditions, but according to the National Safety Council, they aren't really much help on the variety of winter road surfaces on which most of us drive.

Why Studded Tires?

Studded snow tires aren't perfect either, but they're far superior to conventional snow tires, particularly in the critical 25° to 30° Fahrenheit (−4° to −1°C.) temperature range, when roads are twice as slippery as they are at zero. During such warm spells, surface ice is melted by traffic, forming a thin film of water that acts as a lubricant— for better sliding on the solid ice beneath.

As temperatures go down, water lubrication becomes less of a problem, and regular snow tires are almost as good as the studs. At minus 10° Fahrenheit (−12°C.) there's almost no difference between the two in traction and stopping ability, but unless you live in a climate that's consistently this cold, studded snow tires on all four wheels are definitely the tire of choice.

SNOW-TIRE TIPS

1. Snow tires wear faster than ordinary tires; so get them off the car as soon as you're sure it's really spring.
2. The handling characteristics of radial and bias-ply (nonradial) tires differ radically. Don't mix radial snow tires with nonradials on the same axle of the car, though it's okay to use radial snows in the rear and nonradials up front.
3. Letting some air out of your tires does *not* increase traction. It only produces more wear and tear on the sidewalls. Air pressure inside tires goes down as outside temperatures do—at the rate of one pound per square inch for every ten degrees.
4. When you're putting your studded or radial tires away for the warm months, be sure to mark them left and right, then remount them at the same corner of the car they occupied the winter before. Front snow tires should also be separated from rear studded tires and mounted likewise.
5. Snow tires, like any others, should always be stored lying down, since the weight of the upright tire will tend to flatten it permanently in one spot.

King Lear

Winter's not gone yet, if the wild geese fly that way.

—*Shakespeare*

Are They Legal?

Unfortunately, studs have a rather wearing effect on the highways they run over, especially in the absence of snow. New soft studs wear better and are a lot easier on highway surfaces, but they still accelerate road deterioration. More and more states and localities have been moving to ban or severely limit the use of studded tires, and it's best to check both local and state ordinances before you invest in them.

In response to the widespread banning of studs in Europe, a new generation of nonstudded snow tires has been created there and should be readily available from all American manufacturers by the time you read this. These new tires are formulated of rubber compounds that tend to combine with water rather than shrug it off, thus absorbing more of the slippery film under the rolling wheel. They retain their flexibility in cold weather, thus putting considerably more tread on the road than ordinary snow tires.

Tire Chains

Tire chains are rarely seen these days, but they still give better traction—nearly twice as much—as anything else moving in snow, including the studded tires. The trouble with chains, of course, is that you have to put them on when it snows and take them off again as soon as roads are cleared. If you don't, you'll soon have broken chains, which may lead to dents and holes in your fenders as well. And of course you have to jack up your car to mount and remove them.

Strap-On Chains

For driving in snow of any depth, the newer strap-on chains probably provide the best traction. They come in two or three separate units per tire and are simply wrapped around the tire from back to front and cleated securely to the rim with straps that go through an opening in the wheel. Not all wheels have such openings, however, and if yours don't, you can't use these chains. They won't work on oversize tires, either. But at least you don't have to jack up your car to install them. By the way, there are also plastic chains available that are more convenient to carry and easier to use than metal ones.

Proper Fit and Installation

If you're going to use chains of any kind on steel-belted radial tires, make sure they fit properly and are installed snugly. If they're too loose, they'll move around and damage the sidewalls.

A new product known as *Liquid Chain* (also sold under other similar trade names) will provide a temporary, chainlike grip for those slippery moments in the driveway or snowbank. The sticky resins that come out of the can adhere to the tire, greatly improving traction, and wear off quickly on dry roads so that handling isn't affected in the long run.

HOW TO GET OUT OF A SNOWBANK

Should you come out in the morning to find your car sitting in a heap of plowed-up snow or have the bad luck to have skidded into a snowbank, the first thing to do is dig. All other efforts will be virtually useless if you don't have a path that's more or less level with the bottom of your tires and as straight as possible in front of and in back of your tires. It's much harder to free a snowbound car if you have to turn.

Once you've dug deep enough, putting down boards, rags, traction mats, sand, or whatever, will just about always get you out. But you'll probably have to employ one or more of the following techniques as well.

If Digging Doesn't Do It

Before you start trying to move the car, remember: *your first attempt is the most important one.* If you start off by spinning the wheels, you'll quickly lose whatever traction you might have had. Therefore, in a manual-shift car, the best technique is to start gently forward in high (third or fourth) gear. This reduces the torque going to the driving wheels and makes spin less likely. Accelerate slowly, and try to ease the car out. If you have an automatic transmission, use the same technique with the car in the highest drive range.

The Rocking Technique

If this fails, try rocking the car back and forth using the clutch and shift lever. Go as far forward as you can in first gear; then let the clutch in, switching to reverse as the car rolls backward, engaging reverse gear to get yourself as far back as you can safely go, then rolling forward again, engaging first—and so on until you're out of the hole. With automatic transmission, the procedure is easier, but consult your owner's

manual to avoid damaging the transmission.

If rocking the car back and forth fails, try to get a push. It's surprising how often a good shove, done *while* you're rocking the car back and forth, will free a vehicle that seems hopelessly snowbound. If this technique doesn't work, now's the time to use the chains we recommend you carry for such emergencies.

However, if you find that the underside of the car is resting on the snowbank, with the wheels lifted so that *both* rear tires spin, give up and call the tow truck. Or have someone pull you out, using the chain you've providentially stored in the trunk.

Lebanese Cocktail

Four parts gin, two parts scotch, two parts lemon juice, and two parts grenadine, courtesy Robert Stuart Mathews, who guarantees this will thaw out *anything and everything.*

Rum Trinidad Cocktail

Another good warmer-upper for strong-hearted characters is this interesting libation, also from Mr. Mathews:

This requires a brown rum—Barbados or Trinidad—and a strong hand on the Angostura bitters (about ½ tsp. per ounce of rum). The rum and bitters are shaken with ice to about double the initial volume. This is not for sippers.

GET DOWN

Ducks and geese have known for years that down will keep you warm without adding a lot of excess weight. Down, the soft, fluffy, underfeathers, can provide the most efficient insulation material available to the would-be camper, hiker, mountain climber, or outdoor enthusiast.

Lightweight Filler

When insulating sleeping bags, parkas, and other cold weather gear, the object is to fill the maximum space while adding minimum weight. In this capacity, down is champion. This ability to fill space effectively is known as the down's loft. Loft translates into warmth when you realize that a sleeping bag with a six-inch loft is rated for temperatures down to 5° Fahrenheit (−15°C.), while the equivalent loft (and weight) of fiber-fill will only keep you warm if the temperature stays about 15° Fahrenheit (−10°C.). Which would you rather have with you under the stars on a frigid November night?

Springs Right Back

Down's resiliency is another great feature. After laundering or storage, down will spring back to its original density. In addition, down-filled products can be folded more compactly than fiber-filled products, greatly adding to their convenience for travel.

Lanolin, which many people use to keep their hair from becoming dry and brittle, is a natural ingredient in down. This helps down retain its resiliency and insulating warmth after years of use.

The best down comes from healthy geese whose feathers have a high lanolin content. However, in the United States, duck down is more common and less expensive. To judge the quality of the product feel the down through the fabric; it should be soft and springy. Too many feather quills, spines, or other hard objects denote a poor-quality down.

DOWN CARE

1. Occasionally, you may notice a feather poking through the material of your down-filled parka or sleeping bag. Don't pull it out—push it in: pulling the feathers out will only reduce the fill and make the hole larger, allowing more feathers to fall out.

2. When you hang your down-filled garment for the summer, leave space on both sides to avoid crushing the down. Remember, come winter, the fluffier the down, the warmer the garment.

3. Be sure to follow manufacturer's laundering instructions. If the item is machine washable, use a mild detergent (Woolite is a good choice) in low-temperature water.

4. Use the clothes dryer at medium temperature. Throw in an old *clean* sneaker—this will help fluff the down.

5. Use a warm (not hot) iron to press out wrinkles after drying.

DOWN KITS

Kits are available for the construction of down parkas, vests, or comforters. The cost is much less than for a comparable factory-prepared product. Kits come with everything you need, precut patterns, down packets, zippers, cords, thread, and Velcro closures. So, if you're the do-it-yourself type, check out these kits and save some money.

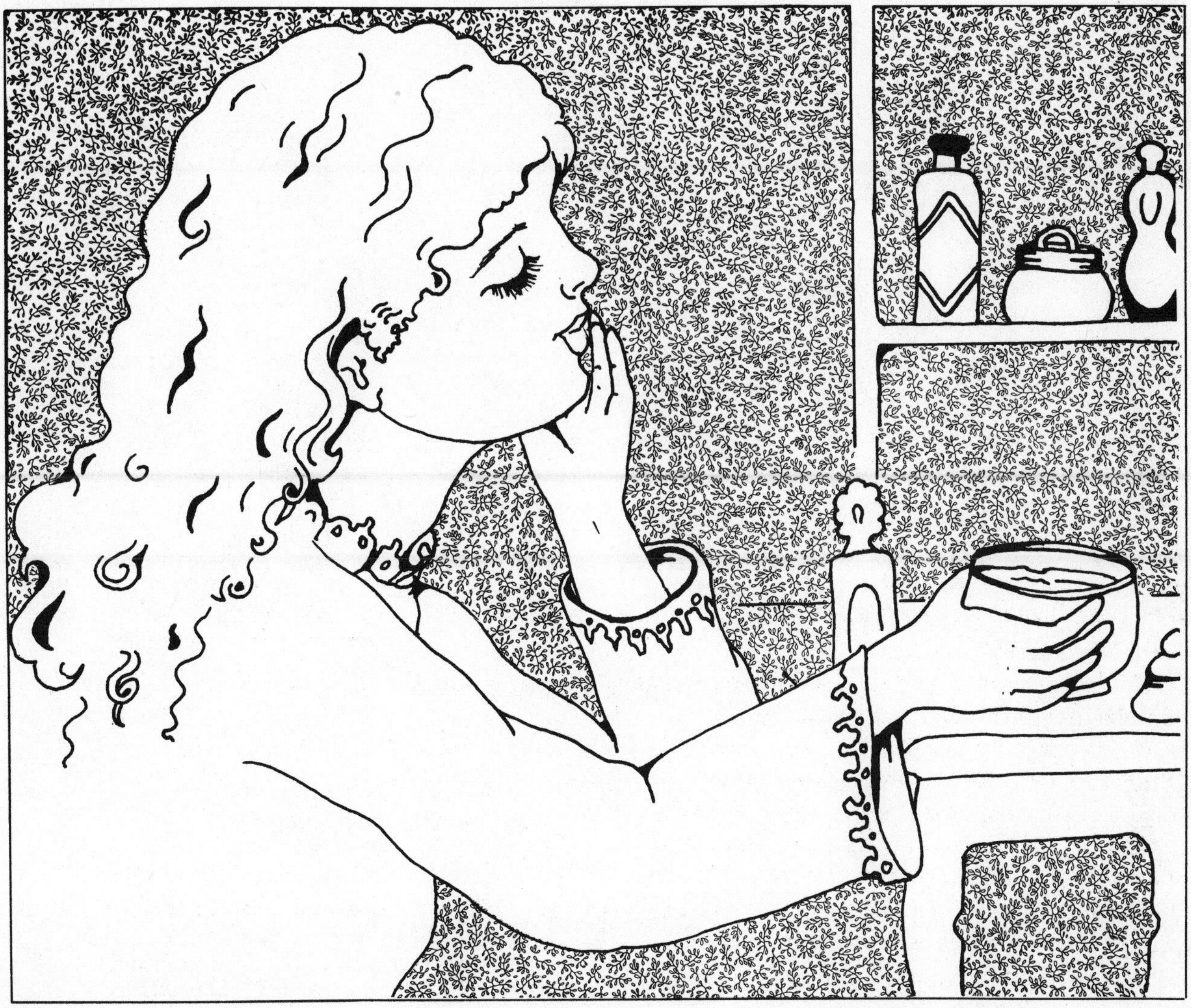

SKIN PROTECTION IN COLD WEATHER

Many living things have their own distinctive ways of protecting themselves against the unpleasant side effects of winter. Furry animals develop thicker coats, many birds head for sunnier climes, and several mammals and reptiles just sleep through the whole thing. Humans, on the other hand, have no such instinctive mechanisms to protect them from the icy grasp of winter. However, we do have the option of providing ourselves with a variety of products and preventive measures that can add to our comfort during the frigid season.

Effects of Cold Weather on Skin

Some people sail through the winter looking as fresh and dewy as spring flowers, others resemble scarlet sandpaper when the thermometer dips below 60 degrees. Cold has a nasty habit of constrict-

Jack Frost Special

3 cups applejack
1 cup sugar
juice of 1 lemon
2 tbsps. Angostura bitters
4 sticks cinnamon
boiling water

Heat the applejack with sugar, lemon juice, and bitters in the blazing pan of a chafing dish over direct heat. Add the cinnamon sticks. Flame up and then add just enough boiling water to extinguish the flames. Serve in warmed mugs.

ing blood vessels, which in turn leads to dryness of the skin, frequently resulting in that familiar and unwelcomed chapped, irritated appearance. Some people develop such a marked sensitivity to the cold that they suffer from winter itch, a generalized (and annoying) itching of the skin. There are a number of procedures that will relieve symptoms such as these, but, as in most situations, an ounce of prevention is worth a pound of cure.

Prevention

A combination of proper skin care, hygiene, and clothing will go a long way toward counteracting the effects of cold weather on your skin. The extent of skin problems will be in proportion to the length of exposure and degree of cold encountered. Tight garments that constrict circulation are to be avoided as are long periods of sitting or standing, particularly when clothing is wet.

Your Face in General

Since your face is most frequently exposed to the cold, and covering it completely isn't practical, it deserves special consideration. It is the loss of water, not oil, from the outer skin layers that causes dryness, and when skin is dry, it becomes chapped and rough. Daily use of an emollient, which is a cream or lotion made of oil and water, is recommended. An emollient restores moisture, and softens and smooths the skin. An inexpensive, bland cold cream or lotion can be just as effective as a widely advertised, overpriced exotic concoction. Just be sure that you use it daily, and for extra help for very dry skin, use it before going to bed at night.

Lips Particularly

As most of us know, lips also become rough and chapped in the cold. Lipstick provides significant protection, as do the many commercial preparations (Chap Stick, Blistex, etc.) available. The impulse to lick your dry, chapped lips should be ignored; skin that is damp chaps easily.

Ears, Too

Ears, which have no fatty layer to insulate them from the cold, are easily affected. The only sure protection is to keep them covered with a hat or earmuffs.

The Rest of You

Even parts of the body that are covered, such as your arms and legs, can become scaly and dry during the cold weather. It takes only a few minutes to massage a bit of lotion into your skin before going out of doors and you'll benefit by having soft smooth skin when those around you begin to resemble a family of alligators.

Many people find that wearing long underwear alleviates all-over itchy skin. Added skin protection is provided by wearing two thin layers rather than one bulky layer. The insulation offered will keep

UNDERNEATH IT ALL

When dressing for cold weather, think in terms of layers. And the first layer should be warm, toasty underwear. Thermal underwear is the best bet on those frosty wintry days, and wearing it will make you comfortable enough to enjoy most outdoor activities.

Three Choices

There are three types of thermal underwear: thermal knit, insulated, and fishnet. The most widely used is the thermal-knit type, which has either a smooth texture or the familiar waffle pattern.

Insulated underwear consists of two layers of thermal knit with an insulating layer between. This type is extremely warm—just great for outdoor activity, but it might prove to be a bit stifling when you return indoors.

Fishnet is precisely what the name implies, and is worn under your regular underwear. Visually, it may appear rather bizarre, but the insulating properties of the air pockets it creates will make you forget about high fashion.

your skin dry and comfortable.

Using oil in your bath will make you feel pampered and help your skin retain its suppleness. If your skin is very dry, however, bathing every day will only aggravate the condition since you'll be washing away your skin's natural moisture. Alternating bath days with oil-rubdown days is the best, and most enjoyable, routine.

Winter Sports

A skiing holiday can be as damaging to you as an interlude on a sun-baked tropical island, especially for those with fair skin. The sun beats down with greater intensity at high altitudes, and additional radiation is reflected by snow, both of which increase the risk of sunburn as well as windburn. There's no need to cancel your week in Aspen, just be sure to use a sunscreen preparation before you hit the slopes. If you're bound and determined to have a golden tan during the winter months (the better to create envy among your friends), a sunlamp, *properly and cautiously used,* can be the answer. Follow all directions; carelessness with this appliance can result in a severe and painful sunburn.

Wintertime skin need not be rough and chapped. A consistently followed program of daily skin care and a fair degree of common sense will keep your skin in great shape all winter long.

FURS

Whether you believe in evolution or divine creation, it would appear to be inarguable that at one point man found himself naked. Not having a warm coat of his own, he began to use the skins of animals to provide cold weather comfort.

Almost immediately thereafter, the furrier skins began to represent signs of status. Early Egyptians, having little use for their warmth, nonetheless used furs in royal households for furnishings and ceremonial purposes. During the Middle Ages, scarcity of this product moved the nobility to enact laws against the possession of furs by the lower classes. With the discovery of the New World and its seemingly limitless supply of pelts, a more democratic approach evolved—all you now need is money!

Fur is warm. Worn on the inside or the outside of a garment (except for trim and collars, extensive use of fur on the outside of a garment is a recent phenomenon), it will insulate your body against the coldest temperatures with little or no help from sweaters and long underwear.

Though a fur coat's heavy weight counts against it for hiking or mountain climbing, it definitely beats the lightweight ski parka for the opera or an opening night.

SMOOTH AS SILK

There's more to nostalgia than meets the eye. All of those lovely silk undergarments and fragile silk stockings did more than make a girl feel pretty—they also kept her warm. Silk is one of the best insulating materials available. Worn underneath cashmere and other woolens, wind and cold are no longer formidable. In addition, silk, being a natural fiber, will breathe and be more comfortable than nylon or polyester.

To stock up on silk clothing, check out department stores—some will make items to order. Or be more adventurous and search out the boutiques carrying old clothes or try your own grandmother's trunk. If you can't find or afford such all-out luxury, do indulge at least in silk liners for gloves. Worn under a simple pair of knitted gloves, you're ready for the coldest of days.

Care and Cleaning

The proper cleaning of a fur piece or coat requires elaborate machinery and processing and is best done by a professional. Following some simple rules in caring for your furs can lengthen their life significantly.

1. Hang furs on wide, padded hangers. Never use wire hangers.
2. Furs need freely circulating air to prevent drying and subsequent loss of hair; so store furs in paper or cloth clothes bags—never plastic.
3. Store furs in a cool place—a closet during winter and special fur vaults (where the temperature and humidity are controlled) during the warmer months.
4. Wet fur should be hung away from direct heat, and when thoroughly dry, it should be shaken well.
5. Do not subject fur to friction, i.e. shoulder straps or purses carried under the arm.
6. Do not pin brooches or flowers to fur.
7. Do not put perfume directly on fur as it will dry out the skin and stiffen the hairs.
8. Do not apply moth-proofing sprays to furs.

FAKE FUR

The look of leopard, zebra, or tiger fur is available without endangering the species or your financial status. There are fake furs that resemble these animals, as well as seal, raccoon, beaver, mink, and many others, and they cost a fraction of the genuine article.

A woven or knitted backing is substituted for the skin, and modacrylic, acrylic, polyester, or rayon fibers constitute the "fur." For the most realistic effect, a quality fake fur will be layered with softer underfur and a coarser layer of guard hairs on top. The imitation can be dyed and patterned to resemble animal markings or to conform to fashion trends.

When shopping for fake fur, check the density of the pile by pushing your fingers into it then brushing it with your hand—no mark should be visible.

If you take care of a fake fur as you would the real thing, you should get at least as much wear out of it as you would the genuine article. There is no danger of a fake fur drying out, so plastic clothes bags may be used for storage. However, extremely high temperatures will burn or melt the synthetic fibers; so never iron the coat or dry too near direct heat. Ample closet space will prevent matting of the fur pile, and while a cool closet is ideal, professional storage is unnecessary.

WHAT ESKIMOS WEAR

Eskimos wear two layers of fur clothing. The inner layer has the fur side turned inward and may be worn alone during warm weather. The outer layer is worn with the fur facing out.

Caribou skin is the most popular material, but seal skin, polar bear skin, or fox hides are also used. Fox fur and beads are often used to decorate these cold weather outfits.

THE SKIN GAME

The inheritance comes through, your stocks split, *and* you find a ten-dollar bill on the street! You are now ready to purchase that dream coat you have always wanted, but which fur is right for you? They all look terrific. Styles and warmth, however, vary from animal to animal. The following chart will help you decide. . . .

Fur	Characteristics	Look For	Uses—Warmth
Beaver	Sheared to reveal dense underfur	Soft, silky	Coats—very warm
Calf	Short, sleek, flat hairs	Light, supple skins; clear markings	Sportswear—not as warm as long-haired furs
Chinchilla	Short, dense, silky fur	Slate-blue color	Coats, jackets, stoles—warm
Fitch	Long, dark guard hairs over light underfur	Clarity of color and silky texture	Coats—very warm
Fox	Fluffy, long hair	Long, glossy guard hairs; soft, deep underfur	Coats, jackets, stoles—warm
Lamb	Broadtail—flat, moiré pattern	Lustrous skins; not too curly	Coats, jackets—only moderately warm
	Persian—silky curls	Lightweight, pliable skins	Coats, jackets—very warm
Lynx	Long fur, white and spotted pale brown	Creamy white tone	Coats, jackets—warm
Mink	Dense underfur with lustrous guard hairs	Silky look and feel; even texture	Coats, jackets, stoles—very warm
Mink Pieced	Gills—spotted Paws—chevron pattern Sides—solid color	Well-matched skins in color and hair height	Coats, jackets (often combined with leather or knit)—warm
Muskrat	Short, heavy underfur with strong guard hairs	Well-matched skins; dense underfur	Coats—warm
Sable	Soft, brown, dense, medium-long hair	Soft, deep pile in dark lustrous brown	Coats, jackets, scarves—very warm
Seal	Short fur, always plucked to remove long, coarse guard hairs	Velvety texture; deep even color; luster	Coats, jackets—very warm

OF FUR AND CONSERVATION (RECYCLING)

A passion for the warmth and sensuality of fur need not involve emptying one's bank account, nor is it necessary to feel directly responsible for terminating an entire species. The feeling of fur may be acquired on a budget and without any further loss of animal life through recycling old skins and/or purchasing a new fake fur.

Recycling

An old fur coat may not be suitable for "dinner with barons and earls" but with some creative cutting and restyling it can be turned into a jacket that *is*. Thrift shops, second-hand stores, and relatives can often be sources of inexpensive or free fur, suitable for recycling into pillows, collars, cuffs, flings, hats, muffs, or bags.

To determine if a fur piece is reusable, first pull at the hair. If it comes out in your hands easily, the piece is not usable. If you plan to make a garment the skin must be pliable so that it will drape properly. Check the skin for brittleness by lifting the lining and pinching the skin be-

BUY NATURAL—BE WARM

Once upon a time you could tell what a coat, suit, dress, sweater, or shirt was made of simply by feeling and sometimes even just by looking at the material. And you knew how warm it would be. This is not true today.

Garments made of 100 percent natural fibers still exist but they are becoming increasingly rare. More often than not, synthetic materials (Acrilan, Orlon, Dacron) are used, either exclusively or blended with natural fibers.

Government regulations require that the materials and the percentage used must be listed on a clearly visible label. When purchasing a winter garment, careful check of this label can prove invaluable. Just remember—the higher the percentage of natural fiber, the warmer the garment.

Fabric	Best Uses	How Warm
Acrylic (Acrilan, Creslan, Orlon)	Shirts, blouses, nightgowns, robes	Soft and cozy synthetic that can look like wool or cotton flannel but isn't as warm
Angora	Sweaters, dresses, hats, gloves	Feather light and warm (often blended with synthetics to control shedding)
Cashmere	Sweaters, dresses, coats, scarves, hats, socks, mittens	Lightweight and warm as a hug
Cotton	Brushed cotton nightgowns and pajamas, thermal underwear	Cuddly-soft nightwear that's warmer than synthetics; thermal underwear traps body heat and is very warm
Mohair	Sweaters, coats, scarves	Fluffy, long-haired knit that traps the natural heat of the body—very warm
Polyester (Dacron, Fortrel, Kodel, etc.)	Shirts, blouses, dresses	Blended with natural fibers, it improves washability but cuts down on warmth
Silk	Glove-silk underwear	Moderately warm—better than synthetics but not as warm as thermal
Wool	Coats, suits, dresses sweaters, shirts, socks	Depending upon weight, wool can be sheer as cotton or heavy enough to keep a sheik warm through the desert night

tween your fingers. If possible, moisten a small section of the skin and try to stretch it—if it stretches without tearing it is not too dry. If the hair is good but the backing is weak, the fur may still be used by reinforcing the skin with lightweight material.

The usable parts may be distributed all over the garment, as once they are sewn together, the seams will be invisible, covered by hair, and it will all look like one piece. Just make sure that the hair all runs in the same direction and that the patterns, if any, match. You can get the maximum mileage out of each usable piece since there is no seam overlap. The skins are taped at the edges with furrier's torsion tape (also known as cold tape), and the parts of your project are sewn together with the seams butted.

The addition of a three-sided, leather-sewing needle and heavy-duty thread to your sewing kit is just about all you need to convert the old to the new and pamper yourself with recycled fur clothes, accessories, and furnishings.

WINTER CLOTHES MAINTENANCE

Winter brings its own set of clothing care and cleaning problems. Fortunately, there are many products available that prevent and remove stains caused by winter's salt and slush.

Waterproofing

Water damage, while not exclusive to winter, is a real problem as snow starts to melt. When waterproofing footgear, a balance must be struck between water repellency and a fair degree of porosity. Rubber footwear offers maximum imperviousness to water, but does not allow the foot to breathe. Leather wear, properly waterproofed, will allow the body's water vapor to evaporate while still

offering a reasonable degree of water repellency.

If They Get Soaked

When boots or shoes become soaked, stuff them with crumpled paper to hold their shape. Keep them in a warm place but away from direct heat. After the shoes dry, castor oil or mink oil applied to the uppers (all of the shoe except the sole and heel) keeps the leather soft and flexible. Regular cleaning with saddle soap keeps the leather in good condition.

Removing Spots

Water spots usually occur on fabric that contains sizing or some other finishing agent (taffeta, moiré, silk, or rayon). Water dislodges this sizing, which then rearranges itself unevenly, forming rings or spots. Removing these spots is simple: dampen the entire article of clothing, and sponge it or shake it in front of a steaming kettle. Another method is to rub the fabric with a stiff brush or to gently scratch the spot with your fingernail.

Minor stains and spots on suede can be eliminated with a rubber, bristle, or wire brush. Clean the garment by gently brushing in a circular motion. When you have finished, smooth the nap in one direction. Major cleaning problems should be handled by a professional dry cleaner.

Salt Stains

One problem exclusive to winter is the removal of salt stains. The rock salt used for snow and ice removal dissolves into the puddles and slush that it creates. Ultimately, the salt winds up being deposited on shoes or splashed onto coats. Waterproofed clothing will require only a quick brushing off—the stain will not set into the material. For other garments, sprays are available that can prevent and remove salt stains. More serious stains, particularly on expensive suede or fur, should be professionally cleaned.

ELECTRIC BLANKETS

An electric blanket can keep you as warm and comfortable as two or more conventional blankets. A consumer testing agency recently declared that every brand examined was found to be essentially safe when used according to the manufacturer's directions. However, many people still shy away from the idea of using an electric blanket—sleeping under an electric current tends to conjure up images of Dr. Frankenstein hard at work.

No Real Danger

It should be of some comfort to know that electric blankets rated 240th when 250 household products were indexed for possible hazards by the Consumer Product Safety Commission. In addition, the National Fire Protection Association

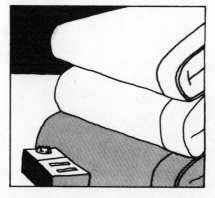

reported only three fires caused by faulty electric blankets in ten years, and none of those fires resulted in personal injury.

Electric shocks, another fear harbored by many consumers, are about as unlikely to occur as fires. The wiring is so well insulated and waterproofed that the user would virtually have to be *trying* to cause an electric shock: ripping the blanket apart, exposing the wires at several points, and clutching two wires at key spots.

Maintenance Tips

If you are convinced that an electric blanket is just what you need, there are certain usage and maintenance tips to keep in mind:

1. Unless otherwise specified by the manufacturer, do not dry clean as the cleaning solvents used can damage the heating wire insulation.
2. Electric blankets are not to be used by infants, disabled persons, or anyone who may be insensitive to heat or unable to adjust the setting properly.
3. While in use, avoid excessive bunching or folding of the blanket, and do not tuck the heating elements under your mattress. Most electric blankets have snaps around the edges as guides to let you know where the wiring is so you don't scrunch it up while making the bed.
4. Never stick pins into the blanket—this is just common sense.
5. Keep the control unit away from direct heat or cold. Since the blanket operates on a thermostatic principle, direct heat or cold will cause the control to incorrectly read the outside temperature.

Using an electric blanket this winter can result in fuel-cost savings since it is an efficient way to warm your body without having to heat the entire house. It is estimated that it costs an average of five cents a night to operate; so, come this winter, plug yourself in and stay toasty.

A CENTURY OF WINTER FASHION

Winter fashions have always been kept down to earth by the fact that they must above all keep the wearer warm. Style changes have revolved largely around the amount, the location, and the kind of fur used.

In contrast to the world of nature, the female of the human species has carried most of the decorative coloration (at least for the last 100 years). Women's winter "plumage" has ranged from the sublime to the ridiculous, involving great displays of furs and flares and folds of cloth. Silver fox scarves and stoles have come in and out of fashion. Muffs appeared at the beginning of this century and again in the 20s and 30s. Fur trim has shifted from the top to the bottom of women's coats and back again.

Turn-of-the-century American men found the full fur coats worn by trappers too flamboyant. Heavy cloth coats came into vogue and remained there, with minor stylistic variation, until the late 1960s. The dark colors, militaristic styling, and conservatism that have been the trademarks of men's winter fashions since the Victorian era were interrupted only by the raccoon and polo coats of the "Roaring Twenties." It was not until the late 1960s that men's fashions were livened up, thanks to the intrroduction—actually the reintroduction—of the "peacock look."

Today, the fashions worn by both sexes draw heavily on the past. The raccoon coat is as acceptable as a rough-and-ready parka, and it is not unusual to see modern man looking like an 1890s fur trader or North Pole explorer. Women's coat and skirt lengths vary to such a degree that the "now" woman may resemble anything from a Victorian matron to a 20s flapper. "Plus ça change, plus ça reste la même chose."

FUR TRADE

The demand for furs and the trading of pelts goes back long before the beginning of recorded history. After being considered the exclusive province of royalty for thousands of years, fur trade started a new chapter with the discovery of the Americas. The bounty of fur-bearing animals living in the New World made furs available to the newly emerging middle class as well as to anyone willing to trap the beasts.

Trappers became the vanguard in the exploration and settlement of this vast new wilderness. French-Canadian fur traders led the way West long before English settlers had reached the Mississippi. The members of the Hudson's Bay Company were probably among the first Europeans to see the west coast of the Americas. The John Jacob Astor fortune was one among many made in the fur trade of the eighteenth and nineteenth centuries.

In harvesting what seemed to be a limitless crop of pelts, the buffalo and the northern fur seal were almost exterminated. Today, conservationists keep a close watch on fur-bearing species in danger of extinction.

Snow Posset

Boil a stick of cinnamon and a quarter of a nutmeg with a quart of new milk, and when it boils, remove the spice. Beat the yolks of ten eggs well, and mix gradually with the milk until thick, then beat the whites of the eggs with sugar and canary wine into a saucepan; sweeten to taste, set over a slow fire, and pour the milk and snow into the saucepan, stirring all the time it is over the fire; when warm, remove from the fire, cover close, and set aside for a little time before being used.

—*Practical Housewife*, 1860

THE GAY 90s

Mother wears muffs of Persian lamb or mink (head and all!).

Father's coat is lined and trimmed with mink or musquash; while it's ermine for little Ernestine.

Matching boa and muff are of black lynx.

THE 20s— FLAMING YOUTH

In the post-war 20s, matching turns to mixing—instead of matching muff and boa combinations, we find coats of leopard cuffed and collared in lynx, seal contrasted with civet. Coats wrap around for that much-sought-after slinky look. Once elaborately trimmed, women's hats are made of simple felt, pulled down over the neck and ears. Men's fashions take a welcome respite from the conservatism of the nineteenth century with the introduction of the raccoon coat.

THE 40s AND 50s
WAR AND PEACE

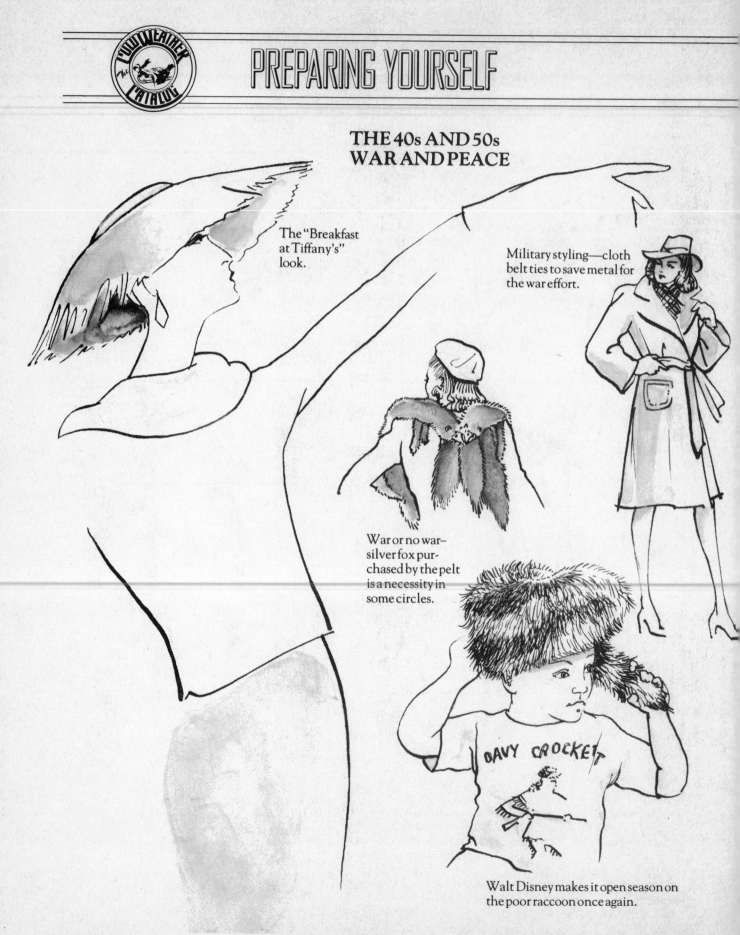

The "Breakfast at Tiffany's" look.

Military styling—cloth belt ties to save metal for the war effort.

War or no war—silver fox purchased by the pelt is a necessity in some circles.

DAVY CROCKETT

Walt Disney makes it open season on the poor raccoon once again.

THE 60s AND 70s
FAST AND FUR-IOUS

Anything goes. It's "flaming youth" revisited. This time around, however, there is a conscience attached. Styles are more outrageous than anything the 20s produced, but those pelts that seemed infinitely available cannot be harvested so thoughtlessly now. Fake furs are "in," coats made from endangered species are "out."

Mink and fox are two thriving species.

Dyed calfskin becomes Pop Art.

A WORD ABOUT THE MYSTERIES OF WINTER

Much of this catalog is devoted to the fruits of our ingenious technology: an enumeration of the joys and comforts that modern man has been able to devise. Ever since man started understanding the ways of science and industry, his response to the change of seasons has been to minimize the effects of the process. No longer the slave of the same yearly cycle that governs the plant and animal world, our particularly human consciousness has been allowed to flourish.

It is becoming clear, though, that modern man is approaching the limit of his useful conquest of the natural world and that the sons and daughters of the generations that have triumphed over nature are now beginning to look for something else. We are beginning to think that we might have overlooked something in our scramble to dominate Mother Nature. Winter is coming, we say, and we take this as a signal to check up on the smooth functioning of our heating systems and energy supply, which give us warmth and light through the long, dark nights. And although we know the vegetative process has stopped, most of us are so removed from it that we rarely question the continuous flow of food for our winter feasts. If looked at slightly differently, however, the approach of winter holds a symbolic meaning, the promise of something significant that goes beyond our capacity to control it.

Ancient man looked upon the winter solstice, that point when the sun has descended to its lowest position on the horizon and shines for

INDIAN WINTER

The South American Mapuche Indians place winter on the left or yin side of their cosmology. Winter is linked with the left hand, the moon, the ocean, north, west, and black among other things. It is opposed to the right side containing, the sun, land, south, east, and white.

The Other Side of the Coin

In the Indians' minds many of the things on the winter side are related to death. The ocean, for example, is the last barrier between their ancestral spirits and the afterworld. In spite of these associations, the winter side is not necessarily considered evil. For the Mapuche, as for many other so-called primitive societies, death is a part of life, the other side of the same coin.

The Social Season

For the North American Apache Indians, winter is a much lighter affair. They consider winter the social season. Winter camp is equivalent to the European "season"; it is a time for fulfilling social obligations, dancing and telling stories.

the least duration, as a time of mystery and reverence. He took pains to offer the proper ceremonies to ensure that the sun, pulling the whole vegetative process with it, would once again begin to mount higher on the horizon and shine for a greater length of time each day.

Historians tell us that human consciousness developed around an awareness of the yearly cycle. Our sense of magic, religion, and poetry developed over the centuries as mankind began to worship the spirit of the seasons, personified by the sun, as it passed through the yearly cycle of birth, initiation, consummation, repose, and death.

Psychologists are beginning to tell us that this observance of an agriculturally based cycle, one that is matriarchal in origin since it is based on the primacy of the Mother Earth Goddess who enjoys a succession of Sun God consorts, is much more than a curious bit of prehistory. It is, rather, the original terms of our psyche. Built up over hundreds of thousands of years and implanted in our genes, we cannot ignore the fact that our whole mental process has evolved in response to the turning of the seasons. We spend half our time in slumber, and like the seasons, are rejuvenated by the alternation between light and dark, activity and rest.

We in our technological age have perfectly expressed our inclinations, and, some would say, sown the seeds of our destruction by our attitude toward nature and her cycles. Modern man strains in a straight line toward progress, but in the process he has created a deadening sameness and has lost the knack of alternating his energies. We seem to be refusing to take advantage of the compensating rhythms of nature. We might learn something from different cultures in the past that have responded to the seasons in a wholly different manner.

Consider the winter custom of many of the tribes of British Columbian Indians. The nobles among these people had two names, one for the summertime and one for the winter. The summer name came from the clan, and its use by royal families in the spring was the sign to begin activities that were public and extroverted, considered proper for the summer: hunting, fishing, trading, governing. The winter name was given to each person individually during his secret initiation into the spiritual societies of the tribe. The use of the winter name signaled the beginning of the private, introverted activities appropriate for winter: story telling, religious meditation, and thinking on one's individuality.

There is more in this companion to the winter season that the abundant proof of our dominance over nature. Chronicled here also are the things that might appeal to your winter name, the particular features of winter, the unique joys, the signals of change, the hints at the mysteries.

STOPPING BY WOODS ON A SNOWY EVENING

Whose woods these are I think I know.
His house is in the village, though;
He will not see me stopping here
To watch his woods fill up with snow.

My little horse must think it queer
To stop without a farmhouse near
Between the woods and frozen lake
The darkest evening of the year.

He gives his harness bells a shake
To ask if there is some mistake.
The only other sound's the sweep
Of easy wind and downy flake.

The woods are lovely, dark, and deep,
But I have promises to keep,
And miles to go before I sleep,
And miles to go before I sleep.

—*Robert Frost*

COLD WEATHER
The
CATALOG

APPENDIX

Mail-Order Suppliers. Clubs and Organizations. Books.

Mail-Order Suppliers

You may be unable to locate some cold weather products in your area, but many can be bought through the mail. Some firms send brochures and catalogs free on request; others charge a nominal fee. When writing a mail-order company for information, enclose a stamped, self-addressed envelope to help speed the reply. Some companies are too small to handle a large volume of mail quickly, so be patient.

CANDLEMAKING

Sears, Roebuck and Co.
National Office
Sears Tower
Chicago, IL 60684

American Handicrafts Co.
3 Tandy Center
Fort Worth, TX 76107

J.C. Penney Co. Inc.
National Office
P.O. Box 2056
Milwaukee, WI 53201

Kaydee Craft Supplies
P.O. Box 8
Ft. Myers Beach, FL 33931

Berje
43-10 23rd St.
Long Island City, NY 11101

Candle Mill Village
Old Mill Road
East Arlington, VT 05252

HERBAL TEAS

Dunkled Acres
Rte. 3
Jersey Shore, PA 17740

Greene Herb Gardens
Greene, RI 02827

Hemlock Hill Herb Farm
Hemlock Hill Road
Litchfield, CT 06759

Taylor's Garden
2649 Stingle Ave.
Rosemead, CA 91770

Capriland's Herb Farm
Silver St.
Coventry CT 06238

Yankee Peddler Herb Farm
Dept. TC, Highway 36 N.
Brenham, TX 77833

Otto Richter and Sons
Box 26, Goodwood
Ontario, Canada L0C 1A0

Bonnie Fisher
Hickory Hollow
Rte. 1, Box 52
Peterstown, WV 24963

McNulty's Tea & Coffee Co.
109 Christopher St.
New York, NY 10014

Lewis & Conger
39-25 Skillman Ave.
Long Island City, NY 11104

SOLAR HEATING

Ken Fischer Sun Systems
716 Main St.
Berlin, PA 15530

Solar Sunstill Inc.
15 Blueberry Ridge Rd.
Setauket, NY 11733

Helio Assoc. Inc.
8230 East Broadway
Tucson, AZ 85710

Zomeworks Corp.
P.O. Box 712
Albuquerque, NM 87103

Fafco Inc.
138 Jefferson Dr.
Menlo Park, CA 94025

Solarator Inc.
16231 West 14 Mile Rd.
Birmingham, MI 48009

Environmental Energies Corp.
Front Street
Copemish, MI 49625

Sol-Therm Corp.
7 West 14th St.
New York, NY 10011

Sunworks, Div. of Enthone, Inc.
P.O. Box 1004
New Haven, CT 06508

Fred Rice Productions, Inc.
6313 Peach Ave.
Van Nuys, CA 91401

DOG SLEDDING

Hall's Alaskan Cache Kennel
5875 McCrum Road
Jackson, MI 49201

Kimiluk
Stanstead, Quebec
Canada

Joe Vennewitz
20370 Ostrom Ave. N.
Marine-on-St. Croix, MN 55047

OUTDOOR GEAR

Adventure 16, Inc.
11161 West Pico
West Los Angeles, CA 90064

Adventure 16
4620 Alvarado Canyon Rd.
San Diego, CA 92120

Alpenlite
29 North Garden
Ventura, CA 93001

Alpine Designs
P.O. Box 3407
Boulder, CO 80307

Alpine Recreation Warehouse
4b Henshaw Street
Woburn, MA 01801

Antarctic Products Co., Ltd.
P.O. Box 223
Nelson, New Zealand

Appalachian Designs
P.O. Box 11252
Chattanooga, TN 37401

Ascente
P.O. Box 2028
Fresno, CA 93718

Eddie Bauer
P.O. Box 3700
Third and Virginia
Seattle, WA 98124

L.L. Bean, Inc.
Freeport, ME 04033

Bishops Ultimate Outdoor Equipment
6804 Millwood Rd.
Bethesda, MD 20034

Thomas Black & Sons, Ltd.
930 Ford St.
Ogdensburg, NY 13669

Holubar Mountaineering Ltd.
P.O. Box 7
Boulder, CO 80302

Eastern Mountain Sports
1041 Commonwealth Ave.
Boston, MA 02215

Frostline Outdoor Equipment
1750 30th St.
Boulder, CO 80302

Frostline Kits
Dept. C
Frostline Circle
Denver, CO 80241

Gerry, Division of Outdoor Sports Ind., Inc.
5450 North Valley Hwy.
Denver, CO 80216

Holubar Mountaineering Ltd.
Box 7
Boulder, CO 80302

Kelty Mountaineering
1801 Victory Blvd.
Glendale, CA 91201
and:
9066 Tampa Ave.
Northwich, CA 91324

Kreeger & Son, Ltd.
16 West 46th St.
New York, NY 10036

Sierra Designs
4th & Addison Sts.
Berkeley, CA 94710
and:
217 Alma
Palo Alto, CA 92667

Algonquin Outfitters
RR 1
Dwight, Ontario, Canada
P0A 1H0

Colorado Outdoor Sports Corp.
P.O. Box 5544
Denver, CO 80217

BULBS

International Growers Exchange
Box 397
Farmington, MI 48024

R.W. Longabaugh
2144 Northeast Lakeview Dr.
Sebring, FL 33870

Van Bourgondien Brothers
Box A, 245 Farmingdale Rd.
Rte. 109
Babylon, NY 11702

Cooley's Gardens
Silverton, OR 97381

Alexander Heimlich
71 Burlington St.
Woburn, MA 01801

Amaryllis, Inc.
Box 318
Baton Rouge, LA 70808

C.A. Cruickshank, Ltd.
1015 Mt. Pleasant Road
Toronto, Ontario,
Canada M4P 2M1

The Daffodil Mart
Box 112
North, VA 23128

HOME SCENTS

Aphrodisia
28 Carmine St.
New York, NY 10014

Caswell-Massey Co., Ltd.
518 Lexington Ave.
New York, NY 10017

Kiehl Pharmacy
109 Third Ave.
New York, NY 10003

Rocky Hollow Herb Farm, Inc.
Box 215, Lake Wallkill Rd.
Sussex, NJ 07461

Bassinnova
18 East 41st St.
New York, NY 10017

WOOD-CHOPPING TOOLS

Sears, Roebuck and Company
4640 Roosevelt Blvd.
Philadelphia, PA 19132

U.S. General Supply Corp.
100 General Pl.
Jerico, NY 11753

Woodcraft Supply Corp.
313 Montvale Ave.
Woburn, MA 01801

Snow & Nealley Co.
155 Perry Rd.
Bangor, ME 04401

Bartlett Manufacturing Co.
3003 East Grand Blvd.
Detroit, MI 48202

Granberg Industries, Inc.
200 South Garrard Blvd.
Richmond, CA 94804

Nasco
Fort Atkinson, WI 53538

RUG-HOOKING SUPPLIES

Berry's of Maine
20-22 Main St.
Yarmouth, ME 04096

Dick Blick
Box 1267
Galesburg, IL 61401

The Handcrafters
1 West Brown St.
Waupun, WI 53963

House of Gould
1290 N.E. 135th St.
Miami, FL 33161

Party Bazaar
390 Fifth Ave.
New York, NY 10018

Jane Olson
P.O. Box 351
Hawthorne, CA 90250

Lee Wards
National Office
1200 St. Charles Road
Elgin, IL 60120

Pins & Needles
P.O. Box 2535
Hialeah, FL 33012

ICE-FISHING SUPPLIES

Michigan Dept. of Conservation
Dept. of Natural Resources
Mason Building
Lansing, MI 48926

Pennsylvania Fish Commission
P.O. Box 1673
Harrisburg, PA 17120

Post Ski & Sports Shops
1323 Third Ave.
New York, NY 10021

Scientific Anglers
Box 2007
Midland, MI 48640

Ministry of Industry & Tourism
Ontario Travel Centre
Hearst Block, 3rd Floor
Queen's Park,
Ontario, Canada M7A 2E3

BOBSLEDS AND TOBOGGANS

Snowcraft Corp.
Oak Hill Plaza
P.O. Box 487
Scarboro, ME 04074

SNOWMOBILES AND SNOW BIKES

House of Minnel
Deerpath Road
Batavia, IL 60510

Herter's Inc.
RR 1
Waseca, MN 56093

International Snowmobile Industry Assoc.
1800 M Street N.W.
Suite 850 South
Washington, DC 20036

U.S. Snowmobile Assoc.
101 Snowmobile Dr.
Eagle River, WI 54521

Clubs & Organizations

Organized groups offer an opportunity to find others with similar interests. Few cater exclusively to winter recreation, but the cold weather aficionado will find plenty of company and information through the clubs and organizations listed.

FOREST SERVICE, U.S. DEPARTMENT OF AGRICULTURE
P.O. Box 2417
Washington, DC 20013

Presides over the 187 million acres of National Forest system. This land is all open to backpacking. For specific information, the government provides these booklets: *Backpacking in the National Forest Wilderness, PA-585, 25¢; Camping, PA-502, 25¢; National Forest Vacations, FS-45, 55¢; The National Forests, FS-25, 15¢; Search for Solitude, PA-942, 65¢; Pamphlets are from Public Documents Dept., U.S. Government Printing Office, Washington, DC 20402.*

By addressing your inquiries to regional **Forest Service** offices, detailed information may be obtained

on National Forests and wilderness areas:

P.O. Box 1628
Juneau, AL 99801

P.O. Box 3623
Portland, OR 92708

517 Gold Avenue S.W.
Albuquerque, NM 87101

1720 Peachtree Road, N.W.
Atlanta, GA 30309

U.S. FOREST SERVICE OFFICE OF INFORMATION
630 Sansome St.
San Francisco, CA 94111

U.S. FOREST SERVICE
11177 West 8th Ave.
Box 25127
Lakewood, CO 80225

FOREST SERVICE, USDA
Eastern Region
633 West Wisconsin Ave.
Milwaukee, WI 53203

DEPT. OF AGRICULTURE
USDA Forest Service
Northern Region Headquarters
Federal Building
Box 7669   Massoula, MT 59807

REGIONAL FORESTER
U.S. Forest Service
324 25th St.
Ogden, Utah 84401

NATIONAL PARK SERVICE
C Street between 18th & 19th Sts.,
N.W.   Washington, DC 20204

Established "exclusively to preserve outstanding recreational, scenic, inspirational, geological, and historical values on the American scene and make them available permanently for public use and enjoyment." The purchase of a Golden Eagle Passport will admit you to areas with an entrance fee. The cost of the passport is $10, it is good for one year.

Booklets concerning camping in National Parks:

National Parks of the U.S. (*map folder*), *S/N 2405-0039, $1.50; Back Country Travel in the National Park System, S/N 2405-0267, 35¢; Camping in the National Park System, S/N 2405-0205, 25¢; These may be obtained from:*

SUPERINTENDENT OF DOCUMENTS
U.S. Government Printing Office
Washington, DC 20402

UNITED STATES DEPT. OF INTERIOR BUREAU OF LAND MANAGEMENT
1800 C Street, N.W.
Washington, D.C. 20204

Contains 457 million acres of undesignated Western lands. More than 2500 Federal recreational areas are open for public use. Golden Eagle Passport is honored. Information about the wilderness areas included in these lands may be obtained by writing to the regional director for your state.

NATIONAL PARKS AND CONSERVATION ASSOCIATION
1701 18th Street, N.W.
Washington, DC 20009

Founded in 1919, at present claims over 50,000 members. Allies private and government agencies interested in issues of environmental protection.

NATIONAL TRAILS COUNCIL
P.O. Box 1042
St. Charles, IL 60174

A center for information concerning trails and recreation associated with them. The organization was founded by Gunnar Peterson with the purpose of supporting the "planning, promotion, and execution of trails systems at the local, county, state, regional, and national levels."

For information on wilderness areas, forests, parks, trails, camping, canoeing, and related outdoor activities, contact state recreation and tourist bureaus:

BUREAU OF PUBLICITY & INFORMATION
Room 403, State Hwy. Building
Montgomery, AL 36130

OFFICE OF TOURISM
1400 10th St.
Sacramento, CA 95814

DIVISION OF COMMERCE & DEVELOPMENT
602 State Capital Annex
Denver, CO 80203

DEPARTMENT OF BUSINESS & ECONOMIC DEVELOPMENT, DIVISION OF TOURISM
222 South College
Springfield, IL 62706

STATE DEVELOPMENT OFFICE
State House
Augusta, ME 04333

CHAMBER OF COMMERCE TRAVERSE CITY AREA
Grandview Parkway
P.O. Box 387
Traverse City, MI 49684

NEW YORK STATE DEPT. OF COMMERCE
99 Washington Ave.
Albany, NY 12245

THE ADIRONDACK FORTY-SIXERS
Adirondack, NY 12808

$2 annual dues. Membership based on successful scaling of Adirondack peaks. Pamphlet: *Mountain Manners.*

THE ADIRONDACK MOUNTAIN CLUB, INC.
172 Ridge St.
Glens Falls, NY 12801

Concern with and promotion of the Adirondack Mountain Preserve.

6,000 members concentrate on year-round outings. $10 yearly dues, bi-monthly publication: *Adirondack.*

APPALACHIAN MOUNTAIN CLUB
5 Joy St.
Boston, MA 02108

Oldest mountain club in America, founded in 1876. Membership over 14,000 with primary concern for preservation and enjoyment of New England outdoors.

THE COLORADO MOUNTAIN CLUB
1723 East 16th Ave.
Denver, CO 80218

Conservation-minded group of over 6,000 members. Promotes all outdoor recreational activities, with an emphasis on hiking and backpacking.

GREEN MOUNTAIN CLUB
P.O. Box 94
Rutland, VT 05701

Protects and maintains Vermont's Long Trail system. Plans related outdoor activities. Publishes guidebooks, and its own newsletter, *Long Trail News.*

NEW ENGLAND TRAIL CONFERENCE
% Kay Barnett, Secretary
629 Florence Road
Northampton, ME 01060

Amalgamation of hiking clubs and related information. Club outings, news, and maps are issued in its publication, *New England Trails* (25¢).

NEW YORK-NEW JERSEY TRAIL CONFERENCES, INC.
G.P.O. 2250
New York, NY 10001
Maintains over 450 miles of trails under the auspices of a federation of New York and New Jersey hiking clubs. Official publication: *Trail Walker.*

THE SIERRA CLUB
Bush Street
San Francisco, CA 94104

A 140,000-member assault on environmental abuse. The club acts through legal representatives, local education via literature and films, and a persistent public-relations campaign encouraging the respectful use of our natural resources. Provides literature on all outdoor recreational pursuits. Publications: *Sierra Club Bulletin, Ascent.*

WILDERNESS SOCIETY
729 15th St., N.W.
Washington, DC 20005

Founded by Robert Marshall, the society is highly conservation-conscious. Offers its members the opportunity to participate in its schedule of wilderness education trips. Quarterly publication: *The Living Wilderness.*

AMERICAN ALPINE CLUB
113 East 90th St.
New York, NY 10028

NORTHWESTERN ICE YACHTING ASSOC.
% Paul Kruger, Secy. Treas. NIYA
3027 Siggelbow Rd.
McFarland, WI 53558

EASTERN ICE YACHTING ASSOC.
% Thomas Nichols
760 ARD # 2
Andover, NJ 07821

NORTH STAR SLED DOG CLUB
Rte. 1 Box 289
Bemidjii, MN 56601

INTERNATIONAL SLED DOG RACING ASSOC.
P.O. Box 55
Watertown, NY 13601

Books

What follows is a partial list of the many books available that pertain to subjects covered in this book. If they are not at your local bookstore or library, write the publisher for buying information.

QUILTING

Bacon, Lenice Ingram,
American Patchwork Quilts.
William Morrow and Company, New York, 1973.

Colby, Averil
Quilting.
Charles Scribner's Sons, New York, 1971.

"Patchwork," Volume 12, and "Quilting," Volume 14,
The Family Creative Workshop.
Plenary Publications International, Inc., New York, 1975.

Gammell, Alice I.,
Polly Prindle's Book of American Patchwork Quilts.
Grosset and Dunlap, New York, 1973.

Green, Sylvia,
Patchwork for Beginners.
Watson-Guptill Publications, New York, 1972.

Gutcheon, Beth,
The Perfect Patchwork Primer.
David McKay Company, New York, 1973.

Haywood, Dixie,
The Contemporary Crazy Quilt Project Book.
Crown Publishers, Inc., New York, 1977.

Holstein, Jonathon,
American Pieced Quilts.
The Viking Press, New York, 1973.

Ickis, Marguerite,
The Standard Book of Quilting and Collecting.
Dover Publications, New York, 1949.

Laury, Jean Ray,
Quilts and Coverlets.
Van Nostrand Reinhold, New York, 1970.

Lithgow, Marilyn,
Quiltmaking and Quiltmakers.
Funk & Wagnalls, New York, 1974.

Mahler, Celine Blanchard,
Once Upon A Quilt: Patchwork Design and Technique.
Van Nostrand Reinhold, New York, 1973.

Wooster, Ann-Sargent,
Quiltmaking: The Modern Approach to a Traditional Craft.
Drake Publishers, New York, 1972.

SCRIMSHAW

Barbeau, Marius,
All Hands Aboard Scrimshawing.
Peabody Foundation for Archeology, Cambridge, Massachusetts, 1966.

"Scrimshaw," Volume 15,
The Family Creative Workshop.
Plenary Publications International, Inc., New York, 1975.

Flayderman, E. Norman,
Scrimshaw and Scrimshanders.
N. Flayderman & Co., Inc., New Milford, Connecticut, 1972.

Linsley, Leslie,
Scrimshaw.
Hawthorn Books, Inc., New York, 1976.

Ritchie, Carson I.A.,
Scrimshaw.
Sterling Publishing Co., Inc., New York, 1972,
Oak Tree Press Co., Ltd.

BOOKS

SACHET AND POMANDER

"Potpourris and Pomanders,"
Volume 13,
The Family Creative Workshop.
Plenary Publications International,
Inc., New York, 1975.

CANDLEMAKING

Collins, Paul,
Introducing Candlemaking.
B.T. Batsford Limited, London,
1972.

"Candlemaking," Volume 3,
The Family Creative Workshop,
Plenary Publications International,
Inc., New York, 1974.

Monroe, Ruth,
Kitchen Candlecrafting.
A.S. Barnes and Company, Inc.,
New York, 1965.

Olsen, Don and Ray,
Modern Art of Candle Crafting.
A.S. Barnes and Company, Inc.,
New York, 1965.

Shaw, Ray,
Candle Art.
William Morrow & Company, Inc.,
New York, 1973.

Strose, Susanne,
Candle-Making.
Sterling Publishing Co., Inc.,
1968, Oak Tree Press Co., Ltd.

HOOKING RUGS

Beitler, Ethel J.,
Hooked & Knotted Rugs.
Sterling Publishing Co., Inc.,
New York, 1973,
Oak Tree Press Co., Ltd.

"Hooked Rugs," Volume 8,
The Family Creative Workshop.
Plenary Publications International,
Inc., New York, 1974.

Frost, Edward Sands,
Hooked Rug Patterns.
Greenwich Village and Henry Ford
Museum, Dearborn, Michigan,
1970.

Kopp, Joel and Kate,
American Hooked and Sewn Rugs.
E.P. Dutton & Co., New York,
1975.

Bowles, Ella Shannon,
Handmade Rugs.
Little, Brown & Co., Boston, 1927.

Parker, Xenia L.,
Hooked Rugs and Ryas.
Henry Regnery Company,
Chicago, Illinois, 1976.

SAUNAS

Viherjuuri, Hillari Johannes,
Sauna: The Finnish Bath.
Stephen Greene Press, Brattleboro,
Vermont, 1972.

FORCING BULBS

Genders, Roy,
Bulbs—A Complete Handbook.
The Bobbs-Merrill Co.,
Indianapolis, Indiana, 1973.

Matthew, Brian,
Dwarf Bulbs.
Arco Publishing Co., New York,
1973.

Miles, Bebe,
Bulbs for the Home Gardener.
Grosset and Dunlap, New York,
1976.

Peters, Ruth Marie,
Bulb Magic in Your Window.
William Morrow and Co.,
New York, 1975.

Reynolds, Marc, and
Meachem, William L.,
**The Complete Book of Garden
Bulbs.**
Funk & Wagnalls Publishing Co.,
New York, 1971.

WOOD-BURNING STOVES AND OPEN-FIRE COOKING

Coleman, Peter,
Wood Stove Know-how.
Garden Way Publishing,
Charlotte, Vermont, 1976.

Curtis, Will and Jane,
Antique Woodstoves.
Garden Way Publishing,
Charlotte, Vermont, 1976.

Franklin, Linda C.,
From Hearth to Cookstove.
House of Collectibles, Inc.,
Florence, Alabama, 1976.

Gay, Larry,
**The Complete Book of Heating
with Wood.**
Garden Way Publishing,
Charlotte, Vermont, 1976.

CAR MAINTENANCE

Harman, Robert Dan,
Minor Auto Body Repair.
Chilton Book Co., Radnor,
Pennsylvania, 1976.

Sclar, Deanna,
Auto Repair for Dummies.
McGraw-Hill Book Company,
New York, 1976.

SOLAR HEATING

Anderson, Bruce N.,
Solar Energy and Shelter Design.
Total Environmental Action,
Harrisville, New Hampshire, 1973.

Anderson, Bruce N.,
**Solar Energy Home Design in
Four Climates.**
Total Environmental Action,
Harrisville, New Hampshire, 1975.

Lucas, Ted,
How to Build a Solar Heater.
The Ward Ritchie Press, Pasadena,
California, 1975.

HOME INSULATION

Adams, Anthony,
Your Energy-Efficient House—Building and Remodeling Ideas.
Garden Way Publishing, Charlotte, Vermont, 1976.

Badinski, Stanley Jr.,
House Construction—A Guide to Buying, Building, and Evaluating.
Prentice-Hall, Englewood Cliffs, New Jersey, 1976.

United States Department of Agriculture,
Wood Frame House Construction.
Forest Service Handbook No. 73.

WINTER WILDLIFE

Gibbons, Euell,
Stalking the Wild Asparagus.
David McKay Co., Inc., New York, 1970 (field-guide edition).

Shuttlesworth, Dorothy,
Exploring Nature with Your Child.
Harry N. Abrams, New York, 1977.

Teale, Edwin W.,
Wandering through Winter.
Dodd, Mead, & Co.,
New York, 1965,
Apollo Editions, Inc., New York 1969 — paper.

NEW ICE AGE

Impact Team Report,
The Weather Conspiracy.
Heron House Publishing International, Ltd., Ballantine Books, New York, 1977.

Ponte, Lowell,
Cooling.
Prentice-Hall, Englewood Cliffs, New Jersey, July 1976.

ICE SCULPTURE

Haskins, Jim,
Snow Sculpture and Ice Carving.
Macmillan, Inc., New York, 1974.

WINTER SPORTS

Arlott, John, ed.,
Oxford Companion to Sports and Games.
Oxford University Press, London, New York, and Toronto, 1975.

Bass, Howard,
Let's Go Skating.
St. Martin's Press, New York, 1976.

Bennett, Margaret,
Cross Country Skiing for the Fun of It.
Ballantine Books, New York, 1973.

Casewit, Curtis W.,
The Skier's Handbook.
Winchester Press, New York, 1971, Arc Books, Inc., New York, 1975.

Evans, Harold; Jackman, Brian; and Ottaway, Mark,
We Learned to Ski.
St. Martin's Press, New York, 1975.

Liebers, Arthur,
The Complete Book of Winter Sports.
Coward, McCann & Geoghegan, Inc., New York, 1963.

Freeman, Courtland,
Ski Touring for the Fun of It.
Little, Brown & Co., Boston, 1974.

McCulloch, Ernie,
Ski Easy.
McGraw-Hill Book Company, New York, 1973.

National Ski Association of America,
Manual of Ski Mountaineering.
San Francisco, California, 1969.

Osgood, William E., and Hurley, Leslie,
The Snowshoe Book.
The Stephen Greene Press, Brattleboro, Vermont, 1971.

Welsh, Robin,
Beginner's Guide to Curling.
Transatlantic Arts, Inc., Levittown, New York, 1971.

WINTER CAMPING AND OUTDOOR COOKING

The Boy Scout's Handbook.
Official Publication of the Boy Scouts of America.
Boy Scouts of America, October 1976.

Bridge, Raymond,
The Complete Snow Camper's Guide.
Charles Scribner's Sons, New York, 1973.

Bunnelle, Hasse, and Sarvis, Shirley,
Cooking for Camp and Trail.
Sierra Club Books, San Francisco, California, 1972.

Colby, C.B., and Angier, Bradford,
The Art & Science of Taking to the Woods.
Macmillan Publishing Co., New York, © 1970 by The Stackpole Company.

Cunningham, Gerry,
How to Keep Warm.
Available (free) from Colorado Outdoor Sports Corp., P.O. Box 5544, Denver, Colorado, 80217.

Danielson, John A.,
"How to Get Started Winter Backpacking."
Back Packer Magazine, #13,
February 1976.

Farmer, Charles and Kathy,
Campground Cooking.
Digest Books, Inc., Northfield, Illinois, 1974.

Reimers, Emil,
Cooking for Camp and Caravan.
Nelson Publishers, London, 1975 (out of print).

Thomas, Dian,
Roughing It Easy.
Brigham Young University Press, Provo, Utah, 1974.